MAKI
PEACE
WITH
NATURE

DUKE UNIVERSITY PRESS   Durham and London   2022

MAKING PEACE WITH NATURE

ECOLOGICAL ENCOUNTERS ALONG THE KOREAN DMZ

ELEANA J. KIM

Printed in the United States of America on acid-free paper ∞
Designed by A. Mattson Gallagher
Typeset in Portrait Text and Helvetica Neue by
Westchester Publishing Services

Library of Congress Cataloging-in-Publication Data
Names: Kim, Eleana Jean, [date] author.
Title: Making peace with nature : ecological encounters along the
Korean DMZ / Eleana J. Kim.
Description: Durham : Duke University Press, 2022. | Includes biblio-
graphical references and index.
Identifiers: LCCN 2021041276 (print)
LCCN 2021041277 (ebook)
ISBN 9781478015727 (hardcover)
ISBN 9781478018353 (paperback)
ISBN 9781478022961 (ebook)
Subjects: LCSH: Human ecology—Korean Demilitarized Zone
(Korea) | Ecology—Korean Demilitarized Zone (Korea) | Biodiversity
conservation—Korean Demilitarized Zone (Korea) | Korean
War, 1950–1953—Environmental aspects. | Korean Demilitarized
Zone (Korea)—Environmental conditions. | BISAC: SOCIAL
SCIENCE / Anthropology / Cultural & Social | NATURE /
Environmental Conservation & Protection
Classification: LCC GF659.K535 2022 (print) | LCC GF659 (ebook) | DDC
304.209519—dc23/eng/20211119
LC record available at https://lccn.loc.gov/2021041276
LC ebook record available at https://lccn.loc.gov/2021041277

Cover art: DMZ wetlands, 2005. Photograph by Kim Seung
Ho. Courtesy of the DMZ Ecology Research Institute.

This work was supported by the Core University Program for
Korean Studies through the Ministry of Education of the
Republic of the Korea and Korean Studies Promotion Service
of the Academy of Korean Studies (AKS-2016-OLU-2250005).

This project was supported in part by the University of California
Office of the President MRPI funding MRP-19-600791.

To my kin, familiar and strange

1

2

3

4

Contents

List of Abbreviations

BFS	black-faced spoonbill
CCL	Civilian Control Line
CCZ	Civilian Control Zone
DERI	DMZ Ecology Research Institute
DMZ	Demilitarized Zone
DPRK	Democratic People's Republic of Korea
GPS	Global Positioning System
HLZ	Handicapped Life Zone
IUCN	International Union for the Conservation of Nature
KATUSA	Korean Augmentation to the United States Army
KCCNNR	Korean Commission for the Conservation of Nature and Natural Resources
MAB	UNESCO Man and the Biosphere Programme
MAPS	Migratory Animals Pathological Survey
MDL	Military Demarcation Line
MIPD	Military Installations Protection District
NBL	Northern Boundary Line
NLL	Northern Limit Line
NSL	National Security Law
PLV	Peace and Life Valley
PLZ	Peace and Life Zone
POBS	Pacific Ocean Biological Survey
RCC	red-crowned crane
ROK	Republic of Korea
SBL	Southern Boundary Line
UNCMAC	United Nations Command Military Armistice Commission

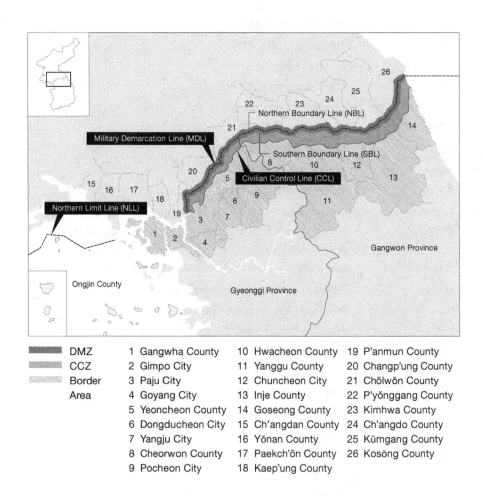

▨ DMZ	
▨ CCZ	
▧ Border Area	

1 Gangwha County
2 Gimpo City
3 Paju City
4 Goyang City
5 Yeoncheon County
6 Dongducheon City
7 Yangju City
8 Cheorwon County
9 Pocheon City

10 Hwacheon County
11 Yanggu County
12 Chuncheon City
13 Inje County
14 Goseong County
15 Ch'angdan County
16 Yŏnan County
17 Paekch'ŏn County
18 Kaep'ung County

19 P'anmun County
20 Changp'ung County
21 Chŏlwŏn County
22 P'yŏnggang County
23 Kimhwa County
24 Ch'angdo County
25 Kŭmgang County
26 Kosŏng County

Map FM.1
Map of the Korean DMZ region. Adapted from E.-J. Park (2013c) and Son (2011).

The South Korean DMZ Region

The South Korean DMZ region includes the Demilitarized Zone (DMZ), the Civilian Control Zone (CCZ), and the Border Area. The Military Demarcation Line (MDL), which is the actual Korean War ceasefire line, is represented by the dotted line. By order of the 1953 Armistice Agreement, the DMZ extends two kilometers on either side of the MDL and is bordered by the Northern Boundary Line (NBL) and the Southern Boundary Line (SBL). The Civilian Control Line (CCL) marks the southern border of the CCZ, and prior clearance is required to pass through checkpoints into the CCZ, which is guarded by South Korean soldiers. The CCL has been adjusted northward four times since 1983 and has shrunk by 75 percent since the 1950s. In 2008, it was legally redefined as the area within five to ten kilometers from the SBL. The Border Area, which incorporates but extends beyond the CCZ, is an administratively defined region that has been targeted for economic development since the 2000s.

The DMZ is a terrestrial border only, which ends at the mouth of the Han River estuary. The estuary, which is defined by the Armistice Agreement as neutral waters, may be used by both North and South Korean civilian vessels. Despite this fact, as of this writing, neither country has used the waters of the estuary. The Northern Limit Line (NLL) off the western coast has been highly contested since the signing of the Armistice Agreement. Several islands in the Yellow Sea belong to South Korea and are part of Ongjin County, five of which are north of the thirty-eighth parallel.

There are eight counties in the border area: Ongjin, Ganghwa, and Yeoncheon in Gyeonggi Province; and Cheorwon, Hwacheon, Yanggu, Inje, and Goseong in Gangwon Province. There are also seven cities: Gimpo, Paju, Goyang, Yangju, Dongducheon, Pocheon, and Chuncheon. Both Goseong and Cheorwon counties, like Gangwon Province, are divided, existing on both sides of the DMZ.

A Note about Romanization and Translation

I use the McCune–Reischauer romanization system to transliterate Korean words into Latin script, except for instances in which a common transliteration is in wide usage, such as Seoul instead of Sŏul. Personal names in Korean follow the cultural convention of family name followed by given name, except for individuals who publish under or who prefer Western conventions. Place names in South Korea follow the South Korean revised romanization system, which was adopted by the South Korean government in 2000. I forgo transliteration in favor of Korean script (*hangŭl*) throughout the text when the meaning might be enhanced for readers familiar with the Korean language. I also forgo romanization for Korean-language bibliographic sources but include the English-language translation. Unless otherwise indicated, all translations from Korean are my own.

Acknowledgments

Because the Korean DMZ is often described as a no-man's land, I sometimes joked that I was writing an ethnography of a place without people. Of course, this was far from the truth, and no ethnography could be written without dozens of interlocutors, colleagues, and friends—human and other-than-human—some of whom appear in the following pages, and others who were crucial in aiding me behind the scenes. Moreover, writing these words of appreciation after more than a year of isolation due to the COVID-19 pandemic, I am acutely aware of the deep sociality and feelingful co-presences that brought this project into being. Countless conversations with generous collaborators, stimulating colleagues, and dear friends suffuse every word. Yet, I alone am responsible for any omissions or inaccuracies.

Of the many debts I've accumulated, by far the largest is owed to Kim Seung Ho (김승호 소장님), founder and director of the DMZ Ecology Research Institute in Paju, South Korea, who welcomed me to join his organization in September 2011. He was the first to introduce me to the endlessly fascinating ecologies of the DMZ/CCZ area, and he continues to be a source of inspiration.

I owe another deep debt of gratitude to Dr. Lee Kisup (이기섭 박사님), who invited me to join the Waterbird Network Korea and Korea Crane Network in 2012, thus opening a host of human and nonhuman connections to me. Dr. Lee's generosity extended to permitting me to reproduce images from his online café for the Korean Waterbird Network. Dr. Lee and Director Kim appear prominently in the chapters of this book as both social actors and theorists of interconnected multispecies worlds. I'm profoundly appreciative of their cooperation and kind patience in allowing me to conduct fieldwork on their fieldwork. I also thank Kim Seung Ho for permission to use his photograph for the cover of this book.

The seeds of this project were first planted when I attended a presentation by then president of the DMZ Forum, Hall Healy, in New York City.

I soon met the founders, Dr. Ke Chung (K. C.) Kim and Seung-ho Lee, who invited me to join the board a few years later. I thank Hall, K. C., and Seung-ho, as well as other members of the board for teaching me about their ongoing efforts to ensure the DMZ's future as a protected area. K. C.'s pivotal role in the history of the DMZ's ecologies and the history of biodiversity conservation is hinted at in the pages of this book, but it deserves much more focused in-depth treatment. Conversations with George Archibald of the International Crane Foundation also helped to situate the work of crane conservation into a longer history of postwar South Korea.

Eunhyei Kim, my intrepid research assistant, was indispensable to me in getting this project off the ground and then to seeing the manuscript out the door and into the wider world. She has continued to keep my ethnographic analysis both concrete and "substantiable," and I look forward to her further ethnographic adventures.

Dr. Park Eun-Jin, formerly of the Gyeonggi Research Institute, was exceedingly generous with her time and provided well-honed insights on the DMZ region and its sustainable future. A fortuitous meeting with Jisuk (Peter) Chung, founder of the Border Peace School, opened up insights into the social worlds of the border area, and I am grateful for his important perspectives on peace and models for moving past the division. I also thank Professor of Anthropology Han Geon-soo, who provided early institutional support at Gangwon National University as well as valuable insights about the region, and Professor of Geology Kim Changhwan at Gangwon National University, who provided crucial information and social inroads to the border area in the early stages of this project. My gratitude further extends to Rhee T'ae-yoon, Heo Young, Kim Kyung-hoon, Ahn Chi-young, Kim Jae Hyun, Kim Kyunghee and Un-nam, whose infectious delight in the CCZ's ecologies made my fieldwork not only fascinating but fun. I also learned crucial details about the environmental politics of the border area from Lee Seung-eun and Myung Ho of EcoHorizon Institute and Chŏng In-ch'ŏl of Green Korea United. Spike Millington, then director of the East Asian Australasian Flyway Partnership in Songdo, provided generous insights about migratory bird conservation in Korea and beyond.

I began this project while an assistant professor in the Anthropology Department at the University of Rochester, and I cherish the intellectual rigor and sincere collegiality that made my seven years there incredibly edifying, nurturing, and productive. Special thanks to Ayala Emmett, Bob Foster, Tom Gibson, Daniel Reichman, Kristin Doughty, Rachel Haidu, June Hwang, Leila Nadir, Cary Adams, Janet Berlo, and Ro Ferreri. When

I arrived at UC Irvine, I found numerous affinities and a wonderful intellectual home. I've been privileged to be among a stellar community of big-hearted and creative thinkers within and beyond the Anthropology Department, including Samar Al-Bulushi, Victoria Bernal, Tom Boellstorff, Mike Burton, Leo Chavez, Chungmoo Choi, Susan Coutin, Julia Elyachar, David Fedman, Kim Fortun, Mike Fortun, David Theo Goldberg, Anneeth Hundle, Angela Jenks, Laura Kang, Jerry Won Lee, Jim Lee, Mimi Long, Lilith Mahmud, George Marcus, Bill Maurer, Keith Murphy, Sylvia Nam, Valerie Olson, Kris Peterson, Justin Richland, Damien Sojoyner, Ian Straughn, Roxanne Varzi, and Salvatore Zárate, and last but not at all least, Mei Zhan. A happy situation became even happier with the arrival of Sherine Hamdy. My daily life as an instructor and academic would be impossible without the countless acts by department staff members who often go above and beyond the call of duty. My thanks to Norma Miranda, Jennifer dos Santos, Mel Brown, Tami Hoksbergen, Cory Hodges, and Olga Dunaevsky for their indispensable work over the years. The Center for Critical Korean Studies, established by the tireless Kyung Hyun Kim, led by Serk-bae Suh and Joseph Jeon, and expertly administered by Amanda Swain, Erica Yun, and Joo Hoon Shin, continues to provide a generative space for linking Korean Studies scholars in the university and internationally.

The many conceptual and literal journeys that this book has taken me on were made more joyful and rewarding by the intellectual companionship of the infrastructure reading group at the University of Chicago, organized by Julie Chu and Michael Fisch, and enlivened by the spirited minds of Brian Larkin, Amahl Bishara, Jun Mizukawa, Bettina Stoetzer, and Andrew Mathews. In 2017, I had the opportunity to organize a workshop on militarized ecologies, sponsored by the UCI Center for Global Peace and Conflict Studies and by a Sawyer Mellon Seminar grant. Thanks to Cécile Whiting and Carol Burke and the participants for sharing their exciting work: Amahl Bishara, Darcie DeAngelo, Lindsey Dillon, Kristina Lyons, Juanita Sundberg, and Leah Zani, with special gratitude to Bridget Guarasci and Simone Popperl.

The writing of this book was made a little less lonely thanks to Kris Peterson and Elizabeth Chin, who created a warm and nourishing space of focused productivity and conviviality at the UCI Steele/Burnand Anza-Borrego Desert Research Center in January 2020. Unpacking the mysteries of the writing process (and then actually writing) with Gloria Kim helped to deliver some focus during a period of maximum distraction. Timely support from the University of California Humanities Research Institute funded a Mid-Career Book Manuscript Workshop in late February 2020, which took place in person right before the pandemic required us all to work from home. The individual care and collective braininess of Jessica Cattelino, Tim Choy, Jennifer J. Chun, Judy Ju-hui Han, Diana Pardo Pedraza, Gabriele Schwab, Christina Schwenkel, and Ina Kim were truly invaluable.

To have Ken Wissoker also present at the workshop to provide his discerning insights and vital advice was more than I could have asked for from an editor and friend. Every coffee, meal, and conference chat over these many years has kept me forging ahead. Thank you also to Ryan Kendall at Duke University Press for expertly navigating the manuscript into production.

I thank the organizers of workshops and talks whose kind invitations provided opportunities to put my thoughts to paper and to refine my analysis: Beyond the Korean War Workshop at University of Chicago, the Asian Environments workshop at the Rachel Carson Center, University of Wisconsin–Milwaukee's C21, University of Toronto, University of Texas–Austin, Cornell University, UC San Diego, Stanford University, UC Santa Barbara, Duke University, Oberlin College, Sarah Lawrence College, The New School, University of Chicago, University of Minnesota, University of California, Berkeley, the UCI Center for Global Peace and Conflict Studies, Wooster College, UCLA, The Nam Center at the University of Michigan, Stony Brook University's Center for Korean Studies, and Melbourne University's Conflict, Justice and Development research cluster. I appreciated the gracious engagement and interest of those who hosted me, provided valuable feedback, and made these events possible: Hannah Appel, Andrew Bauer, Frank Billé, Sean Brotherton, John (Song Pae) Cho, Paula Ebron, Jim Ferguson, Daniel Fisher, Sabine Frühstück, Duana Fullwiley, Tim Gitzen, Mark Graham, Richard Grusin, Ryan Gustafsson, Ursula Hëise, Todd Henry, Karen Ho, Miyako Inoue, Hwansoo Kim, Nojin Kwak, Nayoung Aimee Kwon, Namhee Lee, Sohl C. Lee, Dolly Li, Liisa Malkki, Victoria Massie, Hirozaku Miyazaki, Yumi Moon, David Novak, Robert M. Oppenheim, Youjeong Oh, Shiho Satsuka, Ann Sharif, Gi-Wook Shin, Stergios Skaperdas, Kabir Tambar, Miriam Ticktin, David Valentine, Sarah Vaughan, Sylvia Yanagisako, Charles Zerner, Dafna Zur, and many others who I may be inadvertently leaving unnamed.

Two anonymous reviewers helped me to sharpen the manuscript's contributions, and I thank them for their discerning assessments and guidance. Hosu Kim, Sohl C. Lee, Sarah Luna, Leila Nadir, Albert Park, Jeongsu Shin, Seoyoung Park, and Dafna Zur generously read parts of the manuscript at different stages of completion. Kim Stoker is a true friend who lent expert editorial assistance at the eleventh hour. I thank John Hamrin, Nan Kim, R. Richard Grinker, Robert M. Oppenheim, and Theodore Jun Yoo for sending me relevant clippings and precious research materials. Much appreciation to Laurel Kendall for stimulating conversations that always helped me refine my thinking. The late Nancy Abelmann, with her characteristic generosity and warmth, lent me some of her bountiful enthusiasm whenever we met. She was a force of nature whose energetic spirit, scholarly commitments, and extraordinary mentorship provide a model for me and many others who were fortunate to know her. I am grateful that Jesook Song and Laura Nelson included me in the events that commemorated her tremendous contributions to both anthropology and Korean Studies.

I doubt that I would have completed this book without the loving support of my dear friends, even those I don't see often enough. Thanks to my peeps who, in various ways cheered me on, commiserated with me, and fed me with humor, food, advice, and affection: Elise Andaya, Shanti Avirgan, HyoJung Bidol, Larry Chang, Tammy Chu, Jennifer Jihye Chun, Sarah Fraiden, Sherine Hamdy, Judy Ju Hui Han, Gloria Chan-Sook Kim, Mimi Kim, Sangbeom Kim, Nicola Kountoupes, Molly Larkey, Ing Lee, Deann Borshay Liem, Kat McGowan, Leila Nadir, Kim Park Nelson, Alissa Quart, kate hers-Rhee, Kim Stoker, KimSu Theiler, Sridhar Venkatapuram, Maya Weimer, and Jackie A. Williams. Sue-je Lee Gage passed away suddenly in May 2020, and I mourn her loss and all the conversations we might have had. May she rest in peace.

I'm so grateful to Adria Imada, who had the brilliant foresight to propose that we form a writing dyad at the beginning of our new projects. That we both moved to UC Irvine at the same time was simply amazing kismet. The ups, downs, ins, and outs of the past several years would have been impossible to navigate without the anchor of her friendship and her crystalline intelligence.

The research and writing of this book were made possible by generous funding from the ACLS/SSRC/NEH International and Area Studies Fellowship and the Wenner–Gren Foundation for Anthropological Research's Richard Carley Hunt Postdoctoral Fellowship. In the later stages, the University of California's Humanities Research Institute and the UC Irvine Center for Critical Korean Studies provided additional financial support.

Tremendous thanks to Leah H. Nichols for providing the maps that appear in the book and for lending her impeccable aesthetic to their design. My appreciation also extends to Juwon Lee for his careful proofreading.

Finally, profound gratitude to my family, including my many cousins and extended family in South Korea (and New York), especially Sung-wook, Seonghae, Seongsoog, Hyeryun, and Yohan, who have always been a phone call away whenever I needed anything, from a cell phone rental to a nice meal. My mother and father, Jae Jin and Yung Duk, continue to model for me essential qualities of constancy, flexibility, and integrity. I am so fortunate to feel their love for me every day. I cherish the uncanny ability that my brother, Lawrence, has to help me put things in perspective while still affirming my point of view. And lastly, I dedicate this book to Rick and our strange familiars who have tolerated our doting affections over the years—the cats we call Mao, Boxer, Mommy, Baby, and Coco.

Introduction

It was the advent of the first rice harvest and just before the initial weeks of the migratory bird season. Ubiquitous reeds on the borders of the mature rice paddies created a feathery landscape of light brown and yellowish green that emanated a gold hue against the open blue skies of early autumn. I witnessed grasshoppers mating on the rice stalks, exchanged silent stares with soldiers passing by in military convoys, and relished the textures and fragrance of the overgrown vegetation alongside the borders of small ponds hidden amid the flourishing fields (figure I.1).

I had just stepped out of Dr. Rhee's Jeep to join the others in identifying wildflowers on the side of the road. There was a group of several high school students on this trip who were being taught by the citizen-ecologists to use the field guide and to pay close attention to the specific characteristics of various plants. Dr. Rhee, more anthropological than botanical in his interests, wanted to introduce me to the paradoxes of the area known as the Civilian Control Zone (CCZ; 민간인출입통제구역), the heavily militarized area immediately south of the Demilitarized Zone (DMZ) proper. The CCZ is where the majority of species that constitute the DMZ's famed biodiversity have been identified and studied. Rhee pointed past the barbed wire along the side of the road, directing my gaze beyond a low cement barrier and down a corridor of trees, and said, "That used to be a road connecting to the North!" Jokes ensued about how easy it would be for us to run across the border and who would go first. Another member of our group, an avid nature photographer, made a mock gesture of stepping over the barbed wire and, in the process, snagged the edge of his trousers, which added a dose of reality and physical humor to the moment.

Dr. Rhee was a wiry and wry ethnolinguist in his sixties who had a bad leg from a congenital disability and had written about the DMZ as the Handicapped Life Zone (HLZ), to critique the state-branded Peace and Life Zone (PLZ; 평화 · 생명지대; Rhee 2010). He was intrigued by my earlier

Figure I.1
A combine threshing rice
for the first harvest, CCZ
north of Paju City, South
Korea. October 2011.
Photograph by the author.

research on transnational adoption from South Korea and considered the abandonment of Korean children by the state to be akin to the state's lack of "ecological welfare" (생태 복지) for nonhuman life in the DMZ area (see E. J. Kim 2010). His poetic and analytic mind was continually seeking out connections and conceptual rhymes, such as his beloved vehicle (non-military Jeeps were at the time unusual to see in South Korea), itself a civilian–military hybrid, which was perfectly suited for forays into the CCZ. For him, the "paradox" (역설) of the DMZ was of endless fascination, one that similarly drew me to this research project. Just an hour before, he had articulated strongly worded critiques of US hegemony, but also expressed humility at the tremendous benefits South Korea had received from its Cold War benefactor. Like his biopolitical critique of the state's lack of welfare for both the nation's children and its nonhuman creatures, his views were informed by both cultural nationalism and an anti-state perspective that existed in ambivalent relation to US empire.

Back in Dr. Rhee's Jeep, I was sitting in the backseat with artist Heo Young (Dr. Rhee's spouse) as he drove us south through the checkpoint, along Freedom Road, toward Seoul's expanding satellite cities of Ilsan and

Paju. We passed billboards advertising English-language immersion academies, Peace and Life K-pop concerts, and the most bizarre one of a chubby baby's face sticking out of a hooded Astroturf onesie, promoting the greening of Paju City. There were also mammoth cement tank blockades along the highway, designed to stop North Korean tanks in a future land war, and engine-powered replicas of ancient sailboats that used to ferry people from Seoul to towns along the Imjin River basin.

Several kilometers past the checkpoint, Heo Young pointed out the window past me, toward the mountains, across the expanse of the Han River estuary. "That's North Korea. You can tell because the mountains don't have a single tree left on them." I adjusted my gaze to look beyond the highway guardrails, the barbed wired fences, the guard posts, and the wetlands toward the mountains, which were the color of bark or, more likely, dirt. I knew that fuel shortages in North Korea had led to massive deforestation, with additional ecological and social consequences, including mudslides, soil erosion, and ecosystem vulnerability. Having been asked to view those dark shapes as bare, I took them as visual evidence of the poverty and desperation of the people on the other side. When she asked me moments later what my impressions were, I was caught off guard. Instinctively, I said that the sight made me sad, but it was a pat and generic response to the national division and ongoing war, one that felt acutely inadequate to encompass the affective and sensory excess from my first foray into the ecology of the CCZ, which was still vibrating around and through me with immediacy and novelty.

That first visit introduced me to the CCZ as a heterotopic space of multiple temporalities, ambiguities, and affective possibilities—of premodern and (post–)Cold War histories, future visions of and nostalgic desires for a reconnected if not unified peninsula, as well as ecological timescapes of seasons, annual migrations, and cyclical changes of various nonhuman creatures in the context of climate change. These temporal readjustments, epistemological associations, ontological states, and multiscalar relations soon exceeded the paradoxical framing that had first intrigued me. The disorientation I felt after that first visit was influenced by the peculiar insecurity of knowing that one is in a space of heightened military security. But more importantly, it was also related to my bodily attunement to multispecies landscapes that denaturalized the dominant timescapes of contemporary South Korea—the hyperactive rhythms of capitalist growth, the past-oriented traumas of national division, and future-oriented teleologies of Korean unification.

The proposition that the Korean DMZ, one of the most heavily fortified and militarized spaces in the world, has become a site of rare biodiversity seems, on the face of it, paradoxical. This notion—that war and nature or militarization and preservation, when juxtaposed, coexist in ironic tension—has informed assertions that the DMZ, once representing national division, war, and death, now represents communication, peace, and life. These binaries were difficult to escape during my fieldwork in South Korea, emanating from local and regional governments, tourism ventures, government ministries, environmental nongovernmental organizations (NGOs), and the media.

These discourses and framings are premised on scientific findings that South Korea's DMZ region—including both the southern half of the DMZ and the CCZ and which constitutes just 1,557 square kilometers, or 1.6 percent of the total South Korean territory—is home to 6,168 identified species. According to a 2019 report by the Ministry of Environment, 102 of these species are categorized as endangered, and they constitute 38.2 percent of all such species in South Korea. Based on similar data, the National Institute of Ecology in 2018 asserted that "the DMZ has become an important habitat for endangered species."[1] Scholars, bureaucrats, journalists, artists, and tourists draw on this fact to posit the DMZ's nature as a redemptive force for healing the "scars of war," invariably finding aesthetic appeal in the "paradoxical coexistence of manmade conflict *and* an environment of natural wildlife that is completely indifferent to the surrounding human world of absurdity and violence" (S.-Y. Kim 2011: 397; emphasis in original).[2]

Yet, however alluring it may be, the framework of paradox is conceptually limited, for its rhetorical force depends on an ahistorical logic that holds two ostensible, yet incommensurable, truths in tension: ecology and war or, put another way, nature and culture. Rather than merely dwell in the space of paradox, I became intrigued by what one of my main interlocutors, Kim Seung Ho, calls "biological peace." Biological peace became a key to understanding the life forms of the DMZ, which exist not in spite of the division, as the paradoxical narratives would attest, but alongside and in relation to it. This book examines some of these life forms and relations "in the meantime of division," the peacelessness of almost seventy years of unending war. I analyze ponds, birds, and landmines in the CCZ/DMZ region as networked assemblages to show how each disrupts the temporalities common to South Korean discourses of division and unification and offers other less anthropocentric approaches to "making peace with nature."

The Double Bind of the DMZ's Nature

If paradox is one common cultural trope that frames the DMZ's nature, another could be described as that of the double bind. The double bind characterizes the discourses and concerns of policy makers and environmentalists who debate how to guard these precious landscapes within the purview of international environmental governance and the nation-state system. It originates from a concern that inter-Korean peace and exchange will lead to the destruction of the DMZ as a de facto protected area, and that preparations must be made to ensure against this possibility. The unprecedented détente of the late-1990s Sunshine Policy era (1998–2008) in particular enlivened discussions among conservationists and UN-level organizations, which called for the designation of the zone as a peace park or World Heritage Site. Since the mid-1990s, for instance, the DMZ Forum, a US-based not-for-profit, has sought to raise awareness and rally support for these efforts, which would use existing modes of international governance to recognize the DMZ as a site of global significance and protect it from any future development. As a member of the Forum's board, I participated in conversations centered on these goals, but because the North would not entertain the idea of a peace park in the absence of a peace treaty, we invariably came up against a fundamental impasse. On the one hand, members believed that the DMZ's nature could serve as the vehicle for building peace on the peninsula, but on the other hand, no meaningful progress could be made without North Korean agreement.

South Korean leaders—who, following the language of Article 12, Chapter 2, of the 1992 Agreement on Reconciliation, Non-aggression and Exchanges and Cooperation between South and North, have proposed to "peacefully utilize" (평화적 이용) the DMZ's nature—have been consistently rejected by the North on the grounds that the DMZ does not represent peace and also that, in the absence of a peace treaty, it cannot be transformed into a peace park or nature reserve.[3] Moreover, a unilateral attempt in 2011 by South Korea to register the DMZ as a UNESCO biosphere reserve was fiercely opposed by the North Korean representative to the governing committee as a violation of the Armistice Agreement.

The double bind thus entails two distinct yet interconnected impossibilities: (1) the DMZ's rare ecologies cannot be adequately protected from future development without having achieved peace, and (2) if peace is achieved, its precious nature will be sacrificed in the name of economic development. In other words, nature preservation depends on peace, but

Table I.1
South Korean Presidential Plans for the DMZ (1988–2020)

Roh Tae-woo (1988–93)	International Peace City (1988) Peace Zone (1989)
Kim Young-sam (1993–98)	DMZ Nature Park (1994)
Kim Dae-jung (1998–2003)	DMZ Peace Park (2001)
Roh Moo-hyun (2003–8)	Peace and Life Zone (2006)
Lee Myung-bak (2008–13)	UNESCO Biosphere Reserve (2011)
Park Geun-hye (2013–16)	International Peace Park (2013)
Moon Jae-in (2016–21)	International Peace Zone (2019)

peace, which is more than ever defined as economic cooperation, would destroy its nature. The values of a state-centric, capital-driven peace and a less anthropocentric, more-than-human peace seem to be in an impossible contradiction.

The future of the DMZ is tied to complex and knotty geopolitical negotiations involving multiple state parties, making the probability of any solution to the double bind uncertain at best. The impossibility of this double bind has not, however, prevented multiple South Korean administrations from attempting to leverage the DMZ as the site of future inter-Korean cooperation and peace. In fact, the policies of recent conservative administrations suggest that the more unpromising the prospects of inter-Korean dialogue are, the more the state invests in the DMZ's nature as a symbol of (future) peace, under the guise of preparing for unification, but more likely to shore up its own political agendas (see Table I.1).[4]

Of course, the double bind has led to certain practical measures to be sought by state and nonstate actors. For instance, under Article 2 of the Natural Environment Conservation Act (Act No. 13885), once the DMZ is under the jurisdiction of the Republic of Korea (ROK), it would be designated a "natural reservation area" (자연유보지역) for two years.[5] Bureaucrats in South Korea's Ministry of Environment and the Ministry of Oceans and Fisheries, as well as government researchers in both Gyeonggi and Gangwon Provinces, have spent at least a decade preparing plans for a post-unification DMZ, which include conservation of the DMZ's biodiversity.[6]

During the period of my fieldwork (2011–16), many observers I met were not optimistic that commitments to nature conservation would be able to temper the drive for economic development, and the changes taking place in the CCZ only reinforced their pessimistic views. People such as Dr. Rhee, for instance, abhorred the government slogan "peace and life" (hereafter without quotes) because they viewed it as a thinly disguised project for economic development. The slogan was also problematic in that it ignored the existence of the double bind by wedding two universal categories into a pacified harmony, idealizing life in the DMZ as if it symbolically represents unification itself, while ignoring the actual life forms that have been documented. I conducted this fieldwork during the Lee Myung-bak and Park Geun-hye administrations (2008–16) when inter-Korean hostility was peaking and, at the same time, the sacrifice of nonhuman nature to the dictates of economic development was intensifying. In this context, the optimistic tone presupposed by the slogan of peace and life rang especially hollow. The dynamic of the double bind is one in which, according to Gregory Bateson, the person who is caught within it cannot overcome the situation—it's a no-win situation (2000 [1972]). It was particularly ironic, then, that the PLZ and its related tourism ventures were frequently being framed by its proponents as a win-win situation—not for North and South Korea, but for conservation and development interests.

If Dr. Rhee viewed the discourses of peace and life to be a form of greenwashing, his HLZ refuses to ignore the ravages of history and ongoing violence. Rhee succinctly captures the environmental failures of both communism and capitalism, writing that the DMZ's disability is due to "the dual agonies of poverty *and* development" (2010: 80; emphasis added). The DMZ, as he asserts, is a space not of spontaneous nature but of dependent nature, having evolved in relation to the agricultural activities in the CCZ (see chapter 2). In this way, the DMZ's nature defamiliarizes the present: "From the space of division between North and South, sensing simultaneously the cruel bare mountains to the north and the ostentatious buildings in the south, [the DMZ's biodiversity] restlessly observes, from between the barbed wire fences, the face of humanity" (2010: 80). In Rhee's framing of the HLZ, South Korea's widely celebrated economic miracle is to blame for creating the conditions that necessitate "ecological welfare." Instead of welfare, however, the state offers what disability studies scholar Eunjung Kim might call the "curative violence" of peace and life.[7] Moreover, although the ecology of the DMZ can appear to be refreshingly beyond the reach of state power and global capital, Rhee's HLZ emphasizes that it is not just paradoxically protected by the militarization of the zone; rather, it is threatened by both militarization and neoliberal capital as climate change and development continue to affect multiple lifeways and prospects of survival.

Thinking alongside Dr. Rhee's HLZ, I depart from policy approaches that seek to solve the double bind—that is, by determining whether a peace treaty or a peace park agreement comes first. These approaches are too often tied to conservation imaginaries that scholars have critiqued because they depend on a liberal internationalist worldview that ultimately privileges market-based solutions (Büscher, Dressler, and Fletcher 2014). Instead, I show how the double bind, however intractable it may seem to be, has nonetheless been generative of unexpected and novel possibilities.[8] I return to these possibilities by connecting them to Kim Seung Ho's notion of biological peace after first discussing the DMZ's history and its associations with peace.

Situating the DMZ

Ever since the fateful line was drawn by US Army colonels Charles Bonesteel and Dean Rusk, dividing the newly liberated Korea at the thirty-eighth parallel on August 15, 1945, the Korean peninsula has served as a buffer or bulwark within a Cold War and post–Cold War global order. As artist and theorist Kyong Park writes, the "Korean peninsula was turned into a collaboratively designed buffer zone that predestined and defined the Cold War" (K. Park 2020: n.p.). Policy analysts and political scientists credit the DMZ with "maintaining the peace," even as it is the emblematic site of the unresolved Korean War (1950–53), which was suspended but not ended nearly seventy years ago with the signing of the Armistice Agreement.

The Armistice Agreement set the boundaries of the buffer zone at two kilometers north and two kilometers south of the Military Demarcation Line (MDL), which is the actual ceasefire line. The DMZ runs across the entire 250-kilometer-long width of the peninsula and separates the Democratic People's Republic of Korea (DPRK; North Korea) and the ROK (South Korea; see map FM.1). No heavy artillery is permitted between the Northern Boundary Line (NBL) and Southern Boundary Line (SBL), and this fact is what defines the DMZ as demilitarized, even though there are one million troops north of the NBL and more than 600,000 south of the SBL, along with an estimated one million landmines within the DMZ, and more than one million landmines in the southern half alone.[9]

The 1953 Armistice Agreement was signed by the UN forces, the North Korean People's Army, and the Chinese People's Volunteer Army (represented by the North Korean People's Army), with President Syngman Rhee of South Korea unwilling to sign anything that would fall short of the reunification of the nation. The signatories agreed to the terms under the assumption that a solution to the division would be decided within the year. The 1954 Geneva Conference, which was intended to bring about a peaceful resolution to the war, ultimately served to reinscribe the Cold War biopolarity, allowing the United States to set the terms of discussion while satisfying the desires of Britain and the Soviet Union for the "relaxation of world tensions" (Ra 1999: 403). Haruka Matsuda argues that the conference on Korea, coinciding with the conference on Indochina (which established the division of another country, Vietnam), "was the decisive opportunity for the US to act as a 'new empire' in all of East Asia" (Matsuda 2007: 208), while the influence of the old imperial powers, Britain and France, receded. The DMZ, an uneasy outcome of the armistice, thereby represented the inauguration of a new world order, a provisional solution to the international war, and the radically indecisive suspension of the civil war.

At the DMZ, this indecisive condition has led to the continuous and iterative drawing of lines and assertion of positions in a "zone of undecidability" or space of exception (Agamben 2005: 2). Politically, it is an exceptional, extraterritorial space governed in the south by the UN Command Military Armistice Commission (UNCMAC), directed by the US Army, and in the north by the DPRK Army. For both the ROK and DPRK, however, the division is considered to be unconstitutional, and each state is illegitimate in the eyes of the other. Both agree that the DMZ is rightfully part of Korean territory, but each asserts singular sovereignty over that same territory. Yet South Korean sovereignty ends at the SBL.[10] To comply with the Armistice Agreement, any activities within the southern half of the DMZ require UNCMAC approval, making many South Koreans resentful that their own land is controlled by the United States.

The division and ongoing war justify not only the militarization at the border, but also the militarization of everyday life and the normalization of militarized violence in both societies. It also reproduces and underwrites the expansion of US imperial power in the region. With few exceptions, all South Korean men are subject to mandatory two-year military service, and US armed forces have been a continuous presence since the Korean War. The UNCMAC is supported by roughly twenty-nine thousand Eighth US Army forces as well as members of the Korean Augmentation to the United States Army (KATUSA), English-proficient South Korean soldiers who are granted relatively privileged status as part of the Eighth US Army.[11] It was only in 1994 that peacetime command of the ROK army was returned to South Korea, and despite frequent plans to shift wartime command of South Korean defense forces to ROK leadership, these changes in command have been deferred by every administration, most recently by Moon Jae-in, to 2022. Thus, the DMZ area is caught up not only in inter-Korean contests over political legitimacy, but also post–Cold War tensions over military and territorial sovereignty that now characterize the once unshakeable alliance between the ROK and the United States.

The geographic, political, and economic shifts on the South Korean side of the DMZ take place both despite and in relation to the DMZ's status as a militarized and contested space. Indeed, much of the development feeds off the DMZ's allure as an international tourist attraction. In the global imaginary, the DMZ continues to be seen by many, to quote US president Bill Clinton's memorable assessment, as "the scariest place on Earth." It invites other superlative descriptions: the most heavily fortified border, a symbol of the longest running war, and the last Cold War division. These superlatives highlight the ways in which the two Koreas exist at the margins of what is considered to be normative in the global order of things, calling out the assumptions of a progressive model of history in which we are now in a post–Cold War era, or one in which wars end and postcolonial states are expected to transition into liberal democratic governments, lest they be labeled "failed" or "rogue."

In South Korea, the DMZ's associations have shifted over time, from the dark semiotics of the Cold War era to the progressive peace politics of the post–Cold War period (see chapter 1). It is referred to as DMZ, DM-Zed, or *pimujangjidae* (비무장지대), a literal translation of "demilitarized zone," and in place of the MDL (군사분계선; *kunsa pun'gyesŏn*), Koreans refer to the dividing line as the thirty-eighth parallel (삼팔선; *samp'alsŏn*) or the Armistice Line (휴전선; *hyujŏnsŏn*). The word "border" is rarely referred to as such. Even the "Border Area," an administrative designation, is a rough translation of *chŏpkyŏng chiyŏk* (접경지역), which would be more accurately referred to as "frontier area." The Korean word *chŏpkyŏng* emphasizes contiguity over boundary making. In other words, the Border Area is that which is abutting the CCZ, and does not refer to the border with the North. All of these lines and areas have shifted over time. The environmental organization, Green Korea United, through field studies and satellite image analysis, determined that the four-kilometer width of the DMZ had shrunk by 43 percent in the sixty years between 1953 and 2013, with both ROK and DPRK soldiers moving the barbed wire fencing in toward the MDL (Green Korea United 2013b).

Areas of the northern CCZ are thus actually part of the former DMZ, while the CCL has moved northward, making formerly militarily restricted zones part of the civilian Border Area. As I discuss in chapter 2, the zone is therefore far from being merely the location of an immobile standoff. As more areas are freed from the restriction of the CCZ, the area has witnessed increasing numbers of economic development projects. Valérie Gelézeau's assertion that "the persistence, growth and continued emergence of enclaves around the inter-Korean border suggest that the border is anything but static" (2013: 31) continues to ring true.

For decades, the conventional wisdom of political scientists, military experts, and policy makers was that the Korean DMZ was a success story in that it managed to keep the peace for nearly seventy years. For more critical analysts, however, rather than representing peace, the armistice and the MDL are framed as the grounds on which inter-Korean tensions and the threat of war have been continuously reproduced. Historian Steven Lee writes, "Despite the consistent refrain heard over the decades after 1953 that the Armistice had maintained the peace on the Korean peninsula, in many ways the reverse was true—the Armistice had preserved the state of war, and the constant violations of the agreement on both sides had only accelerated the arms buildup on the peninsula" (2013: 206). This unstable relationship with the North has furthermore served as the basis for the asymmetrical, neocolonial relationship between the United States and South Korea, and the justification for state violence and political repression on the part of both South Korean and North Korean regimes. The absence of war, or what peace scholars refer to as "negative peace," is merely a form of peace premised on militarized and imperial logics and does not address the lack of "positive peace," an open-ended concept encompassing "all other good things in the world community, particularly cooperation and integration between human groups" (Galtung 1967: 12).

Progressive scholars and activists in South Korea and the diaspora believe that the resolution of the civil war and reconciliation based on positive peace can only be achieved with the complete withdrawal of US troops and the cessation of political interference (see Baik and Kaisen 2018). More hawkish perspectives are skeptical of this approach because it aligns with the DPRK's demands, which have been consistent in calling for the "obsolete and outdated" Armistice Agreement to be replaced with a peace treaty, as the first step toward lasting peace on the peninsula.[12] In fact, after more than six decades and after multiple violations of the armistice on both sides, not to mention North Korean withdrawals from the agreement, the question of which parties would actually sign any future peace treaty remains unanswered.

Given this history, it could be argued that, the most paradoxical aspect of the DMZ is not that pristine nature coexists with manmade violence, but rather that the thanatopolitical logics of modern military power were for so long unproblematically equated with peace. This dominant view of the DMZ normalizes a militarized and US-centric world order that indiscriminately produces politically and socially exceptional spaces, which are then further normalized when the ecologies they contain are celebrated as accidental by-products of (post)war. Equating those ecologies with peace is another step in a discursive logic that naturalizes the foundational status of war and empire, and "obfuscate[s] an alternative genealogy of arrested decolonization and demilitarization" (Shigematsu and Camacho 2010: xxxii). Given these imperial periodizations and Cold War epistemologies (J. Kim 2010) that dare to represent the most militarized and war-enmeshed spaces as "peaceful," how can we think of the DMZ's ecology as related to peace? What peace, and whose peace?

Fuzzy Peace

When the story of the DMZ is told as "a diplomatic failure turned into an environmental success," to paraphrase historian Lisa Brady (2008), it can serve as a satisfying allegory for our planetary moment, highlighting nature's resilience over the vagaries of human politics. This is what I refer to as the DMZ's "ecological exceptionalism," and that it is depicted as an ironic outcome of war and indecisive peace makes it an even better tale. This narrative not only satisfies the desire of audiences in the United States and other parts of the Global North, who seek optimistic examples to buttress hopes for the future, it also captures the imagination of people in South Korea, for whom the future has always been entangled with collective dreams of and doubts over peace.

In South Korea, peace invariably is defined as "overcoming division," meaning the division between the two Koreas. As I discuss chapter 1, many discourses of peace in the post–Cold War era extended peace to include the transcendence of all forms of difference, scaling up from peace on the peninsula to cosmopolitan peace among all nations and peoples. This operation transforms Korea's tragic and dark associations with the Cold War into a modern and future-oriented symbol that rescues (South) Korea from the margins of world history and places it at the center. Nature and biodiversity have played a key part in South Korean resignifications of the DMZ, producing a hybrid figure that at once naturalizes peace as universal and also pacifies nature as a symbol of an organic moral order.[13]

When I looked to the anthropological literature for guidance on how to approach peace analytically, I found it to be curiously attenuated. Liisa Malkki, in her ethnography of everyday forms of humanitarianism among Finnish aid workers, writes, "peace…is conspicuously not an anthropological category" (2015: 92). In contrast, peace and conflict studies is a wide and diverse field, but, like anthropology, it has tended to focus on the conflict/post-conflict binary more than it has centered on peace per se. Erica Weiss, in her ethnographic research on Israeli conscientious objectors, notes that "militarism has been far more theorized than pacifism" (2012: 86). Both Weiss and Malkki are ambivalent about whether peace deserves to be theorized, suggesting that this absence of theorization is perhaps "legitimate" (Weiss 2012: 86) and "perhaps for good reasons" (Malkki 2015: 92), but both also insist that peace requires greater ethnographic attention—for Weiss, to ask how it challenges the state's monopoly over legitimate violence, and for Malkki, to understand the cultural specificities of peace and its tendency to be "readily infantilized and thus depoliticized" (104).

I share the ambivalence that both Malkki and Weiss express in their approaches to peace because of its "fuzzy and sentimental" associations (Malkki 2015: 104), which are part of the aesthetics of peace in South Korea, and also because of a well-honed anthropological skepticism to anything purporting to be universal—in the sense of ubiquitous or timeless. Yet, as Anna Tsing (2005) usefully suggests, the ethnographic analysis of "actually existing universalisms" requires grappling with the social significance of universals in the everyday lives of anthropologists' interlocutors as well as in our own knowledge production. As she writes, slyly invoking a universal register, "the universal offers us the chance to participate in the global stream of humanity. We can't turn it down" (1).

The simultaneous universality of peace as a concept and its nonexistence as an anthropological category may be explained by the fact that it has always been hiding in plain sight. War (and peace) has been a feature in the history of modern anthropology since its origins in early twentieth-century Europe, and the disciplinary focus on social organization and kinship in small-scale societies was conditioned in part by the crisis of modernity brought on by the conflict and violence of World War I. Marcel Mauss, who lost many of his friends and colleagues in the war, famously concluded his treatise on the gift with an allegory of King Arthur's Round

Table, and a reflection on the relationship between exchange and peace: "Societies have progressed in so far as they themselves, their subgroups, and lastly, the individuals in them, have succeeded in stabilizing relationships, giving, receiving, and finally, giving in return. To trade, the first condition was to be able to lay aside the spear" (Mauss 1990 [1924]: 105).

Thus, peace may not be an anthropological category like exchange, kinship, or religion, but it exists as part of the implicit comparative epistemologies of anthropology (beyond sociobiological categories of "peaceful" and "warlike" societies). Like conflict and power, moreover, peace is inseparable from colonial and postcolonial histories and the material and epistemological violence anthropologists have abetted and resisted. Peace also partakes of "the universal," that which we "cannot not want, even as it so often excludes us" (Tsing 2005: 1; citing Gayatri Spivak). And in that way, like justice, it informs many of the questions we ask about the relevance of our work to political futures and underlies the progressivist impulse in much of contemporary anthropology and cultural studies.

"Peace" appears most explicitly in the work of Bruno Latour in his rejection of the "perpetual peace" of Kantian cosmopolitanism. Building on the concept of cosmopolitics coined by Isabelle Stengers, he offers a new kind of peace but, unlike Malkki and Weiss, expresses no reservations about peace's legitimacy, sentimentality, or fuzziness. Instead, he posits what he calls a "true peace"—as opposed to the "fake peace" of the liberal, Eurocentric world order—which will be the outcome of what he calls the "war of the worlds" (2002), in which plural sciences (as opposed to singular Science) will overcome the Enlightenment reduction of the pluriverse to a universal logic based on a singular Nature. In a less agonistic vein, Arturo Escobar's offers "peace-with-justice," a central part of his theory of the "ecology of difference," which refers to "a set of economic, cultural, and ecological processes that bring about a measure of justice and balance to the natural and social orders" (2008: 17).

How is it that peace can foreclose theorizing, on the one hand, and also become an object of it, on the other? One answer may be that the peace of humanitarianism and pacifism cannot escape its own impossibility because of the overwhelming evidence in our contemporary world that state violence and human warfare cannot be overcome. It is for this reason, as Malkki observes, that peace can be accused of evacuating history and also can be "readily infantilized" (2015: 104). But the peace of Latour and Escobar returns a hopeful orientation to anthropology through what Ghassan Hage calls "alter-politics," a mode of critical anthropology that centers radical alterity. This is an optimistic view of how the study of difference can lead to new conceptual, political, and ethical possibilities—"we can be other than we are" (2012: 300; see Miyazaki 2006 on hope in social theory).

The peace imaginaries and processes that appear in this book hinge between pessimism and optimism—constituting what might be called a "fuzzy peace." Fuzzy here is not of the cute and fuzzy variety (though it can be that), but fuzzy in the sense of incipient, residual, and emergent formations, affects, and structures of feeling (Williams 1976). It emerges out of a space of (im)possibility—between the impossibility of cosmopolitan peace in the liberal internationalist, militaristic order of things and the possibilities opened by a cosmopolitical peace in the more-than-human modes of relating that I experienced with my interlocutors. Fuzzy peace is, in this way—like ethnography and our (im)possible relationship to our own universalisms—a practice of sensing the outlines of emergent worlds and pulling them momentarily into focus.

In contemporary South Korea, the unstable distinctions between war/peace and conflict/post-conflict are already blurry, and the DMZ region is now a site where military/civilian spaces are hybridizing and physical borders are shifting dramatically. In this context, peace is a ubiquitous yet ambiguous and inherently multiple concept. This is the condition of unending war, in a gray zone of "peacelessness" (N. Kim 2017: 220), what I frame in the following pages as peace under erasure.

~~Peace~~

Despite the persistence of hardline anti-Communist sentiments among some South Koreans, after more than seventy-five years of division, many express an openness to alternative ways of thinking about war, peace, division, and unification, and these visions have embraced a hopeful, speculative, and non-prescriptive logic. Samuel Collins cogently identifies this cultural mood of hope as "simultaneously future-oriented and retrograde." This hope, in his assessment, points to "the achievement of a unified Korea that is at the same time a return to the unified past. But, importantly, this is not recourse to an impotent nostalgia or a refusal to change with changing times" (2013: 140). This shift in the politics of unification marks a turn away from the desire for the restitution of an organic ethnic nation (Grinker 1998) to a more prospective, post-ideological, and potentially generative futurity.

The DMZ is a screen on which these multiple and heterotopic visions and desires have been projected. Whereas in Western representations of the DMZ a simplistic juxtaposition of war and nature frames it as ironic, in many South Korean narratives, there is an added pathos for those who cannot help but value the hopeful vitality that has emerged out of the tragedy and traumas of war and national division. "The DMZ Lives!" (DMZ는 살아 있다) is the telling title of a 2013 MBC television documentary series on the topic. This is the sentimental core of cultural representations of the DMZ in South Korea, where peace has been, for more than half a century, *sous rature*, or under erasure. Following Jacques Derrida's Heideggerian formulation, to consider peace under erasure is to deconstruct its metaphysical presence while also acknowledging its indispensability and inadequacy as a signifier (Derrida 1976). It is an aspiration and an idea that lacks a clear referent or telos.

While there is widespread desire, especially among progressive activists, for positive peace and the values of justice and freedom it represents, within both the pragmatic politics of engagement and the utopian politics of ethnonationalist recovery, it has always existed in dialectical relationship to unending war and capitalist hegemony.[14] In fact, the transformation of the DMZ region into the touristic PLZ in 2007 is part of a wider politics of memory in South Korea. Sheila Miyoshi Jager and Jiyul Kim argue that "South Korea's post–Cold War and post–Korean War consciousness [shifted] from a 'war' narrative to a 'peace' narrative…[which] also brought a fundamental reevaluation of US–South Korea relations" (2007: 264). They link a "peace politics" ushered in by the Roh Moo-hyun administration (2003–8) to a pan-Korean nationalism that reframed the Cold War mutual defense posture of the United States–ROK alliance against the common enemy of North Korea into a pre–Korean War spirit of national defense that allies all Koreans, North and South, against foreign aggressors, including Japanese and US empires. This shift also entailed a change in the commemoration of war—instead of the national remembrance of June 25 (the day that North Korean forces attacked the South), July 27, Armistice Day, has gained in increasing symbolic relevance as an opportunity to foreground a "progressive peace system between the two Koreas" (Cho Hŭi-yŏn, cited in Jager and Kim 2007: 258).

As "peace" became a keyword in South Korean state discourses and resignifications of post–Cold War nationalism, however, it also became commodified and simplified. Seunghei Clara Hong (2015), in her analysis of the war memorial at No-Gun-Ri, rightly asks, "What peace, whose peace?" observing that peace is presented as "an empty, abstract concept, devoid of any political or ideological value" (196). The detached concept of peace seemed to take on more concrete directions with the unprecedented dialogue and engagement between President Moon Jae-in of South Korea and Kim Jong Un of North Korea, starting with the Panmunjom Declaration of April 2018. That mood of euphoria was short-lived, however, and for peace activists in Korea and elsewhere who advance a notion of peace beyond that of the liberal internationalist order, it remains the case that whatever form peace takes for the two Koreas, it will likely exceed that of a state-centric peace treaty and fall short of any idealized vision of national unification.

The political logics of peace and unification have multiplied over the course of the past seven decades of the division, along a wide spectrum of positions, from left-wing to right-wing, from the prewar generation to cosmopolitan millennials. Whether peace precedes or follows unification and whether peace without unification is an acceptable goal are topics of endless debate, even as, for many South Koreans, the status of the division and the threat of North Korea typically exist far from their everyday concerns. Sociologist Hyun Ok Park, however, argues that a capital-driven "transnational form of Korean unification" (2015: 7) has already been achieved, during the Sunshine Policy era. She critiques this form of unification (through neoliberal capital) and trenchantly captures the contemporary moment in which "the appeal for Korean unification has been reconfigured into a transnational form by the new global system of neoliberal capitalism and its utopian politics" (288). For Park, the "national utopia" of mass liberation that characterized the reunification imaginaries for the leftist democratization movement of the 1970s and 1980s (민중운동; *minjung undong*) has entirely given way to the "market utopia" of the 1990s, particularly in light of the Asian financial crisis and the embrace of free trade as the solution for both economic crises: South Korea's crisis capitalism, and North Korea's crisis of economic isolation in the post-socialist world.[15] During the Sunshine Policy decade, the DMZ was the literal site of engagement, where the peace of ethnonational restitution was actively transformed into the peace of unification through capital (H. O. Park 2015: 195).

In fact, one reason that progressive administrations have not been a boon for the DMZ's conservation is because, in the scenario of inter-Korean cooperation, the DMZ's nature could be seen as an impediment to economically driven unification. It is no surprise, then, that during the hawkish administrations of Lee Myung-bak and Park Geun-hye, when the enmity between the two Koreas was at an all-time high, plans to turn the DMZ into a peace park or biosphere reserve were seen as worthy and exciting. Those administrations were also periods in which DMZ ecotourism was actively promoted and pursued at all levels of government, from national to regional levels. As soon as Moon Jae-in's engagement policy gained a foothold, however, the significance of the DMZ as an ecological asset radically diminished. A sense of foreboding among those who value protection of the DMZ's ecology was made apparent to me at a forum on the topic, held at the National Assembly building in July 2018. There, Choe Jae Chun (Ch'oe Jae Ch'ŏn), professor of ecology at Ewha Womans University and the former head of the National Institute of Ecology, described his discordant reaction to the April 2018 inter-Korean summit and the possibility of peace on the peninsula: "In this mood of interKorean 'thawing,' many people are feeling their hearts beating with anticipation (가슴이 벌렁벌렁). Instead, mine was beating with dread (가슴이 철렁철렁). There are twenty roads and rail lines that have been severed by the DMZ—it's a very thin and vulnerable space."

Making Peace with Nature

In the shadow of these global geopolitical dramas and domestic policies, numerous scholars, bureaucrats, environmentalists, and journalists in South Korea and transnationally debate the future of the DMZ and its sustainable development—particularly regarding how to include local residents in the process while creating as small a human footprint as possible. In contrast, I sought to understand how knowledge of the DMZ's nature and the biodiversity that it hosts was being produced, valued, and leveraged.

In chapter 1, I unpack the ubiquity and polysemy of discourses of peace in relation to the DMZ's nature and examine how its ecological exceptionalism opened new conceptual and material possibilities for South Koreans. In these new peace imaginaries, "nature" (자연; *chayŏn*) and "life" (생명; *saengmyŏng*; "life" or "living beings") served to defamiliarize politics as usual and reoriented the scale of perception from the national division to the global or cosmopolitan, and this reorientation was experienced and framed as both progressive and hopeful. Yet, in these discourses, life or nature served a symbolic function that could be instrumentalized for human political preoccupations, particularly through the state's promotion of the PLZ. This market-driven logic simplified and singularized "nature" as a commodity and attached it to an abstract and ahistorical notion of peace.

In contrast to the dehistoricizing simplification and the utopian teleology of the PLZ, the ecologists I worked with were highly attuned to the multiple timescapes and material changes taking place in the CCZ, where the majority of scientific research takes place. When I first met Kim Seung Ho, founder and director of the small NGO, DMZ Ecology Research Institute (DERI), in October 2011, I asked about the relationship between the DMZ's nature and peace, at a moment of heightened tensions between the two Koreas. Kim's answer revealed that peace needn't be only human oriented. According to him, peace had "nothing to do with North or South, leftwing or rightwing." He asserted that those parties interested in the DMZ's ecology were oriented toward political interests that could only understand the DMZ's ecological life as a means, not an end. He went on to say, "Regarding the concept of peace—well, ultimately, if you're talking about science—science is about making things concrete (구체화), so if ideology (이데올로기; i.e., Cold War politics) tries to include science, peace is exceedingly difficult. Therefore, when referring to the DMZ's peace, [politicians] are only talking about political peace. For me, what seems more important is biological peace (생물학적 평화)."

Kim's notion of biological peace offers a key analytic for this book. He highlighted the fact that "peace" is not only a human construct, but also one that privileges human protagonists. My gloss of "biological" is a rough translation of what Kim more literally referred to as "life-sciences peace." In other words, peace as understood through scientific knowledge of biological life forms. Biological peace therefore differs from other peace and life discourses in South Korea, but it also contributes to the heterogeneity of ideas that come together under that banner. These include state-centric discourses that instrumentalize nature for peaceful engagement, environmentalist projects that defend the DMZ's rare nature in the name of a progressive vision of peace and life against the forces of neoliberal development, and the notion of biological peace, which displaces South Korean politics of the national division and reformulates peace by centering nonhuman nature.

In my rendering, biological peace is related to a biocentric vision embodied in Aldo Leopold's "land ethic" (1989 [1949]) and draws on South Korean discourses and practices of life philosophy (생명사상; *saengmyŏng sasang*). It also resonates with the peace of cosmopolitics, as mentioned earlier. Cosmopolitics is oriented around a rejection of Kantian metaphysics and his vision of cosmopolitanism, framed as a perpetual peace grounded in Enlightenment reason and universal science. According to Bruno Latour, Isabelle Stengers, John Law, and others, this "one-world" vision of universal peace has been imposed coercively on the non-West. In contrast, a cosmopolitical response (Stengers 2005) submits a non-ethnocentric, non-Eurocentric, and non-anthropocentric vision of peace that promotes a pluriverse of relations, irreducible to a single cosmos or world. From one world to many, from worlds to worldings, from a singular Nature to multi-naturalism, both the ontological turn and multispecies ethnography have found inspiration in emergent entanglements of humans and nonhumans, which include animate and inanimate forces.

Kim's statement draws a distinction between the peace of politicians and the peace of nature, associating the former with ideology and the latter with science. This statement might suggest that he is invested in the Enlightenment logics of objective science that Latour and his colleagues have strenuously critiqued. As I discuss in more ethnographic detail in the chapters that follow, however, for Kim, science's concreteness is not necessarily derived from an underlying universal truth. Rather, it is the concreteness itself that grounds peace in practices of scientific observation and data gathering in ways that recall Lévi-Strauss's famous discussion of the "science of the concrete" from *The Savage Mind* (1966).

A former member of the DERI complained to me on more than one occasion that the problem with the group was its research was purely descriptive and wasn't guided by any theory. In contrast to his privileging of a certain kind of epistemological value, I found fertile connections between the quotidian practices of my interlocutors in their entanglements with nonhuman others and the contributions of feminist science and technology studies scholars such as Karen Barad, Vinciane Despret, and Donna Haraway, whose notions of "relational ontology" (Barad 2007), ethical "enacting" (Despret 2013), and "becoming with" (Haraway 2008) foreground the intra-active agencies of humans and nonhumans. In her research with natural scientists, feminist philosopher Despret refers to ethical forms of knowledge production as "enacting," and I found that South Korean ecologists engage in practices that could be described in similar terms. Enacting, she writes, "blurs the clear cut divide between knowing subject and known object: Scientists and animals are fleshly creatures which are enacted and enacting through their embodied choreography. This is not only an epistemological issue it is a political one and an ontological one" (2013: 69). A focus on my interlocutors' practices of data gathering, observation, and their quotidian encounters with the nonhumans they study reveals biological peace to be a process that often entails the decentering of human exceptionalism.[16]

The Infrastructure of Division

It is telling that Choe Jae Chun framed his concern for the DMZ's eco-logical protection around infrastructural links between the two Koreas. When people think about development of the DMZ or in the DMZ region, it invariably has to do with transportation infrastructures that will provide the material basis for human connection. The discourses of peace (평화; *p'yŏnghwa*), mutual understanding (소통), and exchange and cooperation (교류와 협조) all depend on these links, particularly roads and rail lines.[17] But this infrastructure is not just about inter-Korean connections—it has also shaped the debate around the CCZ and Border Area when it comes to DMZ-related tourism and economic development.

Although both Gangwon and Gyeonggi Provinces are actively plan-ning for their central roles and locations in a unified peninsula, until that time, their more immediate goals are focused on enhancing economic de-velopment through tourism. To draw more visitors to the Border Area, the central government's 2011 Comprehensive Plan for Border Development (2011–30) has entailed the expansion of roads and rebuilding of defunct rail links as well as a DMZ-wide trail, called the Pyeonghwa Nuri Trail (평화누리길; Peace World Trail) that has been expanded since the 2018 Panmunjom Summit to include Peace Trails inside the actual DMZ.[18]

Early in my fieldwork, I came across the word *inp'ŭra* (인프라) frequently, and it took me a moment to realize that it was a transliterated abbreviation for "infrastructure." *Inp'ŭra* was what the "local people" (지역주민) wanted and what had been denied them during the many decades that they lived under the tightest of militarized restrictions due to national security con-cerns. *Inp'ŭra* referred primarily to transportation infrastructure—roads, bridges, rail lines, and bike paths that would connect their villages to their regional capitals, but most importantly to the flows of capital emanating from the Seoul metropolitan area.

Undeniably, for local residents, the lack of infrastructure development has been central to their feelings of abandonment and isolation, particu-larly for those in the remote villages and mountainous areas of Gangwon Province. In Gyeonggi Province, which has benefited from its proximity to Seoul, infrastructure, particularly trains and railroads, has been a frequently deployed symbol used by local and central governments to represent future unification. But it also reflects the urgency local residents feel about their cultural and social distance from the nation. In the post–Cold War DMZ era, therefore, military infrastructures and civilian infrastructures exist side by side, and they are materially potent symbols deployed by the state in ways that spatially and culturally define the twenty-first century South Korean borderlands.

What I refer to as the "infrastructure of division" was installed during the 1960s and became increasingly fortified during that decade. In coordination with the state's anti-Communist juridical and political projects, it was designed to prevent and disrupt flows—of people, products, media, and ideologies. The physical elements of this peacekeeping spatial order include barbed wire, landmines, guard posts, tank barriers, trenches, surveillance cameras, bases and military installments, firing ranges, training grounds, ammunitions storage facilities, and the like. It has been remarkably successful, but its near impermeability has led to the evolution of other circuits—as North Koreans seek escape via northern routes into China, for instance, or the citizens of Pyongyang rig their television sets to pick up South Korean soap operas (see S.-Y. Kim 2011).

The brutal aesthetics of the division infrastructure, which are easily commodified by dark tourism into romanticized images—such as camouflage paint peeling off the facades of concrete barriers, shallow trenches lined with army-green sandbags, or the ubiquitous barbed wire and landmine warning signs—underscore the past temporality of the DMZ as a Cold War holdover, violently and irrationally impeding co-ethnic amity and neoliberal capitalism's triumphant, borderless world.[19] For the South Korean state, this territorial problem is also an economic problem—infrastructural connections linking South Korea to North Korea would open up more efficient land routes to Eurasia for South Korean products, as well as gas pipelines from Russia into the fossil fuel–starved peninsula. At the regional level, the Military Installations Protection Districts (MIPD; 군사시설보호구역) are defined by their distance from the MDL. The area, which constitutes 5 percent of South Korea's territory, encompasses more than 90 percent of Paju City, Yeoncheon County, and Cheorwon County, which all exist within fifty kilometers of the MDL (Gelézeau 2013: 17). The injunction against infrastructure development is one of the primary restrictions on economic growth in the border areas and produces an outsized sense of distance from the metropolitan center: Paju City Hall, for instance, is just thirty-one miles from Seoul City Hall, and Cheorwon County Hall is just fifty-eight miles.

South Korean president Moon Jae-in's peace economy and inter-Korean engagement policy took on material substance through infrastructure. Removing landmines and the spectacular implosion of a guard post in 2018 were both examples of the South Korean state transitioning from the militarized infrastructure of contested sovereignty, containment, and division to the capitalist infrastructure of transnational flows, or inter-Korean exchange and cooperation. But Moon's highly symbolic moves to demilitarize the DMZ were not a far departure from nearly every previous president since Roh Tae-woo's *Nordpolitik* engagement policy in 1989. As Valérie Gélézeau notes, the "growth of the South Korean Capital Region is now being driven towards the north" (2013: 32), and the infrastructure of division no longer privileges stasis and blockage, but rather promotes the possibilities of connection, like the road connecting the Kaeseong Industrial Complex to the southern side of the DMZ, and the Dongui and Gyeongui rail lines, however restricted or unutilized they may be.

In fact, the lines separating the various military and civilian areas in the DMZ have shifted continually over the years, liberating formerly military restricted areas. Even the barbed wire marking the southern and northern limit lines has been moved by soldiers on either side of the border, narrowing the DMZ itself. Thus, as the South Korean Border Area liberalizes, two overlapping regimes of power and spatial control—sovereign exception and biopolitical discipline (Foucault 2009)—are being materialized through infrastructures of bordering and circulation, of militarization and capitalism. These infrastructures reflect what Wendy Brown identifies as a "series of paradoxes" in a "post-Westphalian order" (2010: 21). Central to these paradoxes are the contradictory values of closure and openness. Despite the globalization of capital, and in light of proliferating transnational flows, states are erecting militarized barriers or installing, in the case of the United States–Mexico border, a "tactical infrastructure" (Jusionyte 2018) to counteract perceived threats from non-state actors.

These tactical infrastructures may be less monolithic than the infrastructure of division at the DMZ, but they make the DMZ seem less anachronistic than it may have in the aftermath of the fall of the Berlin Wall. Indeed, US president Donald Trump's June 2019 invocation of the Korean DMZ as a "real border" and an implicit model for his United States–Mexico border wall suggests how these seeming anachronisms may become reconciled and normalized should protectionist ideologies and xenophobic nationalisms continue to gain political legitimacy.[20] If other states are fortifying their borders against refugees and illicit commodities to make them more akin to the DMZ, the DMZ, over the decades, has become spatially, politically, and symbolically a hybrid military-capitalist zone, with tactical openings to allow for limited exchanges between the two Korean states, especially during periods of diplomatic warming.

Fieldwork in "Naturalcultural Borderlands"

My research for this book was limited to areas accessible to me as an ethnic Korean woman with a US passport. Although tours to North Korea have grown in number over the past decade, most of them are explicit in prohibiting participants from writing about their experiences in scholarly publications. Given my commitment to fine-grained, long-term ethnography, researching the DMZ from the North Korean side could only offer data of a fly-by-night nature. This book therefore focuses on the South Korean side of the DMZ and, more specifically, on what might be called the South Korean "naturalcultural borderlands" (Kirksey and Helmreich 2010: 548), the areas immediately abutting the southern side of the DMZ.

The data that inform my analyses were gathered between 2011 and 2016, primarily in the CCZ, the area immediately south of the DMZ proper. These limitations of access are also ones that constrain South Korean ecological researchers, only one of whom has explicit permission from the UN Command to conduct intermittent ecological surveys inside the DMZ (K.-g. Kim 2010). It was not until 2014 that annual surveys of the DMZ were conducted by the National Institute of Ecology. Despite this fact, the DMZ brand had been building into a powerful one that dozens of DMZ-related organizations, NGOs, and projects were capitalizing on for several years, referring to their work on the DMZ, even as their actual purview was restricted to the CCZ. This slippage is reinforced in recent policy discourses that include the CCZ in what is designated as the "DMZ region," which encompasses the CCZ and the Border Area (접경지역).

The entire region is directly affected by the national division, militarism, and the shifting political economy related to the DMZ as it has been defined over the past six decades—as both the military forward areas (전방지역) and as a neoliberal economic frontier, generating increasingly hybrid spaces of division and connection, of militarized security and capital flows. This invention of the DMZ region in South Korea has very little to do with North Korea and everything to do with particular economic, political, and social conjunctures on the southern side of the border, in the contexts of national and transnational environmental movements and economic neoliberalization.

Considering the large expanse of the DMZ region, I had to make choices about what I would do and where I would spend my time. It would be impossible to achieve a holistic survey of the DMZ. There are eight extant villages in the CCZ and two inside the DMZ proper—one South Korean, the other North Korean. Regular access to any one of those villages would have been very difficult, if not impossible, to secure. I therefore sought to align my fieldwork with that of ecological researchers conducting regular fieldwork in the DMZ region. The DMZ Ecology Research Institute was the only NGO that regularly monitored the ecology in the CCZ, with a focus on the western coast, north of Paju, where the organization's office is located. I participated in nearly all of their weekly research and educational activities between October 2011 and June 2012, as well as during shorter visits between 2013 and 2015. I draw on this research in chapter 2, where I discuss the small irrigation ponds that they analyzed in the spring and summer months.

I also spent time in Cheorwon, a county in Gangwon Province, which, due to its position in the center of the peninsula and its history as a rice-growing region, was a political and economic nexus in the premodern and colonial eras. Because of its proximity to the border and former inclusion in the militarily restricted CCZ, Cheorwon, along with other northern counties in Gangwon Province, has been viewed as culturally inferior and economically stagnant. High-speed transportation infrastructure has recently made Cheorwon a convenient day trip from Seoul and a destination for domestic tourists from the capital. It offers a rich and multilayered history as the ancient capital of Taebong, a state ruled by King Gung Ye during the later Three Kingdoms period (892–936), a central transportation hub during the Japanese colonial period (1910–45), a highly contested battleground during the Korean War, and, today, a primary wintering site for endangered birds.

Multiple stays in Cheorwon between 2012 and 2015 permitted me to witness rapid changes to infrastructure as well as to learn of how the lives and lifeways of residents were being caught up in state and regional projects related to the PLZ. Plans for ecotourism and conservation have been heavily promoted as promissory notes for the economically depressed areas in Gangwon Province, where the category of "local people" has become a key term in policy and tourism discourses. Whereas ecologists focused on nonhuman biota in the DMZ region, I learned from residents about the contested meanings of "environment," which is more closely associated with military waste and landmine pollution than with the pristine picture of the PLZ (chapter 4). In addition, because of Cheorwon's significance as a winter habitat for endangered birds, I came to know Dr. Lee Kisup, an ornithologist and expert on cranes and waterbirds. I participated in his Waterbird Network Korea and Korea Crane Network, overlapping groups of South Korean bird lovers that promote research on the birds and public awareness about their highly endangered status.

The period in which much of this research took place was marked by heightened tensions between the two Koreas. A conservative turn in South Korean politics in 2008 had effectively dismantled the previous decade's Sunshine Policy. The reversal—from engagement to sanctions and from rapprochement to rebuke—also witnessed the inflation of the stature and value of the DMZ's nature in South Korea, as the hawkish and neoliberal government actively leveraged the zone's symbolics of peace for both political and economic ends. During this dark period of political stalemate, if not crisis, centrists and progressives alike continued using the phrase "peaceful utilization of the DMZ" to advance unification efforts. At the same moment, an ecological turn in South Korean environmental movements, as well as the "green agenda" of then president Lee Myung-bak (2008–13), created new funding opportunities for studies of the DMZ, especially in 2011, when he pushed for the southern half of the DMZ to be designated a UNESCO biosphere reserve. That effort was ultimately stymied by North Korea, but Lee's successor, Park Geun-hye, continued to pursue the possibilities of peaceful utilization when she announced her plans to turn the DMZ into an international peace park in 2013.

In contrast to policy makers and bureaucrats who sought to "make peace with nature" by instrumentalizing the DMZ's ecologies in the name of fundamentally nationalist or statist projects, others who engaged directly with the ecologies of the DMZ were "making peace with nature" through other means—by elevating the significance of nonhuman life and foregrounding reconciliation, not between North Koreans and South Koreans but between humans and their environments. In these diverse ways, the existence of the DMZ's rare biodiversity provided the material and symbolic basis for a heterogeneous and collective peace imaginary that ultimately defied tidy binaries of anthropocentric and biocentric, anthropomorphic and multispecies, nationalist and cosmopolitical. In fact, part of the persistent allure of the DMZ's nature is that it is inseparable from the national division and the geopolitics of the (post-)Cold War, yet the biodiversity that lives there can never be fully captured by human knowledge practices and ideologies.

Eventually, my ethnographic gaze homed in on three assemblages: ponds, avian flyways, and landmines. I frame these assemblages as alternative infrastructures in that they are human–nonhuman–technical networks that exist in relation to the infrastructure of division, while generating other flows, circulations, and temporalities. These flows, circulations, and temporalities, in turn, often exceed the material and imaginative bounds of capitalist logics, sovereign power, ethnonationalist teleologies, and anthropocentric metaphysics. These alternative infrastructures reveal the DMZ's nature to be impure and endangered but also cosmopolitical. In contrast to prevalent discourses of ecological exceptionalism in South Korea and internationally, which frame the DMZ's nature as pure, timeless, and symbolically representative of a future Korea, ponds, avian flyways, and landmines offer modes of imagining peace beyond the human.

The Chapters

Chapter 1, "In the Meantime of Division," analyzes how the DMZ's nature came to be recognized as valuable for a diverse range of social actors, particularly in the early 2000s. If discourses of ecological exceptionalism abstracted the DMZ's nature as a symbol of peace, what I call the "the meantime of division" designates a specific spatiotemporality in the late–Cold War era. South Korean desires for peace and the impossibility of imagining geopolitical amity outside of capitalist relations created the conditions in which the DMZ and its rare nature took on significant symbolic and material value. With the waxing and waning of inter-Korean détente and cooperation, the actually existing biodiversity of the DMZ drew ecologists and others to the border areas, precisely because of its "substantiality" (구체성). The CCZ in particular became a site of encounter, with metropolitan environmentalists, state bureaucrats, local people, tourists, and others meeting each other in the borderlands and, in effect, discursively and performatively producing the DMZ's nature. These performances take place in a meantime that is not static but oscillating—between aspirations and hopes for forward movement out of the present impasse and a resigned acceptance of the continuous deferral of peace. Chapter 1 frames the chronopolitics of actually existing biodiversity in the DMZ in a present and near future (Guyer 2007) that stands in contrast to revanchist Cold War ideological binaries that continue to influence division politics and dispensationalist imaginaries focused on a utopian future to come.

Chapter 2, "Ponds," introduces the Paju DMZ area, where agricultural fields dominate the landscape but where security restrictions require farmers to rely on premodern irrigation technologies in the form of *dumbeong* (둠벙; small rainwater-fed irrigation ponds). These ponds are highly biodiverse, but the landscapes of the Paju DMZ area are also shifting, under economic pressures to open the CCZ area to further inter-Korean coopera-tion and tourism and to exploit the land for more highly profitable crops. I frame *dumbeong* as negative infrastructure, in that they, and the knowledge produced about them, would not exist were it not for the infrastructure of division.

If these ponds help us to understand the DMZ's value as more than the site of inevitable inter-Korean economic cooperation and development, then chapter 3, "Birds," takes the avian flyways of black-faced spoonbills as a particular human–nonhuman–technical infrastructure that intervenes into the timeless ethnonationalist myths of primordial Korea. Like the ponds, the habitats of birds are protected by the division, but it does not mean that the birds transcend human politics through their eternal migratory journeys. Against unification imaginaries that frame the Korean nation as a family divided, I show how the division opens up spaces for "strange kinship" (Merleau-Ponty 2003: 214) between humans and avian creatures. This is accomplished through arduous conservation efforts of ornithological researchers and bird lovers who use visual technologies to understand and protect endangered birds who suffer from the effects of development, land reclamation, and climate change, even as they find tem-porary refuge in the militarized spaces of the DMZ area.

Lastly, chapter 4, "Landmines," shifts attention to a different kind of nonhuman assemblage through the framework of rogue infrastructures—these are constituted by the widespread problem of landmines in the CCZ area—where dozens of minefields exist and where the longevity of land-mines terrorizes local residents. The long life spans of landmines introduce another chronopolitics of the meantime, against post-war narratives that frame mines as a problem of the past, or else as being safely contained within the DMZ. As peace and life discourses circulate through state policy and tourism ventures, the existence and persistence of landmines reveal how US policies that maintain the "Korea exception" to keep mines on the Korean peninsula in the name of military security attempt to resignify landmines as humanitarian "peacekeepers," even as they extend the effects of the war into the present. Mines have widespread consequences for local people, killing and maiming residents, destroying families and livelihoods, restricting land use, and generating fear. At the same time, I suggest that a framing of mine victims as only abject subjects of the state's thanato-politics misses the more complex ways that people exist within landmine-contaminated landscapes. The mines "protect" nature from human development, but they also have multiple and heterogeneous effects.

The Epilogue reflects on the DMZ's ecologies as an occasion to consider how to conceptualize peace as more-than-human. Viewed from a certain distance, de/militarized ecologies have become more normative than exceptional in the context of post–World War II military and capital expansion at a planetary scale. With this in mind, I suggest that biological peace is a necessary framework for appreciating the impure, polluted, and endangered life that exists. It is from this situated location that we can begin to reconfigure our relationships to nonhuman others and the Earth and begin to imagine peace beyond merely human politics.

IN THE MEANTIME OF DIVISION

When I first entered the CCZ in autumn 2011, I was immediately struck by this image (figure 1.1), which appeared on the dashboard of Dr. Rhee's Jeep. After our IDs had been checked and verified, we were waved through the military checkpoint at the interchange of Reunification Road (통일로) and Freedom Road (자유로). Now inside the CCZ, we were just a few kilometers from the Joint Security Area, where soldiers face off across the MDL, the official boundary between North and South Korea. In this part of the DMZ region, the main topographic points of reference are the Han River estuary to the west, the Imjin River to the east, the Gongneung stream to the south, Chopyeong Island to the northeast, and Songak Mountain (North Korea) to the northwest. Once past the checkpoint, however, the bottom half of the car's Global Positioning System (GPS) turned white, like a flat empty beach on a virtual planet, with only a strip of ornamental blue mountains appearing on the digital horizon.[1]

The empty terrain on the GPS was less secret than sites of other covert military activity, what geographer and artist Trevor Paglen calls "blank spots on the map" (2010: 11), but its sudden appearance nevertheless identified the area as highly sensitive to national security. This flat, white expanse representing the most heavily militarized border in the world was also a visual reminder I was now in a space of exception, seemingly incommensurable with the hypercartographic spaces of cosmopolitan South Korea, where nearly every intersection and alleyway have been mapped and plotted and where urbanites are tethered to technologies that are continuously augmenting and extending the grid. Here, the capitalist-driven informational infrastructures of urban South Korea were replaced by a security regime of militarized control and sovereign exception.

When I pointed out the blank GPS screen to Dr. Rhee, who was driving, he laughed, assuming that I was worried that we wouldn't have it to guide us. He sought to reassure me by saying, "We don't need the Navi; we know this area better than anyone else." In-

Figure 1.1

The flat white expanse on the GPS upon entering the CCZ. October 2011. Photograph by the author.

deed, while I looked to the GPS for epistemological certainty or representational grounding in what Henri Lefebvre called "conceived space" (1991), I soon discovered how Dr. Rhee and his colleagues navigated their own paths across this landscape, co-producing, in Lefebvre's terms, the "perceived spaces" and "lived spaces" of the DMZ's nature—through socially embedded knowledge practices and engagements in intimate landscapes with nonhuman life forms. As I learned about the DMZ area through my interlocutors, I began to understand its multiplicity, particularly as it was abstracted into a kind of tabula rasa or even terra nullius, making the white expanse on the Navi an apt visual metaphor for how it has served as a screen for the projection of multiple desires, hopes, experiments, and visions.

In 1995, Richard Grinker described the "living museum" of the DMZ as distinct from other national museums in that it does not refer nostalgically to an idyllic past nor does it project a bright future. Instead, it gains symbolic force from the ongoing tensions between the Koreas (32). In the decades following Grinker's assessment, the DMZ has continued to depend on the national division, but its symbolism has also undergone radical revisions, spatially and temporally. Today, "ecology" (생태) and "nature" (자연) project a utopian future-past, in which the DMZ's nature has been "restored" (자연복원), and thereby symbolizes "peace" (평화) in the present that can model a future peaceful unification. This resignification is key to the DMZ's ecological exceptionalism, which gains symbolic power from the unexpected juxtaposition of war and ecology, categories that, like those of culture and nature, are often conceptualized as mutually exclusive, if not oppositional. This exceptionalism imbues the DMZ with a kind of natural sovereignty, idealizing nature as transcendent of war, violence, state sovereignty, and indeed all human politics.

Before moving on to the next chapters, which bring to the foreground the human and nonhuman enactments and alternative infrastructures that constitute the DMZ's ecologies, this chapter assembles an archive of texts and ethnographic evidence that together show how various social actors "made peace with nature" by associating its natural restoration with inter-Korean peace and cosmopolitan peace across the Cold War and post–Cold War periods. These associations were so ubiquitous in the 2010s that it was sometimes difficult to parse their polysemous significance. When first I began my fieldwork in late 2011, I alternatively dismissed or recoiled at their sentimental and romanticizing connotations, viewing the syrupy sweet aesthetics of things such as the DMZ Peace Train as hollow symbols (figure 1.2). This was easy to do, particularly during the hawkish Lee Myung-bak administration, since actual peaceful engagement with the North had become so remote. But I had to grapple with the fact that many times, when my interlocutors referred to the DMZ as "the land of peace and life," they were not doing so cynically or ironically, even if they, like Dr. Rhee, critiqued the idea of the government's PLZ as another example of the failures of the state and the excesses of neoliberalism.[2]

Because North Korea has always predicated a peace park on a peace treaty, the relationship between peace and nature has been primarily a South Korean concern. Whereas policy makers focused on green détente, or seeking apolitical environmental cooperation (usually through international bodies such as the UN) as the means toward establishing political peace between the two Koreas, during the Lee Myung-bak administration (2008–13), the connection between the DMZ and inter-Korean peace was

often utterly absent. This was reflected in the intentional "blank spots on the map," namely, North Korean territory, left as an unmarked space or fuzzy margin on the numerous maps of the DMZ area published by government ministries and tourism boards. This fact does not mean that North Korea has not been part of the larger picture, of course. One of the early South Korean representations of the DMZ's natural richness is a 1973 propaganda film produced about the border zone, which touted the transformation of the DMZ as a "paradise" (낙원) for wildlife.[3]

Representations such as these permitted the South Korean state to claim patrimony over the DMZ, particularly through the Office of Cultural Properties, which used designations such as "cultural property" and "natural monuments" to define (South) Korea's national heritage (Pai 2013). In similar ways, the moves by President Lee Myung-bak to gain international designation for the DMZ could be seen as part of a repertoire of "peace offensives" (평화공세) that acted as provocations to the North by using peace as a token in the broader geopolitical scene (see chapter 2).

Figure 1.2
The DMZ Peace Train was inaugurated in 2014 along the newly extended Gyeongwon rail line, which now extends from Seoul to Baekmagoji Station, a location in Gangwon Province close to the DMZ. Before the division, the rail line ran from Seoul to the northern city of Wonsan. Today, the Gyeongwon and Gyeongui lines are part of a larger state-promoted infrastructural project to link the border areas more efficiently to Seoul. The cars of the train represent peace, love, and unity, and exemplify the sentimental aesthetics of the PLZ, which seeks to rebrand the DMZ as a tourist destination and also resignify the DMZ as a site of inter-Korean peace and economic cooperation.

Given all the civilian activity in the border region since the 2000s, it might be difficult to comprehend how off-limits the DMZ area had been for the first several decades of South Korea's existence. During my fieldwork, I often heard reminiscences among middle-aged South Korean men who had served their mandatory military service along the DMZ, but few had reason to return because it was a space that represented intense fortification against an enemy that threatened South Korea's very existence.

Professor Kim Chin-hwan of the Reunification Humanities Research Center at Geonkuk University paints a stark picture:

> On the one hand, the peninsula has been divided for more than sixty years, which has been a very long time. On the other hand, and astonishingly, the time for citizens [of South Korea] to attend to the material symbolism of division, has been rather short. Before the democratization of South Korean society [in 1987], the DMZ was a space monopolized by the state (정부). The private use of the DMZ likewise had to follow closely the dictates of the state. At the time, the only opportunity non-military citizens had to access the DMZ was through mandatory national security education (안보교육), which defined the DMZ as a symbol of North–South hostility.
>
> Because the state determined the epistemological framework of the DMZ as the frontline of North–South enmity, any interest in the DMZ that deviated in the slightest from the national security education framework was itself treasonous (불온) and [ideologically] contaminated (불순). At that time, if anyone were to wander around the DMZ area (일원), or even worse, have a camera around the neck, asking local people various questions, what would have been that person's fate? One would be suspected of trying to cross the border, or, if one couldn't prove that one wasn't a spy, locked up in jail. If not that, then one would be treated like a mentally-ill person who, like the unification activists (통일 운동권), thought that one could directly communicate plans for peace and unification to the North–South authorities. (C.-h. Kim 2012: 154–55)

Kim pinpoints a shift in the DMZ's epistemological framework that pivots around the democratization of South Korean society, which took place in 1987 as the culmination of more than a decade of activism by students and workers against the anti-democratic authoritarian dictatorships of Park Chung-hee and Chun Doo-hwan. The state's monopoly over both physical access to and cultural meanings of the DMZ loosened at this point, transforming the ideological overdetermination of the DMZ area into an intellectual and affective space for experimental political imaginaries.

In conjunction with the DMZ's forbidden nature, from the beginning of the Republic of Korea, the state also monopolized the discourse on re-unification, mobilizing anti-Communism and ethnonational purity alike in the name of economic development and nation building. Even following the achievement of formal democracy in 1987, with the unending war on the Korean peninsula, the state of exception has been the rule through-out both Korean polities since the establishment of the opposing states in 1948. Seung-ook Lee, Najeeb Jan, and Joel Wainwright (2014) assert that "sovereignty and geography are co-implicated in Korea" precisely because "the spatial structure of modern Korea—the divided peninsula—has cre-ated conditions favorable to the violent operation of sovereign power" (653). For Lee, Jan, and Wainwright, South Korea's National Security Law (NSL) is a primary example of what they call the "quasi-permanent state of exception" (657). The NSL has been in effect since 1948 and is the central legal technology that has maintained the hegemony of anti-Communism in South Korea. Its indiscriminate application to suppress dissent of any kind could render any person a *ppalgaengi* (빨갱이) or a Commie and a "sub-citizen" (659), or akin to Giorgio Agamben's *homo sacer* (1998). Paik Nak-chung calls the NSL a "covert back-page constitution" (2013: 162), and Namhee Lee argues that from its origins in the 1950s as "an emergency measure in an emergency situation," it continued to be renewed, strengthened, and applied in ways that suggests that "this 'emergency situation' lasted more than five decades, throughout South Korea's existence" (2007: 83).

The liberal governments of Kim Dae-jung and Roh Moo-hyun failed to remove it, and during the conservative administrations of Lee Myung-bak and Park Geun-hye, it was applied to dissolve a political party framed as pro–North Korean and to deport a South Korean citizen who spoke favorably about a visit to North Korea and about her desires for peaceful reunification. These events and performances of state power remind all South Koreans that the Cold War is not over in Korea, and for right-wing conservatives, known as the New Right, they legitimize their vigilant anti-Communism even in the post–Cold War period. For progressives, on the other hand, they fuel a resistant politics that views peaceful engagement and eventual reconciliation, if not unification, as necessary for true de-mocracy, not one beholden solely to free market principles.

In place of "post–Cold War," anthropologist Jin-Heon Jung refers to the "late–Cold War era" to describe "a hybrid, heterogeneous, and shifting historical juncture in which the established values, norms, ethics, and subjectivities that were produced and reproduced in the Cold War context have come to struggle, contest, and negotiate with each other in envisioning a reunified nation" (2015: 33–34). Especially with the election of Kim Dae-jung in 1998, South Koreans became empowered to "join in discussions as to what the reunified nation should look like" (2015: 34), from multiple aspects—economic, cultural, and now ecological.

The 1992 Agreement on Reconciliation, Nonaggression and Exchanges and Cooperation between the South and the North was the first to propose, in Article 12, "peaceful utilization" of the DMZ.[4] It would not be until the historic June 2000 summit between Kim Dae-jung and Kim Jong Il, however, that "peaceful utilization" (평화적 이용) would become a key phrase in inter-Korean cooperation as plans for reconnecting road and rail infrastructures began in earnest. This is the origin of the double bind in which conservation of the DMZ and unification first came into conflict. Peaceful utilization also brought into relief how closely peace, the necessary precondition for unification, had come to be associated with capital (H. O. Park 2015). After the collapse of the Soviet Union, South Korea's rapid economic development, particularly as it achieved advanced nation status, was viewed by conservatives as the apotheosis of capitalism's superiority, which made it not only hegemonic but even universal. In this context, historian Namhee Lee describes the New Right as having engaged in the "willful ordering of the disappearance of North Korea, whose divergent trajectory for South Korea symbolized the North's failure as a civilization, which then justified its anticipated demise" (2019: 21).[5]

The DMZ and its nature emerged as a solution to what was becoming an evolving problem space in post-1987 South Korea—what Paik Nak-chung calls the "division system in crisis" (2011 [1995]). With the achievement of democracy and the end of the authoritarian dictatorships that ruled the nation since 1960, as well as the collapse of the Soviet Union in 1991, the late–Cold War era presented new possibilities. Yet, the division of the peninsula itself persisted. The rise of the New Right intensified Cold War bipolarity in South Korea as they vilified the Old Left as "North Korean sympathizer-lefties" (친북 좌파; N. Lee 2019) and disparaged the Kim–Roh decade of détente between the two Koreas as the lost decade.[6] Meanwhile, on the progressive left, the socialist dreams of former revolutionaries were set aside as movement politics shifted into a post-political register, focusing on a range of policy issues, particularly environmental protection.

The abandonment of the radical politics of the democracy movement (국민운동) in favor of the accommodationist politics of the civil society movements (시민사회운동) embodied the transformation of what Hyun Ok Park calls "mass utopia" to "market utopia" and coincided with the state's embrace of neoliberal economic policies imposed by the International Monetary Fund and World Bank during the Asian financial crisis (1997–98). These economic trends, which were institutionalized during the liberal governments of Kim Dae-jung and Roh Moo-hyun, intensified during the conservative administrations of Lee Myung-bak and Park Geun-hye. The major political shift took shape around their combative approaches to the North—particularly in light of Kim Jung Un's provocative nuclear weapons testing—which represented a turn away from peaceful engagement as a national goal. Although the victory of Lee Myung-bak was attributed to the popularity of his economic platform rather than his inter-Korean policy, he made engagement with the North contingent on denuclearization. The New Right considered the Sunshine Policy of Kim Dae-jung and Roh Moo-hyun to have been a failure, serving only to feed the coffers of the Kim dynasty in the North with South Korean taxpayer money while the DPRK further developed its nuclear capability. Especially under Roh Moo-hyun's presidency (2003–8), which was founded on anti-Americanism and the empowerment of the so-called 386 generation, the rise of the New Right came to dominate conservative politics. Ideologically, many on the right became staunchly beholden to the Cold War bipolar mentality and fiercely supportive of the United States–ROK alliance.

In 2012, these late–Cold War ideological dynamics were crystallized by an anecdote told to me by Dr. Jung Jiseok (Peter Jung), a peace activist and founder of a peace studies academy in the border area of Cheorwon. He had established the academy on Quaker principles to help train future peace builders in South Korea and internationally, and he was deliberate in selecting its name: Border Peace School (국경선평화학교). He did not use *chŏpkyŏng* to refer to the "border," which is more akin to "frontier," or an internal space, abutting another territory. Instead, he used the word *kukkyŏngsŏn* (국경선), the Korean word most often used to denote national borders (lit., national borderline). As he recounted to me, with some incredulity, this decision generated suspicion and concern among local residents and bureaucrats, many of whom are politically conservative and staunchly anti-communist. For these South Koreans, referring to the border with North Korea as *kukkyŏngsŏn* implies that one views both the division and the North Korean regime as legitimate and prompts suspicion that one is a *ppalgaengi* (Commie). Progressives, on the other side, also criticized his use of "border" because it fixes the division between the two Koreas. According to Peter, local leaders, provincial officials, and regular citizens have all suggested that he change the Korean name of the school to a more politically neutral one, namely, "DMZ Peace School" (DMZ 평화학교).[7]

As I mentioned, the fact that my friend could be considered a pro-North Commie suggests how alive the Cold War division continues to be in late–Cold War South Korea. But within this context, the DMZ has paradoxically become an apolitical term, which speaks to the persistent politics of the division. In light of the intractable political contests between progressives and conservatives in South Korea, particularly the New Right's recapitulation of Cold War divisions within the nation, the DMZ has emerged as a solution to a new war—not one between North and South Korea, but one between left and right within South Korea. Political scientist and DMZ specialist Kim Chae-Han suggested as much in 2006, during the last few years of the Sunshine Policy era, when he noted that the reduction in antagonism between the two Koreas had not resulted in concomitant reduction in tensions *within* South Korea, where domestic conflict over the national division (남남갈등; lit., South South conflict) was as severe as it had been immediately following liberation in 1945 (2006: 5). For Kim, one solution to both internal tensions and inter-Korean tensions is to center a shared perception grounded in the actual division, the DMZ. Kim asserts that the DMZ does not represent war, as is commonly believed, but peace—because it has successfully deterred war for more than a half century and can thus provide a space for reconciliation. Kim proffered the DMZ as a counterintuitive, neutral meeting ground, and its ecological exceptionalism only enhanced this resignification. How this had come to pass is outlined in what follows.

The Creativity of Nature

An early attempt to link the DMZ's nature to peace appeared in March 1980 in the art, culture, and architecture magazine, *Space* (공간).[8] The editors proposed the creation of a "monumental peace park" in the DMZ (DMZ 를 기념 자연 공원으로). A few months before the horrific massacre of thousands of civilians in Gwangju by the military government of Chun Doo-hwan, which marked a turning point in the struggle for democracy, the proposal appeared as a kind of utopian missive, counterintuitively framing the

DMZ as the grounds for new conceptual and material possibilities. *Space* expressed a desire for a different national future by laying the groundwork for a collective, people-oriented path to unification. In the following issue, the DMZ peace park campaign proposal was reprinted, explicitly linking global environmental crises, including the population explosion, nuclear weapons, and environmental pollution, to the DMZ and national reunification, which the authors describe as the "greatest wish of the 50 million people living on the peninsula" (*Space* 1980: 14).

Appearing in those two consecutive issues in 1980, and revisited multiple times in the decades to follow (1989, 1990, 2014, and 2017), the monumental DMZ park campaign depended on the DMZ as a space of nature. The magazine featured reprints of ecology study reports that had been undertaken in the mid-1960s and early 1970s by the first generation of South Korean natural scientists.[9] In fact, the prominent zoologist Kang Yung Sun, who founded the Korean Commission for the Conservation of Nature and Natural Resources (KCCNNR) and headed those early ecological studies, had first articulated the connection between the DMZ's nature and the possibility of its peaceful utilization in the mid-1970s. In a 1975 essay for *North Korea*, the journal of South Korea's North Korea Research Institute, Kang directly connected his ecological research to the "human and policy related connections" (접촉) between the two Koreas (Kang 1975). Around the same time, he recommended the founding of a national park that would link Geumgangsan (금강산, also known as Diamond Mountain) in the North and Seoraksan (설악산) in the South through the Hyangro Summit area. This protected area would, he suggested, be "the most superb (우수한) national park in Asia" (1974: 29).[10]

What is remarkable about the 1980 manifesto and these publications by Kang from the 1970s is that they appeared during a period of intense anti-Communism and state repression, when any discussion of unification was just cause for investigation or arrest under the NSL. Perhaps because scientific research of nature was considered to be disconnected from Cold War geopolitics, Kang could express his hope that "not too far in the future actual (본격적) research could arise out of academic cooperation between scholars in North and South Korea" (1974: 29).[11]

For its part, the *Space* magazine manifesto featured a proposal by editorial board member and professor of philosophy So Hŭng-yŏl, in which he invoked the phrase "when that day comes" (그 날이 오면; 1980: 16), a highly stirring invocation of nationalist yearning, which originated in the poem by the same name, written by Sim Hun during the Japanese occupation of Korea. The phrase continued to hold resonance for activists during the democratization period—those who longed for the end of military dictatorships that used the Cold War division of the Korean nation to justify their undemocratic rule. In this way, So linked postcolonial desires for national self-determination with the teleological temporality of inevitable unification—leaving as an open question whether unification would be peaceful or violent, and what the role of human desire and action would be. In the absence of power or agency among everyday Koreans, the DMZ presented an opportunity for what So referred to as "substantive, creative action" that would permit those who participated to develop hope and positive thinking about the reunification of the homeland (조국 통일) (1980: 18).

In 1989, two years after the successful transition to parliamentary democracy, *Space* republished the manifesto and recommitted to its call for a monumental DMZ park in a postscript that reflected the optimistic spirit of the post-democratization moment. The authors embraced the "infinite creativity of nature" (자연의 무한한 창조력) as a guide for peaceful reunification. The DMZ as an accidental natural sanctuary was appropriated as a symbol of the inalienability of ethnonational identity and the inevitability of unification: "Like the roots and stems growing entangled with each other in the DMZ, our people (민족; *minjok*) cannot be divided. Let's create our space to reflect this idea to the utmost. Moreover, let's preserve the paramount space that will enable us to learn about life and wisdom with a humble mind before nature's infinite creativity" (*Space* 1989: 35). One year later, these nationalist yearnings were combined with more cosmopolitan visions. In the May 1990 issue of *Space*, the second of two issues dedicated to the DMZ park campaign, Lee Bann, an artist who had been visiting the DMZ since June 1987 and who was collaborating with members of the *Space* group to form the Federation for Artists and Naturalists for the DMZ Conservation and its associated Institute of the Fine Arts Movement for the Abolishment of the Demilitarized Zone, wrote a manifesto that framed the DMZ in terms that continue to resonate today:

> It is necessary to prepare and plan for interest in the DMZ before the day comes for unification (통일의 그 날이 오면). When that day comes, the pressure of the event will make it seem like it's already too late. Moreover, this is not just in our interest, but it's something that all of humanity cares about.
>
> Domestic and international media reports are creating global interest in the DMZ as a unique and one-and-only space in the history of humanity.

This interest concentrates on two aspects. First, the necessity of preservation by turning the DMZ into a nature park to prevent the destruction of its nature (자연물) due to construction or industrialization activities. Second, the necessity to preserve it as a space that symbolizes world (human) peace (인류 평화).

In the process of satisfying this expectation of the world community (인류 사회), we must plan for and preserve the DMZ as a symbolic space that takes up the painful and disgraceful history of our people (민족) toward a creative and dignified history.

Toward this end, artistic and cultural planning must take priority over political or economic schemes. Raising a historical monument that doesn't destroy the natural environment but builds harmony would sublimate the tragedy of the national division through artistic creation. This job of commemorating the history of the DMZ cannot be entrusted to political or economic interests. (Lee Bann 1990: 60)

Even as the romanticism of "when that day comes" has lost its potency today, Lee's manifesto articulates several themes that have continued to inform how the DMZ's nature has been framed in South Korea since the early 2000s. It foregrounds the moral responsibility of South Koreans to universal humanity—that is, protecting the DMZ's ecology connects national to global interests and its symbolic relation with peace links both "our people" and the world community. It also can reorient collective memory from what Lee refers to as a "painful and disgraceful" history to a "creative and dignified" one. Like the 1980 campaign ten years earlier, the DMZ nature park is framed by Lee as a necessary step toward unification and welcomes (South) Koreans of all walks of life, but Lee emphasizes the role that artists and cultural producers must play over bureaucrats and businesspeople. These calls for collective action also share a common characteristic with contemporary ones in the conspicuous absence of North Korea. As such, these psychological and cultural preparations for the day of unification were addressed to South Koreans, even if implicit in this discourse of peace is the unification of the divided nation.

Lee's movement became formalized as the Front DMZ Art and Culture Movement in 1991, and at the August 1995 International Forum, literary scholar and theorist of division politics Paik Nak-chung spoke with some optimism about the ecology of the DMZ. He was inspired by Front DMZ and what he called its "ecological imagination," one that offered a paradigm shift of "qualitatively new thinking...that goes beyond all existing logic" and that could lead to transformations across local, national, and global scales (2011 [1995]: 73). He stated:

> Preserving some nearly 1,000 square kilometers of a truly demilitarized green strip...in the middle of the peninsula neither accords with the interests of the division regimes nor makes practical sense in terms of the logic of the world market. Yet such impracticality has a decidedly practical meaning for a movement that attempts to creatively use the assets of the division period and thus genuinely overcome the division *system*, refusing to accept a unification that leaves the logic of that system intact. So impractical a goal attained through a broad movement of popular solidarity inside and outside Korea will have inflicted on the world-system the utmost damage possible in the given time and place....(Paik Nak-chung 2011 [1995]: 75–76; emphasis in original)

For Paik, it was the very *impracticality* of movements such as Front DMZ that has a "decidedly practical meaning," in that they attempt to use creatively what the division has organically sown—namely, its ecology—to overcome the logic of the division system. Nature conservation was what offered the literal ground for thinking differently about peaceful unification.[12]

Although Front DMZ no longer exists, according to Lee, the movement gathered a thousand participants (mostly South Koreans), including professors, politicians, fine artists, poets, novelists, actors, musicians, journalists, historians, architects, and ecologists (Lee 1996) into dialogue over the DMZ's future as both the grounds for planting the seeds of unification and as a natural space that had to be conserved, whatever changes unification might bring. Under Lee's curation, a new vision of the nation took on cosmological and spiritual dimensions, but most importantly, it offered an alternative "mental" space for "previously unthinkable thoughts and, at best, preposterous dreams," in the words of Front DMZ collaborator, playwright, philosopher, and art historian Hong Kai (1996: 22).

Since the heyday of Front DMZ in the 1990s, the fecundity of cultural production surrounding the DMZ in South Korea and internationally has been remarkable. In this way, the utopian and entrepreneurial spirit of Front DMZ continues to persist through the work of other artists, scholars, and ecological activists, who are also attuned to the DMZ's symbolic and economic currency in the global art market due to its recognizable associations with borders, political division, and Cold War retro aesthetics.[13] Hirokazu Miyazaki argues that "reorientation itself is a key operation of hope" (2017: 9), and the DMZ's nature offered precisely this kind of reorientation for a host of elite actors in South Korea—from the tragedy of civil war to the promise of post-national peace, which could pivot from the scale of the nation and make Korea central to the world.

Given South Korea's rapid modernization in the 1970s and 1980s, it is no wonder that the *Space* campaign anticipated in 1989 that industrialization would be a likely threat for the DMZ's future. Their manifesto therefore called for the "de-militarized zone to turn into a de-construction zone" (비무장지대는 비건설지대로), asking whether the "huge mistake of invasive industrialization, infringing on the limits of nature's regenerative and creative powers" would be "waiting for the DMZ tomorrow" (*Space* 1989: 35). This prescient question would become more pressing following the 2000 summit between Kim Dae-jung and Kim Jong Il, when the DMZ and border areas became viewed as the next frontier of economic development. The Sunshine Policy under Kim and Roh led to greater peaceful utilization of the DMZ. Civilian transformations of the area were directed toward the promotion of inter-Korean "peace and prosperity." Since then, every positive diplomatic step taken by the two Koreas has led to rampant land speculation in the CCZ, as South Korean investors place their bets on the border areas, not as a spatial limit and frontier outpost, but as the beating economic heart of a unified peninsula.

As I show in the following pages, once inter-Korean peace became tied to economic exchange and cooperation in the late 1990s, the cultural expansiveness and democratic potential of the DMZ's nature as the basis for peace ceded ground to state-centric visions. Across a range of venues, discourses, and policy proposals, state actors and bureaucrats linked the DMZ's nature to a form of peace that downplayed unification of the Korean ethnonation in favor of a cosmopolitan vision that foregrounded the universality of capitalism.

From Inter-Korean Peace to Domestic Battlegrounds

Two words that frequently appeared in *Space* magazine with respect to the DMZ's nature were "creativity" (창조) and "substantiality" (구체성). What these words suggest is not only that the existing situation calls for something radically new, but also that the DMZ's nature can ground these ideas in actual reality. As Paik's "ecological imagination" suggests, Front DMZ and similar discourses present the DMZ's nature as a creative force of symbolic transformation—from an impossible situation (a Cold War division that persists beyond the Cold War) into a collective future of peace for Korea and the world. *Space* magazine and Lee directed their manifestos to everyday people in South Korea, but with the 2000 Summit, the DMZ became the actual site for inter-Korean cooperation and exchange. The peaceful utilization of the DMZ included the reconnection of prewar railroad lines—the Gyeongui Line on the western side and the Donghae Line on the eastern side—and the opening of the Kaeseong Industrial Complex in 2004 in the northern city of Kaeseong, a few kilometers from the MDL at Panmunjom (판문점).[14]

Even if these were state-level decisions and agreements, through NGOs in particular, participation of South Koreans in imagining unification and peace was unprecedented under the Kim and Roh presidencies. Moreover, the interest in the DMZ extended internationally, with networks of NGOs, international organizations, local governments, and others collaborating actively to strategize a sustainable future for the DMZ's rare ecologies. (In fact, despite inter-state commitments made by the two Koreas, the only collaboration around environmental issues has been through forestry cooperation to address the severe deforestation of the North [Song and Hastings 2020].) Ke Chung (K. C.) Kim, a Korean American professor of entomology at Penn State, had already been involved in the first ecological study of the DMZ as a consultant for the Smithsonian Institution in 1967–68. Nearly three decades later in 1995, he founded the DMZ Forum, which was able to gain the interest of media mogul Ted Turner as well as conservation organizations such as the International Crane Foundation. Cofounded by Kim and fellow Korean American Seung-ho Lee, the Forum seeks international protected status for the DMZ. Kim was particularly concerned that the Sunshine Policy would lead to greater destruction of the DMZ's ecologies and believed that a global conservation effort would be needed to protect the area before further steps toward unification could be taken. For more than two decades, the Forum has advocated for the DMZ to be designated a transboundary conservation area, peace park, or a UNESCO World Heritage Site. In doing so, it continued conversations that had begun in the 1970s among South Korean scientists, politicians, the UN Command, and conservationists at the International Union for the Conservation of Nature (IUCN) and UN Environment Programme (Miura and Bak 2011: 498).

In tandem with these transnational efforts and activities of international organizations, environmental issues had become mainstream in South Korea, and environmental groups proliferated rapidly in the post-1987 era, particularly after the 1992 Rio Earth Summit. By the 2000s, NGOs and local governments were focusing attention on the DMZ. The number of events and conferences that dealt with issues central to the DMZ mushroomed, as did the number of DMZ-related NGOs, which the editors of *Space* magazine estimated to be close to two hundred in 2014. Miura and Bak (2011) attribute the shift in focus from development to conservation to the transnational networks, which have "gradually induced a policy shift" (515) in the 2000s.[15]

While this may be accurate, the authors draw a stark distinction between practices of conservation and those of development. In fact, this period saw the DMZ's nature become monetized, branded, and used to enhance the nation's green credentials. Local governments at the provincial and county levels also participated in promoting the PLZ. From around 2010, President Lee Myung-bak's version of sustainable development, Low Carbon, Green Growth (known as "Green Growth"), was being heavily disseminated at home and abroad through the new South Korea–based international organization Global Green Growth Institute. Lee had already been recognized internationally for his eco-friendly governance while the mayor of Seoul, in large part because of the restoration of Cheonggyecheon, a stream in the downtown area that had been buried under a highway three decades earlier during the postwar urbanization of Seoul. Winning awards and accolades for this restoration project, Lee extended this eco-friendly image by promoting his signature Green Growth platform, which included the DMZ's preservation as a central goal. For this reason, when I began my fieldwork in late 2011, it was difficult to keep up with the conference and event circuit, especially as South Korea hosted at least three high-profile international environmental conferences during his tenure. Under Lee, international recognition for South Korea's environmental commitments was being actively sought, which was to culminate in the designation of the southern side of the DMZ as a UNESCO biosphere reserve, and this was a frequent topic of conversation in the network of DMZ-related actors.

The DMZ agenda also included the promotion of the PLZ, inherited from his predecessor Roh and centered on economic development of the Border Area. Extending twenty kilometers south of the SBL, the Border Area has been defined by militarization and economic and social marginalization.[16] Prospects of peace during the Sunshine Policy years brought unprecedented media and government attention to these areas as the front lines of development after existing for decades as the military's "rear areas" (후방지역) behind the front lines of a future war. In 2011, the Special Act on Border Area Support was passed, which led to greater funds to support economic development. Villagers increasingly were framed and framed themselves as "local people"

(지역주민) whose "local culture" (지역문화) was tied to tourism development in the form of special foods, cultural festivals, and historic sites. The village that I refer to as CheongJeon-ri in chapter 4 provides a case in point. It was named an eco-peace village in 2007, and its importance as a winter habitat for endangered cranes, its location near the Korean War battleground of White Horse Hill (백마고지), and its signature rice variety Odae-ssal were all mobilized by bureaucrats and locals to diversify DMZ tourism around multiple tastes and interests—military, historical, ecological, recreational, and even agricultural, in the form of farm stays. As these views of peace and nature multiplied under the neoliberalizing economic regimes, new divisions and conflicts emerged, especially as urban environmental NGOs descended on the Border Area to police these newly valued environments. Among the state representatives, environmental NGOs, and local people who comprise the network of actors engaged in the DMZ's ecological futures, a predictable pattern of competing interests began to emerge.

These were readily apparent to me at a public hearing regarding plans for a bicycle path across the eastern part of the DMZ region. Convened by the DMZ Peace Forum at the South Korean National Assembly in October 2011, the opening panel featured bureaucrats, academics, and environmentalists who discussed the pros and cons of the proposal, reproducing conventional discourses of conservation and development. Three male villagers from rural Hwacheon County, Gangwon Province, had come to attend the meeting but were not included among the expert panel of speakers.

In the presentations, the centrist position was represented by an official from the Ministry of Environment, who foregrounded PLZ tourism as a "win-win" opportunity for both conservation and development interests. This market-based vision was profoundly anathema to the deep-ecology views of the activist presenters, who insisted that the cycling route was not only illogical and difficult to traverse, given the area's mountainous terrain, but also threatening to habitats of endangered mammals such as the goat-like amur goral (산양; *sanyang*). These male representatives in their thirties, from the DMZ research teams of Seoul-based environmental NGOs, warned that naïve desires for economic development among local residents would lead to dire ecological consequences. One environmentalist concluded his presentation by deploying the charged creole word *nodaji* (노다지) to describe the CCZ as a natural "bonanza" (*nodaji*), and admonished locals and the state to abide by the rule of "no touch!"[17]

During the discussion period, the older men from Hwacheon were incensed by the environmentalists' declamation, in English, of "no touch!"

These villagers, who identified themselves as local people, asked with heightened emotion, "Are the *sanyang* more important or the humans living in these areas?" They were offended that their intimate knowledge of "nature" (자연) was being summarily discounted, and by the condescending insinuation that they were ruining nature out of ignorance. As I came to understand, the category of local people, which may have once been a technocratic vehicle for including villagers as so-called stakeholders in DMZ schemes, now also serves as a politicized identification for residents in the border areas who are critical of state and NGO projects that seek to capitalize on or conserve the DMZ's nature.

Yet, even as local people rejected the notion that the DMZ's nature is untouchable or pristine, many could not deny that the DMZ's amplification in the national and international ecological imaginary had brought significant economic investments to border-area counties. The resignification of the DMZ since the end of the Cold War from a "scar of war" to a "green belt" had "softened the atmosphere," as one of my informants described it. The fear and anxiety that it may have provoked in the past had dissipated, in part because of digital technologies that brought the actual DMZ into public visibility. This was a period in which K-pop stars began promoting the DMZ in festivals, concerts, and tourism.[18] For local communities, tying the DMZ to K-pop and other consumer ventures was an important lifeline linking them to the megalopolis of Seoul and the rest of the world through tourism revenue. Agricultural profits had been declining due to free trade agreements and ecological stresses attributed to climate change, and some locals were beginning to align their views with provincial and county officials who actively promoted the DMZ brand.

As mentioned in the Introduction, the MIPD encompasses huge portions of both Gyeonggi and Gangwon Provinces, and the restrictions imposed on civilian life have been profound. The plans for the DMZ have always included political plays for those local districts, which competed with each other whenever the state announced a peace park plan. As Shim Youngkyu notes in an issue of *Space* devoted to the DMZ peace park in light of Park Geun-hye's speech at the UN General Assembly in 2013, "In spite of its emphasis on 'peace,' 'win-win situations' and 'demilitarization,' the Peace Park has already become a 'battlefield without gunfire' staged between local governments" (2014: 77). Many of the events that I attended had to do with what Shim calls "clueless competition for conceiving of the park" and were all hosted and funded by provincial and local governments. The DMZ became a major political talking point during the 2014 midterm election season, and continued to be one throughout Park's embattled presidency, which ended when she was impeached in December 2016 and removed from office in March the following year.

National Assembly representatives of the ten Border Area counties have proposed for years that an east–west peace highway linking the western and eastern coasts across their territories is necessary to revitalize their stagnating economies. In their minds, roads are not just links to the metropolitan center but also engines of development. At a policy forum in September 2016, impassioned speeches by members of the Association of Border Area Leaders underscored their shared sense of neglect and abandonment. The population of 1.2 million in their ten counties is rapidly aging and often outnumbered by soldiers. Before getting to his presentation about the East–West Peace Highway, Kim Kyu-sŏn, the chief of Yeoncheon County said:

> We've been endlessly patient and yet we're constantly having to knock, continually demanding, constantly imploring. Since that's not working, we need to find another way. We ten leaders along with all of our constituents, are we not citizens of ROK? We didn't choose to live in the Border Area. The state is always the first to help with local economy, culture, arts, and education, so why are we the only ones to be discriminated against? Is it right that our children leave at an early age for Seoul and come out to the city? Border residents live in suffering, carrying such a heavy economic burden.

Local residents center their desires for modernity and development in the "promise of infrastructure" (Anand, Gupta, and Appel 2018), particularly transportation links, but also economic hubs and educational institutions, which would connect them economically, socially, and politically to the rest of hypermodern South Korea. Local politicians and residents often refer to their position "at the front lines" of a future war, but also "at the center" of a unified peninsula. From this location marked by both danger and hope, they depend on the DMZ and its rebranding as a space for the consumption of peace.

Leaving behind a "Gloomy History"

In July 2013, the Gyeonggi Province celebration of the sixtieth anniversary of the Armistice Agreement featured this statement in their event brochure: "Dusting off the image of war to ring in a new day—from gloomy history to peace, life, understanding, reconciliation." Along with the event's

tag line, "DMZ Is Now Life!" (DMZ 이제 생명이다!), metaphors of regenera-
tion, growth, and peace dominated the event. The celebration kicked off
with a large conference at KINTEX (Korean International Exhibition Center), the nation's largest such venue, composed of KINTEX1 and KINTEX2,
massive futuristic glass and steel complexes completed in 2011 in the "new
town" (신도시) of Goyang on the outskirts of Seoul. Other events included
a photo exhibition, Veterans' Day commemoration, a marathon, film festival, farm tour, and bike tournament, giving credence to the description
of the DMZ as "a multi-space" (멀티공간) and a "land pregnant with life."

Just the year before, the sixtieth anniversary of the Armistice Agreement had been anticipated in the very same halls at the fourth World
Ecotourism Convention (WEC) hosted by the Gyeonggi Tourism Center.
Reinforcing then president Lee Myung-bak's Green Growth platform, the
Minister of the Environment, Lee Maan-Ee, linked ecotourism to Green
Growth as well as world peace, reminding the audience that Korea is the
"only nation that has been divided for sixty years," and that despite its
tragic history, it is now a "valuable space for wildlife" and the "last Gala-
pagos on the planet." The Korea Tourism Organization (KTO) had already
promoted 2012 as the Year of DMZ Tourism, and at the event, the DMZ
was presented as "one of the world's greatest ecotourism destinations" and
"Korea's #1 Brand." All of this was part of a multiyear effort on the part of
the Lee administration to make high-profile contributions to issues of the
global environment.

In 2012 alone, South Korea hosted the WEC, as well as the Korea EXPO
in Yeosu, whose theme was "The Living Ocean and Coast," and the qua-
drennial World Conservation Congress (WCC) for the IUCN, the world's
oldest such organization. All of these events were framed as laying the
groundwork for South Korea to be an environmental leader in the region.
Its hosting of the IUCN WCC was touted as the first time the WCC had
been hosted by a Northeast Asian nation. Lee's Green Growth agenda and
the DMZ took center stage, while, behind the scenes, South Korea awaited
the decision of the UNESCO Man and the Biosphere Programme on its application for the southern half of the DMZ to be designated as a biosphere
reserve, which many spoke of as if it were fait accompli.[19]

Since the 1980 *Space* magazine manifesto, the symbolism of the DMZ's
nature has linked peace between the two Koreas to world peace. Ecological exceptionalism mediated a cosmopolitan vision that opened up a new
moral vision that would permit the Koreas to finally overcome the division *and* transform Korea's abject history into a positive, progressive future.

This jump from the dire situation on the peninsula to a post-national cosmopolitanism could be seen as reflective of the proactive turn to globalization and soft power since the Kim Young-sam administration in the early 1990s. These strategies have only become more institutionalized since the national branding of everything from K-pop to kimchee became a state policy in the early 2000s. The DMZ became part of South Korea's branding industry by being aesthetically repackaged so that it was not merely a dark relic of the Cold War and never-ending war, but also something bright, alive, and forward looking—fecund, not sterile. Its nature provided the raw materials for this makeover. Indeed, nature purified peace, shifting its associations from the opposite of war to a generic, even cute, world peace.

This symbolic transformation is illustrated by the so-called business identity (BI) of the KTO, which printed a brochure, "A Special Journey of Connecting Souls, DMZ" (마음을 잇는 특별한 여행 DMZ), published in both English and Korean for its Visit Korea 2010–12 promotion. The butterfly-shaped logo, with a green wing and a blue wing, represents the divided peninsula, with the letters D-M-Z in white across the middle, where the butterfly's body would be. The final page in the brochure provides a detailed explanation of the "DMZ BI story" and the "DMZ characters," which constitute an extraterrestrial, heteronormative butterfly family: father Didi (for "dream"), daughter Mimi (for "middle"), and mother ZeZe (for "zone"). The BI story tells us that the butterfly family arrived from "Planet Nabi" (*nabi*; butterfly), and cartoon illustrations depict them as puffy, white, bipedal figures with pastel-colored wings in blue, green, and pink strapped to their backs. As it states in the Korean version, "The DMZ, the space in the middle of the peninsula overflowing with vital life force (생명력)—this is the land from which the butterfly family starts its beautiful journey, dreaming of world peace." The BI story strongly suggests that the "souls" being connected in this "special journey" are those of South Koreans and English-speaking foreigners, mediated by the fantastical butterfly family, but not those of Koreans on either side of the division.

This narrative represents one direction in which the value and meanings of the DMZ's nature had diverged from its origins in *Space* magazine and the ecological imagination that excited Paik Nak-chung in 1995. Here, the DMZ's ecological exceptionalism has been evacuated of its original moral vision and of its connection to any earthly politics. Instead, the butterfly family represents the South Korean state's complete erasure of the North and the reduction of the DMZ to a pure symbol. This is a form of stealth nationalism disguised as cosmopolitanism, which uses soft power to assert

South Korea's position as the rightful steward of the DMZ and its nature. The Korean language brochure, which brands the DMZ as ROK DMZ (대한민국 DMZ), states in its prefatory notes, "The DMZ BI embodies the intention of 'Peace and Life.' The title of this guidebook, 'A Special Journey Connecting Souls,' expresses the hope that the DMZ will overcome the symbol of division and connect the hearts of all people who wish for peace."

As this example suggests, state branding of the DMZ as a zone of peace and life conflated different agendas. On the one hand, it promoted domestic and international tourism in the Border Area, and on the other, it gave the appearance of the state's interest in division politics at a time when there was virtually no communication between the two Koreas. But perhaps most importantly, it had the effect of symbolically colonizing the DMZ's nature as South Korean. Indeed, very little was known about the ecology on the North Korean side, apart from geographic information system images that offered a picture of land use, and the information about the general state of the country, which was still recovering from the "arduous march," the 1997–98 famine in which an estimated half a million people died.[20] Nature, in this instance, serves to grant peace a universal register that scales from the South Korean DMZ to the Earth, bypassing the North altogether, neutralizing the politics of the division and pacifying inter-Korean politics.

No, Not That Peace and Life!

It was easy enough to see through the state's branding of the PLZ as a proliferation of signs meant to capitalize on and leverage the ecological exceptionalism of the DMZ. Yet, for this reason, it was surprising to find that the very same slogans were being used by progressive environmental NGOs in their DMZ programming and campaigns to protect the Border Area from developments such as the peace bike trail described above. When I asked representatives about the overlap, they insisted that their peace and life was wholly different from that of state branding.

One reason for this overlap may have to do with the state of funding in 2011 and 2012, as the Lee administration put a chokehold on NGOs who were at war with Lee, a former Hyundai Construction Corporation CEO known as the "bulldozer." He was roundly accused of greenwashing when he pushed through the highly contentious Four Rivers Restoration Project, which was touted as a necessary flood-mitigation measure, but which was revealed, shortly after he left office, to be what most critics had long suspected—a bloated and corrupt construction project that fattened the wallets of his cronies while destroying the ecosystems of South Korea's rivers and riverine communities. Likewise, investigations into the famed Cheonggyecheon revealed that the stream had hardly been restored; rather, municipal water was being pumped in to offer the bucolic image of a stream.

The progressive NGOs Eco Horizon Institute, Korean Federation of Environmental Movements, and Green Korea United all had DMZ teams or research departments, as well as educational programs for youth. As PLZ tourism and peace park–related politics ramped up, the Border Area became an economic frontier and a site of encounter, contestation, and collaboration between urban environmentalists and local people (E. J. Kim 2014). Peace and life projects, instead of creating "mutual communication" (소통) and amity, were generating new divisions and differences. If the state and regional governments were using the DMZ's nature to brand the PLZ, environmental NGOs were seeking to protect these areas from development. Yet, both the state and NGOs drew on the symbolism of peace and life, and both frequently enhanced their projects by calling on the generative power of nature. For environmentalists, however, the slogan "peace and life" was an expression of radical pacifism and deep ecology and resonated with a key phrase popularized during the 1980s environmental movements.[21] Thus, environmental activists insisted to me that despite the superficial similarities, *their* peace and life was distinctly different from the peace and life of the PLZ. From their embrace of peace and life, they called out the spuriousness and hypocrisy of the developmental logic driving much of the state's peace and life rhetoric. But beyond this, peace and life was a sign of their left-wing politics, in support of the peaceful engagement policies of Kim and Roh, which had been dismantled under Lee.

The generativity of the peace and life discourse was most pronounced for me when I visited the DMZ Peace and Life Valley (PLV), an NGO located in Inje County, in a remote mountainous area on the eastern side of Gangwon Province very close to the DMZ. The PLV's slogan is "DMZ, Peace, Life!" In the PLV's promotional video, the associations among nature, peace, life, and reunification are created through a kind of metonymic incantation: "The DMZ, a space of peace and life. The DMZ transforms war to peace, division to unification, aggression to cooperation, closure to communication, destruction to restoration, death to life. It is a space where the Korean people (민족) and humanity can be reborn. A land (나라) of peace, life and culture, this is the future image of a unified Korea and the future begins at the DMZ."[22] The video ends with a satellite image of the globe, zooming into the Korean peninsula and fading into an image of the Korean unification flag, featuring the Korean peninsula in blue against a white background. The video made explicit what were oftentimes vaguely expressed attributes of the DMZ's ecological exceptionalism and what its very status as a liminal threshold could accomplish symbolically, and perhaps substantively, to unify the Korean nation and people.

When I visited the PLV in 2012, I met with Director Hwang Ho-seop, who had been a researcher at an environmental organization in Seoul before moving to the remote town of Seohwa-myeon (서화면) in Inje County, more than a hundred miles east of the capital city area of Seoul. He explained to my research assistant and me how the area could be considered economically backward because of its location within the MIPD. The center's goal was to provide a model of change by engaging with local people, including residents and soldiers. Even though the locals had an "allergic reaction" to preservation, he hoped to teach them how to make a "beneficial space for peace and life, out of a space of division and conflict."

He painted a sorry portrait of Seohwa-myeon, where the three thousand residents were greatly outnumbered by the military. After the Korean War, much of Inje County was located in the so-called recovered areas, north of the thirty-eighth parallel but south of the Armistice Line. These villages, which were North Korean territory from 1945 to 1953, became depopulated so that only 10 percent of the original inhabitants remained. Seohwa-myeon, for instance, had thirty thousand residents before the war. He explained to us:

> After the war, people from the North were subject to surveillance and targeted by government investigations into their family background (출신성분). Because of that, they found it difficult to live here, and many people left. In this village [Seohwa-myeon], there is only one [original] household; everyone left, and there was abandoned property, including rice paddies and fields. Even though the war ended in 1953, after that, the military reigned.... People from other places heard that there was land that had been abandoned and came up. This is why the village members don't have any cultural traditions. If you go to other villages, there are elders [heads of families], clans, festivals, but those don't exist here. The villagers lost their distinctive traits. Most of the Border Area is like that.

Director Hwang's description privileged authentic customs over invented traditions, but he also noted that there was a militarized culture, reflective of the majority of the population, which included young men serving their two years' mandatory military service and career soldiers and their families. The local economy had therefore been growing and developing, mostly around services and nightlife for the soldiers, but then in the 1990s, these young men began to get their own cars and travel to Seoul to avoid scrutiny during their leisure time from their battalion leaders.

He explained that the dominance of the military meant that associations with the DMZ were overwhelmingly focused on the North as an enemy, even if the mindset in broader society had changed to be more "future-oriented." As he put it, "when you go to the tunnel [dug by North Korea into the South, and now part of "security tours"], they show you an anti-Communist video, and visitors don't like it. It's still oriented to the past." He acknowledged the diversity of people's thinking around the DMZ, between conservatives and progressives, but the PLV's goal was to bring a different, more progressive, if not modern, way of thinking to the residents of the border.

When I asked him why DMZ-related organizations all referred to peace instead of unification, even as it seemed to serve as a proxy for unification, his answer seemed to reflect the same logic as the video: "Unification (t'ongil) will be based on peace and life. Unification without peace isn't good. They go together. And life, ecology, these two things also must be considered together." At the time, the words blended in my mind with other vague abstractions that were commonly associated with the DMZ.

A few months later, I visited the center for the Peace and Life Festival, which was tied to Gangwon Province's larger tourist bonanza around the DMZ. I anticipated that the same key words would be bandied about, but I was curious to see how they diverged from the typical touristic fare. When I arrived, I found myself disoriented by the aesthetic pastiche. The grounds of the center were set up like a traditional village festival, with the erection of ceremonial poles (솟대), representing peace, life, and unification. A full ritual spread, including a roasted pig head on an altar, was on display. In this simulacrum of a village festival, in a place that Director Hwang had told me was characterized by a lack of distinctive customs, "tradition" took the form of the PLV's vision of the good life: peace, life, and unification. Performances of traditional music, dance, and drumming followed, with many elderly residents happily joining in.

After watching the performances, I meandered to another part of the grounds in search of lunch. I came upon a set of food vendors, and I was surprised to see both Vietnamese and Chinese fare. When I spoke with the women behind the counter, I realized that they were so-called marriage migrants, who had come to this remote part of South Korea to marry

South Korean men. This had been a trend for at least a decade, in which middle-aged or older Korean men would go on tours across Asia or use brokers to find foreign wives. Economic stagnation and population decline in rural areas were partly a result of hypergamy—South Korean women were abandoning men in the rural countryside to seek greater freedom and opportunity in the cities. These left-behind men would then marry women from the Global South seeking to marry up (M. Kim 2018). The result: "multicultural families" (다문화 가족) as they were referred to by government bureaucrats who were designing programs to facilitate the cultural adaptation of the migrant wives, who were also the mothers to a new generation of Korean citizens. Scholars viewed these programs and the logics behind them as problematically assimilationist, reproducing patriarchal and ethnocentric values, instead of celebrating the actual hybridity of these families and Kosian children (a term used to refer to children who have one Korean parent and one non-Korean Asian parent; H. M. Kim 2012).[23]

After lunch, as I made my way back to the main stage, I was suddenly intercepted by two energetic and excited young women, whose appearance and demeanor were far from what one would expect of twenty-something wives in South Korea. They introduced themselves in a mix of Korean and English words once I told them I was from the United States. They were recent migrant brides from the Philippines. One had been married in South Korea seven months ago, and based on her recommendation, her friend joined her just two months later. They were, of course, huge fans of K-pop, and were carrying very large Samsung smartphones. We couldn't communicate well enough for me to get a detailed sense of what they thought of the event or of living in a remote place in South Korea, but they were exuberant and seemed joyful to be there and to be together.

At the time, I wrote in my field notes that the event was "not really" about unification but more about bringing unity to the local community. My disappointment was tied to expectations of what I thought unification should look like. The closest referents I could find were trite and predictable images of peace that had been drawn by children to represent future unification.

On further reflection, however, I realized that my own expectations about peace as the proxy for t'ongil and my own resistance to the sentimental and ethnonationalist word salad of peace, life, unification, communication, and cooperation had hidden from view what Director Hwang had been attempting to explain to me. I had heard him corroborate my sense that peace was a proxy for *t'ongil*, but in fact, he had said that peace and life are its preconditions. And when I looked back on the scene of the PLV, a different, fuzzier vision of peace came into focus among the heterogeneous, discrepantly cosmopolitan, people of the Border Area—migrant brides and their mixed families, young military conscripts, and an aging, non-indigenous population. This was not the ecstatic liminality of Victor Turner's *communitas*, but rather a dispersed collective, brought together into a momentary copresence, if not unity. What made this event confusing to me at first was that it was a far cry from the myth of ethno-national recovery that often accompanies state-centric photo-ops of (re) unification—heads of state shaking hands or announcing joint declarations that assume, if not assert, coethnicity.[24]

There is much more that could be explored with respect to the PLV's role in Seohwa-myeon, particularly in its relations with the resident community of migrant brides. Scholars and NGOs have documented the common experiences these women have had with gender discrimination, racism, and domestic violence (H. M. Kim 2012). In my brief encounter, however, what came into focus was my own difference as a diasporic Korean American woman of considerable cosmopolitan privilege. I was already aware that my research was participating in the branding of the DMZ's ecological exceptionalism by contributing my social and academic capital to spaces in which my global credentials were valued. What became crystallized for me at the PLV event, however, was an entirely different reflexive awareness of difference—my own racialized assumptions about which South Koreans count as the proper subjects of unification.

T'ongil is more often translated these days as "unification" rather than "reunification," indicating the pragmatic acceptance among South Koreans of the indefinite temporality of any peace process, and the undeniable cultural differences that exist between the people of North and South, divided now for more than seven decades. The notion of the "Korean race" (한민족; *hanminjok*) as a singular entity, however, is still a powerful explanatory scheme that feeds both notions of South Korean superiority to a North Korean other, and the inevitability (even if not necessarily desirable) of a politically unified Korea (Grinker 1998). International relations scholar Iain Watson (2014) asserts that the peace park discourse of state actors and NGOs "confirms rather than questions beliefs in racial and ethnic homogeneity as a response to multiculturalism" (110), and he critiques the romantic investments in the rural as a repository for Korean ethnic nationalism (107). The PLV offered a different vision of a possible future, grounded in the borderlands of South Korea: the women from China, Vietnam, and the Philippines, frequently racialized in dominant South Korean representations as "foreigners" from the Global South, are part of the (current) future of the nation. Meeting these women shifted my own time and space of unification. Despite my personal and political ambivalence about *t'ongil* and the sentimental invocations of peace, my own diasporic assumptions about who and what constitutes the Korean nation were revealed to be rooted in conservative and unreflective ethnocentrism. Rather than using the DMZ's ecological exceptionalism to naturalize the ethnonation, then, perhaps the DMZ PLV was making peace with nature to create an inclusive community that, through and with "nature," could challenge the myth of racial purity.[25]

Conclusion

The double bind of the DMZ's ecology and its creative potential is embedded in two competing frameworks of peace: an internationalist liberal peace among nations and a more peaceful relationship between humans and the Earth. As I have shown, the peace imaginaries inspired by the DMZ opened a hopeful set of conceptual possibilities, reorienting politics away from the knotty problems of geopolitics and war toward the universal desire for harmony among all things. Yet, as my last example suggests, peace within Korea is not just about right-wing and left-wing politics, but rather about a diverse human population in which multiple differences— not limited to race, ethnicity, gender, sexuality, family origin, and region— present ongoing struggles over justice and equality. Thus, the dynamics raised by the DMZ's double bind can be generalized—what is the relationship between human amity and more-than-human peace? Must one come before the other?

Philosopher Michel Serres begins his book, *The Natural Contract* (1990), with an image of Goya's *Duel with Cudgels, or Fight to the Death with Clubs* (1820–23), to draw attention away from the two embattled protagonists and toward the literal ground, the "marsh into which the struggle is sinking" (1) (figure 1.3). Buried up to their knees, yet still attacking, they are stuck in a battle that neither will win and that, in their blind futility, renders them both equal—equally doomed. Serres asks that we shift our gaze away from the human figures to focus on the ground on and in which their agonistic drama unfolds: "Quicksand is swallowing the duelists; the river is threatening the fighter: earth, waters, and climate, the mute world, the voiceless

Figure 1.3
Francisco de Goya, *Duel with Cudgels, or Fight to the Death with Clubs* (1820–23). Museo del Prado, Madrid, Spain.

things once placed as a décor surrounding the usual spectacles, all those things that never interested anyone, from now on thrust themselves brutally and without warning into our schemes and maneuvers. They burst in on our culture, which had never formed anything but a local, vague, and cosmetic idea of them: nature. What was once local—this river, that swamp—is now global: Planet Earth" (1990: 3). From this view, local human conflicts are not only trivial compared to larger, universal, species-level struggle with Planet Earth, they are likely hastening our collective demise. Following Serres's logic, we must imagine any future peace treaty as one involving more than just the state signatories, the former enemy nations. As he wrote in an essay, *Revisiting the Natural Contract* (2006), "In the past, we signed temporary peace treaties between belligerents: today, we must sign the contracts of symbiosis between the global Earth and the totality of actors. For, in spite of their hatred and the force of their blows, these actors actually struggle, in agreement and in unison, with their habitat" (n.p.).

This refocusing on our habitat could not be any more necessary than it is now, and yet the dynamics of "making peace with nature" that I outlined here—allegorizing the DMZ's nature in the name of its universal symbolism while sacrificing its actual ecologies in the name of peace and profit—continue to intensify. Part of the reason that this is possible is because of the common cosmopolitan epistemologies among South Korean intellectuals, environmentalists, and state actors, inspired by the notion of the DMZ as "untouched" and the scientific data of its biodiversity. Appearing as an unexpected counternarrative to the story of ongoing Cold War enmity and national division, the DMZ's nature became attached to war's opposite—offering a surprising "peace dividend" that allowed its significance to jump scales from national to global, from a divided Korean people to a universal humanity. In these narratives, Nature serves as the vehicle by which humans can imagine a solution to human political problems. Moreover, through this very process of instrumentalizing Nature, anthropocentric political forms, whether state or anti-state, become naturalized.

The story I have told so far is one in which the men fighting in Goya's painting are not just allegories of Koreans separated by the DMZ, but also South Koreans fighting among each other. It is a drama whose protagonists symbolically scale from the local to the global, and the dynamics and the drama replicate at all scales—we (South Koreans, all Koreans, all humans) are reproducing lines of difference and division, sinking together, instead of cooperating to find a way to live peaceably with each other and the Earth. The DMZ as an allegory for our planetary condition does not therefore offer an optimistic view—the two Koreas remain at war, and the fragile biodiversity of the DMZ region is facing increasing threats in the name of peace-as-development rather than what Arturo Escobar calls "peace-with-justice" (2008: 17). Humans in Korea are sinking fast, and while the prospects of a peace treaty among humans can recede just as quickly as they appear, life, as it is, lives on, in the meantime of division. The question remains then, how can we make peace with nature, not by using nature as a vehicle to solve human problems, symbolically or materially, but rather by attuning to specific landscapes and relations among humans and nonhumans?

Coda

In recent months, environmental crises in Korea have increasingly "thrust themselves brutally and without warning into our schemes and maneuvers," as Serres warned (1990: 3). Revising this book manuscript in southern California, while historic and unprecedented wildfires burn across California and the Pacific Northwest, I am unable to travel to South Korea because of the novel coronavirus pandemic. Even if I had been in South Korea in late 2019 before the pandemic reached South Korea, however, I would not have been able to travel to the CCZ because of an outbreak of African swine flu, which had crossed over from North Korea through wild boars and infected domestic pigs being raised in Paju, close to the DMZ. Hundreds of pigs were slaughtered, leading to blood-red rivers and bans on DMZ tourism for more than nine months. South Korean efforts to contain this highly contagious virus were hampered by Pyongyang's refusal to respond to multiple missives from Seoul. By August, the monsoon season, which had begun early and served the Korean peninsula with nearly fifty days of continuous rain, had swelled the riverbanks of the Han River, leading to massive flooding in Seoul. In the border regions, thousands of people were displaced when North Korea suddenly released tons of water from its dam without warning and inundated military and civilian areas in the South. Landmines were dislodged, and an explosion along the Imjin River in Paju led to a massive military effort to locate mines before civilians were killed or maimed.

All of these issues—flooding, infectious diseases, global pandemics, and even landmines—require inter-state cooperation, and the declarations that had been signed by Moon Jae-in and Kim Jong Un at their summits in Panmunjom in 2018 and Pyongyang in 2019 explicitly agreed to such cooperation, particularly with respect to the management of infectious diseases. Yet, the heady days of April 2018 have faded, and inter-Korean politics are normalizing back to stalemate, with the geopolitics of the peninsula tied up with the US sanctions regime and the regional power balance ever more influenced by China's economic and political dominance.

The dramatic detonation of the North–South liaison office by the DPRK in June 2020 marked the definitive end to high-level meetings, and despite the dramatic highs and lows of the summits between President Donald Trump and DPRK leader Kim Jong Un in Hanoi and the DMZ, the peace process quickly stalled. These stumbling blocks may have further motivated the Ministry of Unification to continue with ongoing plans to transform the southern side of the DMZ and CCZ into a "peace zone" (평화 지대), by promoting both DMZ tourism and infrastructure development as part of Moon Jae-in's peace economy agenda.[26]

These moves were made in response to the huge numbers of domestic tourists who streamed by the tens of thousands to the observatories along the DMZ to gaze on the North and reflect on the state of division in the euphoric aftermath of the April 2018 Panmunjom Declaration. By 2019, the DMZ was being touted as the site of "peace tourism," which would be, along with K-pop, the driver for expanding the moribund tourism industry. Even as the Pyongyang Declaration of September 2018 included a commitment by both states to promote inter-Korean "environmental cooperation so as to protect and restore the natural ecology," peace tourism, to the dismay of ecologists and environmental groups, largely attempted to bypass nature conservation in its drive to bring the two Koreas closer.[27]

Despite opposition by environmental groups who demanded a comprehensive conservation strategy and roadmap, the government announced plans to open three trails inside the DMZ itself. The first was opened to visitors in April 2019 and was described by the Ministry of Culture, Sports, and Tourism as an opportunity "to enjoy a pristine ecosystem that has been off limits to people for decades. This kind of tour can promote peace on the Korean Peninsula and move away from the usual security-centered sightseeing trips the country had provided in the past."[28]

In Paju, these plans have taken shape around the expansion of Freedom Road (자유로) into the "Munsan–Dorasan Expressway." Even as environmentalists and local residents have expressed vociferous opposition, plans by the Ministry of Land, Infrastructure, and Transport are moving forward. Journalists critical of the project have coined it the Terrestrial Four Rivers Project, referring to the disastrous and corrupt dredging of the four major rivers touted as eco-friendly by the Lee Myung-bak administration. If it were to be built, this expressway project would fragment and sever connections between the marine and land ecosystems of the Han River estuary. Despite demands by ecological activists for an environmental assessment, the Ministry of Land, Infrastructure, and Transport announced in January 2021 the impossibility of conducting one due to safety concerns related to the presence of landmines. Instead, it determined that the assessment would be conducted post facto, once the project was completed.

In the chapters that follow, I focus attention on the "life" part of "peace and life" to ask how knowledge of the DMZ's ecology is produced and valued. I found a different, less anthropocentric, practice of making peace with nature in the work of DERI, where Kim Seung Ho theorized and practiced what he called "biological peace" (see Introduction). As chapter 2 shows, small agricultural ponds in the CCZ offer one example of a peace process, decentering the anthropocentric approaches to division politics in South Korea, which have largely instrumentalized the DMZ's nature in the name of peaceful utilization.

PONDS

Why do so many diverse creatures make this place their home? We couldn't make out the secret. In simple terms, it's because people aren't allowed to move about freely here. But this explanation is broadly insufficient and unsatisfactory. DMZ Ecology Research Institute has frequented this place for five years to decipher this code. We witnessed (보았다). We felt the vitality (기운) of the creatures with our whole bodies and understood the ways to communicate with them (이들과 소통하는 방법을 알았다). And thus, we discovered things. The secrets of maintaining a healthy ecology were concealed in spaces so commonplace as to be simply dismissed out of hand.

Dumbeong, Natural Streams: Cracking the Secret Code of the DMZ's Ecology (DMZ Ecology Research Institute 2009: 9)

I am submerged nearly to my waist in a large pond, wearing waterproof rubber coveralls and holding in front of me a wide net attached on either side to two long rods. I aim the tips down into the water and try to scoop up some of the muck below, dragging the net up along the overgrown, grassy edge of the pond to bring up whatever aquatic organisms may exist, somewhere beneath the murky surface. It requires some strength to get into the weeds where the creatures like to hang out. I don't have the skill, or perhaps the upper body strength, to get the right angle. The first couple of pulls come up empty, and I decide to leave the task to the stronger and taller male students who have mastered the technique. I switch instead to a handheld sieve, panning the same general area, sifting through the dregs for any wiggly shapes that might be dragonfly nymphs (애벌레), or tiny *kkae almul pang'gae* (깨알물방개; lit., "sesame seed beetle"), a small water bug of the *Laccophilus* genus. Easier to spot are the water scorpions (장구애비; *Laccophilus difficilis* Sharp), with their long tails and predatory mien.

Figure 2.1
A *dumbeong* in the Paju
CCZ area. Photograph by
the author.

The pond I am in is one of dozens in the western CCZ being studied by the DERI, a small NGO based in Paju City, north of Seoul (figure 2.1). They refer to the ponds as *dumbeong* (둠벙), adopting a local word for "puddle" used by farmers for whom these ponds serve as mini reservoirs to irrigate rainwater-sourced rice paddies (천수답).[1] Before the consolidation of rice-paddy farms and large-scale irrigation systems in the 1960s, *dumbeong* were important to agricultural development in Korea, which lacks large lakes for reliable sources of fresh water.[2] They are still in use in some remote or mountainous regions and are gaining recognition as traditional ecological knowledge (TEK; G. Kim et al. 2019) in the context of the state's promotion of environment-friendly agriculture (M. Kim et al. 2016), but they have nearly disappeared outside of the Paju CCZ area.

The reasons for their persistence in the CCZ have everything to do with the military infrastructure and the restrictions imposed on building and development. Setting aside questions of land ownership in the Paju CCZ, where two thirds of the land is privately owned, building in the CCZ is subject to multiple laws and restrictions, in particular the Military Bases and Installations Protection Act, which prohibits the construction of canals or waterways.[3] According to a 2011 Paju City government report, only

11 percent of rice paddies in the Paju CCZ area were supplied with water from the municipal pumping station, the rest (89 percent) relied on natural streams or *dumbeong* (cited in S. H. Kim, J. H. Kim, and J. G. Kim 2011: 277). Although some artificial waterways have been built in the western CCZ, in most areas, it lacks the concrete berms and channels that would not only make the *dumbeong* obsolete, but also fragment the CCZ landscape and disrupt the lifeways and habitats of untold numbers of creatures, including those that have yet to be documented. The militarization of the DMZ area has thus created a "multispecies opportunity" (Tsing 2014: 108) by unintentionally preserving a premodern agricultural system within a diverse mosaic landscape of patches and ecotones.

From a high modernist perspective, *dumbeong* might be considered to be, like the Moroccan irrigation system described by Clifford Geertz, "technologically embarrassing" (1972: 36). In the context of division infrastructure and the DMZ's nature, however, they lend truth to Ashley Carse's contention that infrastructures "produce environments" (2014: 6). I frame *dumbeong* as the negative infrastructure of the CCZ—they are not infrastructures in the modern sense, but they function as important elements supporting the ecological structure of the CCZ's agricultural landscapes, and their existence is conditioned by the division and legal injunctions against building infrastructure in the CCZ. Against the dominant political temporalities in South Korea, I argue that they exist "in the meantime of division," in a spatiotemporality in which the relentless drive for progress and efficiency—qualities that have long characterized South Korean economic and cultural logics—has been somewhat lessened.

Even if capitalist development of the most rampant variety is relatively absent from the DMZ region, the discourses that circulate around its future, and the future of the peninsula, are difficult to disentangle from capitalist imaginaries. Since the Sunshine Policy era, inter-Korean "peace" rarely appears without its doppelganger, "prosperity," which is overwhelmingly economic in its connotations.[4] Thus, the negative infrastructure of *dumbeong* is not anti-infrastructure but, rather, a kind of negative space where modern infrastructures might exist, if not for the division. In a sense, they are technological holdovers, necessary for agricultural production, until the "peace and prosperity" promised by the state's discourse of inter-Korean cooperation finally make them obsolete.

Despite their importance to the ecological structure of the DMZ's landscapes, it has only been recently that *dumbeong* has become a scientific term in South Korean environmental studies. And it's likely that most

South Koreans have never heard of the word, even as the South Korean National Institute of Ecology, when it opened in 2013, installed a *dumbeong* on its grounds, called the Ecorium Pond.[5] A *dumbeong*, however, cannot be so easily abstracted from the agricultural landscape it serves, as *dumbeong* habitats rely on the monoculture of rice growing. Ecological studies have shown that a paddy irrigation pond in isolation would eventually be colonized by vegetation and, in the course of about ten years, turn into woodland (C.-s. Lee, You, and Robinson 2002: 312), and rainwater-fed wet-rice paddies rely on *dumbeong*.[6] Although the watery landscapes of flooded rice paddies can be habitats for aquatic species, they are only wet for about three to four months per year (J. H. Ahn et al. 2017), whereas *dumbeong* provide more stable ecosystems and can be considered "permanent wetlands" (M. Kim et al. 2016: 156). For these reasons, my colleagues at the DERI see *dumbeong* as crucial to ecological connectivity among paddies, fields, and forests and as sites of multiple edge effects that help to produce the diversity of landscapes and species in the CCZ.

In what follows, I approach *dumbeong* as "emergent ecologies" of humans, water, and the creatures that live within them (Kirksey 2015). Next to the endangered cranes, bears, tigers, and other megafauna that represent dramatic stories of extinction and survival in the DMZ, the microscopic and invertebrate life-forms of *dumbeong* are certainly less charismatic.[7] Ponds defy iconicization or enrollment in the "Spectacle of Nature" (Brockington, Duffy, and Igoe 2010: 176). Nevertheless, they provide the grounds for experimental encounters that generate both biodiversity and biological peace, a decentering of the (anthropocentric) peace discourses that characterize South Korean division politics.

In the DERI's 2009 book on *dumbeong* ecologies, they describe them as "the spaces that appeared to be commonplace" (혼하게 보이던 공간; DMZ Ecology Research Institute 2009: 9). The epigraph narrates the humble *dumbeong* as holding the secrets to the DMZ's ecology, and it frames the members of the DERI as crucial interlocutors who used their bodies and senses to communicate with the pond's life-forms. However mystical or romantic this narration may seem, the pond work of the DERI that I participated in reflected modes of attunement and attention that hewed closely to this ethos of multispecies care. Based on fieldwork between September 2011 and September 2012, as well as intermittent visits between 2013 and 2016, this chapter suggests that the DERI's *dumbeong* have the potential to decenter hegemonic and anthropocentric approaches to division politics in South Korea, including the dispensationalist utopianism of nationalist peace imaginaries, the "when that day comes" (그 날이 오면) temporality of unification, or the state-driven politics of "diplomatic peace offensives" (평화공세), all of which would instrumentalize the DMZ's nature in the name of peaceful utilization as a means to an end.

(Post-)war Ecosystems and Peace Offensives

In the ongoing policy discussions and public debates over the DMZ's future—as a site of rare nature conservation or a space of future development—skeptics of the conservation agenda often lodge the critique that the ecology of the DMZ is hardly pure. Military activities, which involve frequent forest fires, landmines, and herbicides, are mobilized to mar the picture of pristine nature. But instead of subjecting the DMZ to a test of ecological purity, former research associate at the Gyeonggi Research Institute, Dr. Park Eun-Jin, argues that it should be framed as a "post-war ecosystem":

> It's true that the DMZ was ravaged by the war, and this ecosystem, due to military conflict for over sixty years, has been subject to damage by fires and herbicides, as well as ecological adversity from alien species. Yet it is a nature (자연) that has produced a unique ecosystem from war and hardship, adapting and recovering in its own way. Even though the forests that have emerged are short in stature due to the effects of military operations, in the lowlands, wetlands have formed and abundant nature has materialized. Areas previously used by human inhabitants have been colonized by plains, and without the influence of humans on [former] farmlands, they have transformed through processes of ecological succession. (E.-J. Park 2013b: 33)

She further describes how the military fires and cutting of timber may have interfered with natural succession, but asserts that an effect of these disturbances is an increase in landscape diversity.[8] Framing the DMZ as an "unintentionally unique landscape," Park argues that this militarized "post-war ecosystem" has permitted endangered species and many other diverse forms of life to exist (34). This view was shared by other researchers I met with, including Professor Kim Kwi-gon, a landscape architect and professor of environmental planning at Seoul National University, who explained to me that despite the fires set by North Korea and countered by the South, the DMZ was well protected. Kim was the only researcher to have regular and direct access to the DMZ proper, having permission from the South Korean government and the UN Command. When we met in 2011, he had recently published a massive 470-page, large-format book summarizing his research in the framework of landscape ecology called "DMZ: Land of Peace and Life" (2010; 평화와 생명의 땅: DMZ) based on eighteen years of intermittent ecological surveys in the DMZ and CCZ.[9]

The mountainous eastern region of the DMZ is the most well protected, mostly due to its steep terrain and the sparse human populations in northern Gangwon Province. The western DMZ area, north of the city of Paju, however, boasts greater landscape diversity, given its mosaic landscape of woodland, farmlands, wetlands, grasslands, low hills, and the rivers and streams of the Imjin River corridor and the Han River estuary. This high level of connectivity across these patches is due, in part, to agricultural land use, which supports the biodiversity in this part of the CCZ. At the same time, agricultural activities have introduced pesticides, herbicides, and fertilizers, which, in combination with military activities and industrial runoff from the Kaeseong Industrial Complex (in North Korea, just across the western DMZ), have contributed to the pollution of the area's water and soil. Furthermore, the canalization of waterways, the construction of roads, and the proliferation of ginseng fields and apple orchards are increasingly fragmenting the landscape (K.-g. Kim 2010; Park and Nam 2013; S. H. Kim, J. H. Kim, and J. G. Kim 2011).[10]

Nevertheless, after decades of scientific research documenting the landscapes and the species that exist there, the DMZ area's status as a habitat for diverse forms of life is indisputable. In the western CCZ, this biodiversity is connected to the rice-paddy fields that dominate the landscape. The migratory birds that sojourn there between October and March feed on the leftover rice grains in fallow rice paddies, and the majority of the peninsula's dragonfly habitats are in the CCZ's *dumbeongs*. As Kim Kwi-gon explained to me, the "DMZ ecosystems are a product of agricultural culture," meaning that former rice paddies had transformed into wetlands, but also that agricultural use of the CCZ is part of the area's landscape and species biodiversity.

For both Park and Kim, the DMZ's ecological protection was less concerning than the CCZ, which had been increasingly liberalized and open to civilian activities since the shift at the national level from centralized to local autonomous governance in the late 1990s (see Chang, Bae, and Park 2019). When I interviewed Park in 2015, she felt strongly that the CCZ was the place where sustainable development of the DMZ had to be implemented first, in advance of any peaceful utilization of the DMZ. Through her research on eco-peace villages in the Gyeonggi CCZ, she foregrounded the necessity of building positive relationships between "people and nature." In her view, much of the policy discussion and debate was overly focused on the DMZ and not on the CCZ, and was often appropriated for political ends, particularly with respect to the inter-Korean politics and the competitive "peace offensives" (평화공세) between the two Koreas.

The peace offensives in late 2011 included Lee Myung-bak's promotion of the DMZ as "the land of peace and life" (평화와 생명의 땅) and massive bureaucratic effort to promote the DMZ as a UNESCO biosphere reserve. As described in chapter 1, Lee's green agenda had effectively disarticulated the DMZ's nature from inter-Korean diplomacy in surprising ways. Rather than seeking to protect the entire DMZ and using that proposal to entice North Korea into a joint conservation effort, Lee—who had cut off all communication with the North in a rebuke to his predecessors' Sunshine Policy—proposed that only the southern half of the DMZ be designated as a UNESCO biosphere reserve. South Korea's proposal to the UNESCO Man and the Biosphere Programme was rejected, in large part due to a counter-offensive on the part of the North to Lee's peace offensive, but Lee's successor, Park Geun-hye, revised the idea by announcing at an address to the US Congress in 2013 that she would build an international peace park in the DMZ. Over lunch in 2015, Dr. Park Eun-Jin told me that from the perspective of ecological conservation, these political maneuvers distracted from the problem at hand. For her, the most practical questions to be tackled centered on how to research and preserve the DMZ's environments. With politicians having seized on the DMZ's ecological exceptionalism and associations with wilderness for decades, Park worried that everyday South Koreans would have false expectations and would later come to think, "Oh, it's actually not true."

As she noted in a 2013 essay, "despite many arguments and suggestions, the debate between conservation and utilization of the DMZ that has been at the heart of the inter-Korean cooperation agenda has been going around in circles" (E.-J. Park 2013a: 244). At the local and regional level, the conservation versus development debate has exacerbated divisions, pitting local residents against metropolitan environmentalists. Park suggests, "Rather than viewing the DMZ as a 'treasure trove of ecological resources,' the symbolism of the DMZ should become the source of a new paradigm to move beyond the separation of man and nature and fixed division created by modernization and developmentalism" (2013a: 247). Park, however, leaves the outlines of this paradigm and how it might be formulated unaddressed.

In the following pages, I analyze the political ecology of the Paju CCZ and then focus on the pond work of the DERI, which offers the embryonic outlines of a new paradigm.

The Paju CCZ

Kim Seung Ho founded the DERI in 2005, after moving to Paju to work as a public-school science teacher. An avid fisher, he was frustrated by the fact that he couldn't catch any fish in the upstream part of the Imjin River, which runs through Paju. He did some research and discovered that it was due to water pollution. In 2000, he started an environmental studies project for his students to study the river, which runs downstream from the northeast, across the CCZ. The study of the river eventually led him to the CCZ, where he set up a study of the migratory cinereous vultures (독수리) in 2004, before expanding the scope to include the general ecology of the area.

Kim's arrival in Paju coincided with major transformations to the Paju City and CCZ areas. In particular, the third stage of the Seoul Metropolitan Area's development plan (2006–20) has focused on "Paju becoming a north–south exchange industrial belt" (Chang, Bae, and Park 2019: 481). Cultural geographer Valérie Gelézeau describes Seoul's urban expansion in the 2000s as a northward "frontier drive" (2013: 25), which involved so-called new town (신도시) developments in Gimpo, Goyang, and Paju, all of which are located northwest of Seoul, with Paju as the northernmost city between Seoul and the DMZ. Although the capital area has been expanding since the first decade of mass rural-to-urban migration in the 1960s, with these new towns, it has effectively come to include nearly all of Gyeonggi Province, which makes it the most populous province in the country. The twenty-five million people who live in the capital area constitute nearly 50 percent of the total national population. Paju alone doubled in population in three decades, from 1983 to 2012, and had an annual 6.3 percent growth rate in the first half of the 2000s. Gelézeau attributes this exponential growth in Paju to the implementation of the 2011 Border Area law (which directed government investment and development to the region), as well as the inter-Korean cooperation that characterized the Sunshine Policy era (2013: 24).

Former agricultural areas in the Gimpo and Ilsan Plains, which the Japanese colonial government consolidated through the building of embankments and irrigation systems (Ch'ang-hwan Kim 2011), are now urbanized extensions of Seoul, barely distinguishable from other Seoul neighborhoods—a homogeneous built environment of high-rise apartment complexes, chain stores, and mass consumption that is efficiently connected to the metropolitan center through highways, regional trains, and Seoul subway lines. Between the DMZ and this encroachment of urban development from the Seoul Capital Area, the political economy of the western CCZ has also witnessed important changes.

As the new town developments displaced farmers from their agricultural lands in the mid-2000s, they began purchasing land in the CCZ, cutting down forests and reestablishing rice paddies. Land prices began rising with demand, and land speculation increased particularly with the optimism about unification during the Sunshine Policy era. Soon many non-farming "outsiders" (외지인) purchased land for what would become long-term investments. Unable to build on the property, they rented to tenant farmers, and during the time of my fieldwork, an increasing number of relatively eco-friendly rice paddies were being converted into high-profit environmentally damaging ginseng fields.[11] Ginseng fields were particularly pernicious in the eyes of the DERI because they were proliferating quickly, with farmers illegally clearing forested areas or recovering rice paddies to grow the highly profitable medicinal root. Ginseng requires six years to mature, with plastic tarps stretched over wooden sticks to create the shade necessary for the delicate plants to grow. Because migratory birds, particularly the endangered red-crowned and white-naped cranes, feed and rest on fallow rice paddies, when these rice paddies are replaced by ginseng fields they reduce or encroach upon valuable bird habitats (see E. J. Kim 2019).

I learned much of this history from Kim Seung Ho in the DERI offices in Paju Book City. Built near the banks of the Han River just south of downtown Paju in the 2000s, Paju Book City was designed to be a literature utopia, with more than two hundred publishing companies and "twenty books for every human."[12] Book City is famous for its architecture, much of which is LEED certified, and which often appears as the ultramodern backdrop for television dramas. Kim explained how the Sannam wetland, which was drained to build Paju Book City, had once been twenty meters deep, with silty sedimentation from the Han River. It served as the annual winter habitat for 2,500 white-naped cranes, a spectacular number that was hard to visualize at the time of our conversation in 2012, when it would have been remarkable to see a flock of more than ten white-naped cranes together.

My fieldwork was facilitated by these shifts in the border area political economy and expanding transportation infrastructures as I resided in Seoul and could easily take the 2200 commuter bus thirty kilometers north from the neighborhood of Hong-Ik University in central Seoul to the DERI offices. My early morning companions would invariably include workers going to LG's flat-screen display factories, now called the High-Tech Display Manufacturing Complex, the largest such entity in the world.[13] Returning in the late afternoon, I would be surrounded by university students, young Seoulites, and Asian tourists returning to Seoul from the Lotte Premium Outlets, a massive consumer complex with 270 stores that opened in March 2011, six months before I began conducting fieldwork.[14] Our monitoring excursions into the CCZ started at 8 a.m., and once I arrived in Paju Book City, it was another thirty kilometers to the entrance of the CCZ. With Director Kim at the wheel, I would join other DERI members in his minivan, driving past the wetlands around Gongneung Stream where we would count the waterbirds, onto Route 77, Freedom Road, past the Odusan Reunification Observatory and the wetlands where the Han and Imjin Rivers meet.

Entering the CCZ for the first time can be viscerally jarring because one moves from the familiar built environments of urban South Korea into a borderland space of division. This is a space where modern infrastructures of connection and public works recede and are replaced by military infrastructure.[15] Freedom Road ends at the juncture with Unification Road, symbolically underscoring the transition point from one political system to another, from a space of liberal democracy to one of sovereign exception.[16] Yet, these Cold War semiotics disguise the actual relations of state sovereignty and market penetration: Although the southern half of the DMZ is controlled by the UN Command, the CCZ is under South Korean jurisdiction and is increasingly a hybrid space of both military restriction and capital flows.

This mix of civilian and military use in the context of ongoing war becomes immediately evident at the checkpoint—outside the guard post, announcing the military authority of the area, is a sign that reads "Invincible Dagger Battalion, 1st Infantry Division," with their tag line, "first to enter Pyongyang" (평양 선봉 입성 무적칼 부대), referring to their storming of the North's capital during the Korean War. One DERI member, artist Heo Young, would often comment on what she called the "baby faces" of the privates checking us in, perhaps because she was struck by the incongruity of their stiff demeanor and their innocent youthfulness. Her comments also conveyed an implicit commentary on the irrationality of the whole situation—ongoing war, mandatory military service, and securitized borderlands. Adding to the incongruity were other signs at and around the checkpoint, such as these that I recorded in my field notes in September 2015:

> Agricultural entry/exit times: 6:00–19:00
> Paju, Ready for Unification
> ROK's City of Hope
> Paju Bicycle Tour, 14:20–15:00

One of the first people to identify the ecological possibilities of the DMZ's nature was American conservationist Harold Coolidge, in 1965, when he remarked on the ecological vitality of the area, where former rice paddies had transformed into woodlands (see E. J. Kim n.d.). By that time, however, agricultural activities in the CCZ were already being permitted by the US Armed Forces, and "CCL north-facing villages" (만통선 북방마을) were being established by the South Korean government (see chapter 4). In the Paju area, the first reunification village, Tongil-chon, was established in 1973 with eighty households. And in 1998, during the Sunshine Policy era, the resettlement village of Haemaru-chon was founded. According to 2008 numbers, the total civilian population of the Paju DMZ area is around eight hundred individuals, across 321 households, including Tongil-chon, Haemaru-chon, and Daeseong-dong (also known as 자유의 마을, or Freedom Village), the only South Korean propaganda village inside the DMZ itself.[17] For these reasons, someone expecting to witness pure nature in the Paju CCZ might be disappointed to learn that nearly one-third of the land is used for agricultural production and that the forests (38.6 percent of total land cover) have been shrinking as more land is converted to farmland (Park and Nam 2013).[18]

Siting Biodiversity

Shortly after founding the DERI, Kim was asked by a friend to teach an extramural course on ecology for his daughter—a "unique activity" (독특한 액티비티) that would improve her chances of getting into an elite college, especially in the United States.[19] This was a period in which the discourse of "spec" (스펙)—which referred to a student's specifications (GPA, English-language ability, extracurriculars, and the like)—began to circulate among students and parents, registering a new intensity in South Koreans' fervor for educational advancement, long viewed as the key to cosmopolitan status at home and competitiveness at a global level (Seth 2002; Park and Abelmann 2004). The friend's daughter attended one of the most elite high schools in the country, known as *t'ŭkmok'go* (특목고), or "special purpose high schools," which are akin to preparatory academies in the United States. Kim agreed, and soon other parents with children at the *t'ŭkmok'go* were eager to enroll their students once they saw that some of the alumni of the program had gone on to top South Korean and Ivy League universities.

By the time I began working with the DERI in late 2011, they were running a program for high school freshmen, some of whom continued to the advanced track as sophomores and juniors. The program culminated in an essay and public presentation, and their experience studying the DMZ's ecology often became the basis for their US college entrance essays. The paradox of the DMZ's nature and its ecological exceptionalism was proving to be persuasive content for the students' personal statements. One DERI alumnus was admitted to Cornell University and was even mentioned by the university president in a welcome address to the incoming class. With these successful graduates of the program, the DERI was expanding the program to include second-tier private high schools, aware that they would be helping to reproduce the class system if they only allowed students from the *t'ŭkmok'go*.

The DERI's program provided many students with their first in-depth experience conducting natural science fieldwork and their first opportunity to directly contemplate the national division. Parents appreciated the program because it helped to strengthen their children's college applications while also exposing them to the outdoors. This integration of the DERI's scientific research and its educational programs was central to Director Kim's long-term view of planetary change, environmental crisis, and human responsibility. The students received an education in basic science as well as critical frameworks for analyzing the state's policies and the area's political economy. Moreover, they came to care about the CCZ ecologies and their precarious futures through various research projects related to the flora and fauna of *dumbeong* as well as the habitats and wintering behavior of endangered cranes. Kim reasoned that the elite students at the top high schools in South Korea would grow up to become influential people in South Korean and global society. As such, they could use their social, cultural, and economic capital to promote environmentally sustainable agendas with respect to the DMZ and more generally. He expressed his greater faith in the potential of high school students than he had for university students, for whom, he stated, this kind of ecological awareness building would be too late.

When I first began tagging along on the students' research forays, I probably knew as much as or less than they did about basic ecology or how to identify flora and fauna, in English, and certainly in Korean. I was aware that my social capital as a Korean American professor enhanced their educational capital, particularly in the eyes of parents who enrolled their children in the DERI's program. Furthermore, the irony was not lost on me that I too was leveraging the DMZ's ecological exceptionalism and its paradoxical nature to secure funding and entry into elite academic networks. Indeed, Director Kim likely saw me as similar, in some ways, to these students, many of whom were transnational and had been partially schooled in the United States. He viewed them as lacking Korean identity (한국인의 정체성) and therefore hoped that the program could instill in them an understanding of the current reality of Korea (한국의 현실), which, in turn, could help them successfully pursue their future goals.

When I began my research in late 2011, the core members impressed me with their fun-loving gregariousness and their obsessive attention to the aesthetics and techniques of photographic documentation. Fieldwork with them was an intensely social process of ecological knowledge production. They spoke of the group as a *sikku* (식구), a term meaning "family," but one that connotes kinship based in commensality rather than blood.

Kim's daughter, Jae Hyun, was a key member of the group, and was completing her BA in biology at Seoul Women's University when I first met her. She would go on to complete her MA and PhD in biological sciences education at Seoul National University. She was kept very busy gathering and organizing data for the DERI and also took a leadership role in the educational program. The other members included Mr. Oh, a former government scientist with a master's degree in marine biology who owned a pork-stew restaurant in Paju and whose son was one of the first students in the program. Dr. Rhee, an ethnomusicologist and part-time lecturer, left South Korea for Spain in the 1960s, disgusted with the extreme discrimination he faced because of a congenital disability. He stayed abroad for twenty years before moving back to South Korea with his spouse, painter and sculptor Heo Young, who was also a member of the group. Y. S. Kim, who went by his pen name Un-nam, and his spouse, Sun-young, were retired schoolteachers and amateur naturalists. Kang Han-kyu, in his thirties, had grown up in neighboring Pocheon and was a naturalist who was training to become a botanical researcher for a government agency. Director Kim's wife was also highly knowledgeable about flora, and she frequently joined to lead a group of students in studying the plant life of the area.[20] The members were politically left and identified as environmentalists, but they were not environmental activists, nor were they aligned with the Ministry of Environment or local bureaucracies, although they received funding from the Paju metropolitan government.

I was initially drawn to the group because, although none of the members were local residents of the CCZ, their consistent research activities gave them a kind of local knowledge that other DMZ-related NGOs lacked. Despite the fact that there are reportedly more than two hundred organizations in South Korea that focus on the DMZ (*Space* 2014), few, if any, were engaged in ongoing and regular research. Most tended to generate policy reports, organize environmental actions, or hold conferences and discussions related to the DMZ. In contrast, the DERI conducted their research year-round, at least once a week, focusing on migratory bird counts during the wintering season (October to March) and on *dumbeong* from the spring to the early fall.

The group asserted authority over the DMZ region's ecologies through their long-term commitment to the area and intimate relationships with the landscapes and its nonhuman inhabitants. Indeed, the DERI's identity was affectively charged with a sense of shared intellectual mission based on their expertise derived from a direct knowledge of place. They were wary of professors and other scholars who would often try to piggyback on their work or use their data, which required them to be protective of them, if not secretive. For instance, when I was first introduced to their research on *dumbeong*, I asked Dr. Rhee whether they had a map of the ponds, and he said that they did but refused to share it with anyone out of concern that it would be used without attribution, particularly by foreign scientists. In the hierarchy of biological sciences (in South Korea and elsewhere), which tends to privilege laboratory studies over field studies and genetic analysis over species surveys, graduate students are often the ones who conduct fieldwork, while their professors remain in their university offices and oversee the analysis of the data. Given this hierarchical system, the map, along with DERI's other data, could easily be relegated to the status of context, without being granted value as original scientific research.

As governmental and public interest in the DMZ and its ecologies has increased over the past decade, however, the DERI's scientific reputation and standing have grown in tandem, in part due to Director Kim's active role as a "spokesperson" for the CCZ's nature (Latour 1999). Kim frequently made public presentations and media appearances regarding the DMZ's ecological welfare, and since 2015, the DERI has become a regular presence in government and NGO policy discussions regarding the DMZ's ecologies. In addition, Director Kim and Kim Jae Hyun have coauthored numerous articles with other scientists and DERI researchers on *dumbeong* classifications, hydrological and geomorphic characteristics, and conservation value (Kim S. H., J. H. Kim, and J. G. Kim 2011; Kim J. H. et al. 2016; H.-y. Chung et al. 2020).

Even as the DERI published reports, species lists, and biodiversity studies, the enchantment of discovery conveyed in the epigraph—tied to witnessing, feeling, and communicating with creatures in commonplace *dumbeong*—was still central to their practices of knowledge production. As Geoffrey Bowker's (2000) incisive analysis of biodiversity databases illuminates, one of the stumbling blocks to establishing a global database of biodiversity is that standardization across different national systems and disciplinary data sets is impossible. Similar to other modeling systems, those in ecology are falling short of the spatial and community-level complexity of a given area and the temporal complexity of a changing planet. As he explains, "The importance of site indicates a fact about biodiversity science of central importance for its mapping: it is the science of the radically singular, and so its maps will always enfold—in complex ways—traces of their community and site of production. The underlying question is what diversity there is in this world now—not what diversity there may be in earth-like planets under different sets of conditions" (744–45).[21] *Dumbeong* came into being as sites of biodiversity through embodied, affective, and social knowledge production. In this sense, the diversity of the *dumbeong* was conjoined with the singularity of the encounter between the researchers and the flora and fauna that they observed.

Dumbeong Worldings

We are at *Mulch'an Chebi dumbeong* (물찬 제비 둠벙), a delightful play on words that Director Kim is particularly smitten with. He asks two high school freshmen if they can guess why the *dumbeong* is named *Mulch'an Chebi*, and one of them ventures a bit cheekily that it's because it's a place where swallows come to drink water, which is the literal meaning of the phrase. He chuckles and tells them that the *dumbeong* was given the name because they noticed that there were so many swallows feeding on the plentiful insects here. The phrase in Korean describes the way that swallows drink water, diving and swooping quickly to fill their beaks, but it is also a figurative expression that is used to describe physically slender and nimble people such as athletes who move with grace and fluidity. The name therefore could be both Nimble Pond and Swallows Drinking Water Pond. Not all of the *dumbeong* had such charmingly polysemous names, but most had been christened by members of the DERI in ways that indexed their location, shape, characteristics, or species that were found there: Alder Tree, Half Moon, Seoul Frog (금개구리; *Pelophylax chosenicus*), Shelling Area, Roadside, Dragonfly Nymph (애벌레), and Crane Lily (두루미 천남성; *Arisaema hetero-phyllum*) are just some examples of *dumbeong* that I visited.

Studying *dumbeong* with the DERI, I was struck by how infrequently we would encounter other people, despite the fact that farmers depended on them for their rice cultivation. A tenant farmer once came to a *dumbeong* with her young daughter to look for snails, but that was a rare occurrence, and it was infused with status hierarchies and territoriality on the part of the DERI. It was easy to ignore property lines or public/private distinctions because they are not marked—apart from the military facilities and mine-fields, we were able to travel freely once inside the CCZ. We traversed the spaces as if it were a national park and we were its rangers, moving here and there, along familiar routes. Each of us wielded expensive DSLR cameras and macro lenses to capture the best angles on the yellow petals of *aegi ttong p'ul* (애기똥풀; baby's-poo grass; *Chelidonium majus var. asiaticum*), a common perennial, or the eyes of the endangered Seoul frog. We were almost never interrupted in our close inspection and documentation of the flora and fauna. It was easy also, therefore, to watch over the space as if it were ours. Only on one occasion did we encounter ROK military officers who were curious about our bird-watching activities in a somewhat sensitive area.

The goals of the research were to understand what existed in the CCZ through meticulous and regular documentation of nonmilitary areas. Most of the publications of the DERI have focused on species lists and photographic evidence of plants, birds, mammals, insects, and so on. The *dumbeong* themselves were difficult to represent photographically, and in the DERI's 2009 publication on *dumbeong*, the images of these ponds are placid and absent of any humans—farmers or researchers. Moreover, the fact that military installations or training grounds were, in some instances, just around the corner was difficult to discern, apart from the booming sounds of shelling or artillery that would sometimes punctuate the ambient backdrop of trees rustling and bird calls.

The DERI used the English word "monitoring," a term commonly used in Korea to refer to ecological surveying. And the connotation of "keeping an eye on" was apt—they were engaged not only in seeing what was out there, but also in documenting changes to the landscapes and relations among the species that they studied. Monitoring was predominated by practices of visual documentation, but it was also multisensory. My first visit with the DERI brought us to "roadside *dumbeong*" (길가온 둠벙) where I was enrolled in this process of direct sensory attunement to the DMZ's nature. Armed with their field guides, cameras, clipboards, and pens, the researchers walked the periphery of the *dumbeong*, naming the plants, writing them down, and often stopping to show me the particular characteristics of a plant's leaf structure, the taste of its fruit, or its peculiar texture or smell. I came to see them as akin to Lévi-Strauss's bricoleur, seeking patterns and order in what was in front of them, rather than seeking universal categories or fixed classifications (1966). For Director Kim, the DERI's advantage over scientists with PhDs was that they had "direct experience" (현장 경험): "We understand and grasp species in situ (현장에서), much more so than those people who [just] study in libraries. Through our senses."[22]

On an overcast morning in October 2011, with the fiery colors of the fall leaves filtered by a soft gray mist, Kim pulled over on the side of the road to take a photo of the autumn scenery and was overcome by the sublimity of the changing landscapes. He ruminated on the limits to human knowledge of nature (자연) and its transformations. Even as they continued to monitor this area, returning week after week, the complexity of nature and its transformations continuously eluded him. Jae Hyun added that science is continuously under revision, and that "science is not the truth." For Kim, scientific explanations were insufficient to understanding nature. He subscribed to something akin to E. O. Wilson's theory of biophilia (Takacs 1996), which posits that humans have an innate instinct to enjoy and appreciate the natural world. As he put it, it is enormously inefficient for people to be stressed by work and then be forced to travel on the weekends to enjoy nature. He attributed the decline in public health to the decline in green spaces and the foolish agendas of the government, which was acceding to the basest desires of citizens for convenience and consumption, rather than the moral responsibility to create livable worlds. But his greatest concern was for the nonhuman creatures—not only the rare and endangered migratory cranes, but also the common residents such as magpies and wild boars whose habitats and food systems have been systematically destroyed.[23]

The scientific method embodied in the pond work of the DERI was inseparable from this sensuous biophilia. Moreover, Kim articulated a theory of knowledge that resonated strongly with Lévi-Strauss's "science of the concrete"—essentializing the observation of patterns in nature as a human instinct. But in his view, these observations were "extremely subjective." As he put it, "Studying and classifying is only from my point of view. This is in the name of science, and it's put forth in an objective way. [But,] it's very true to your instincts. It may sound strange, but it's a fundamental [human] problem…so if you seriously consider this, then like me, you won't be able to be certain any longer. Just thinking in terms of generalizability can make you uncertain." This epistemological uncertainty regarding universal science didn't prevent Kim from asserting the fact that changes were occurring in the CCZ, for the ongoing destruction of habitats from the expansion of "new towns" and tourism development in the CCZ was creating unambiguously negative effects on nonhuman habitats.

The DERI's research discoveries were thereby framed in relation to the CCZ's changes. They posited correlations between the increasing number of ginseng fields and the decline in numbers of wintering cranes and measured the effects of concrete water channels on the lifecycles of frogs (Ju, J. H. Kim, and S. H. Kim 2016). They investigated the species diversity of microinvertebrates and various endangered species in *dumbeong* rice-paddy wetland landscapes (e.g., Chung et al. 2020). In addition to these findings related to land use and agricultural activities, they also were detecting evidence of shifting ecological baselines that they connected to the warming of the planet. The first endangered species found in a *dumbeong* habitat was identified in August 2011, shortly before I began my fieldwork. The flowering aquatic plant, *Caldesia parnassifolia* (둥근 입택사), which is categorized as being of "least concern" on the IUCN Red List of Threatened Species, had only been documented in Jeju Island, at the southern tip of the peninsula, which has a subtropical climate. In 2015, DERI researcher Chung Hyunyong discovered *Lethocerus deyrollei* Vuillefroy (물장군, or water admiral), a species of giant water bug found more commonly in tropical and subtropical climates such as Vietnam, which is listed in South Korea as a second-order endangered species.

These discoveries not only underscore the biodiversity quotient of the DMZ region, but also suggest that the CCZ is hardly returning to a primordial nature of endemic species. Rather, its mosaic landscape is now serving as a refuge for species that are migrating northward due to climate change. In contrast to those who would frame the DMZ as a repository of Korea's nature or, as scientists in the 1960s did, as a baseline for understanding change in rapidly industrializing South Korea, the DMZ area instead has become a tenuous lifeline for endemic and non-endemic species alike.

Commoning *Dumbeong*

Navigating through the CCZ area with the DERI, I learned to see the landscape as a palimpsest. Willow trees represented a stage of natural succession, indexing places where wetlands or *dumbeong* had once existed. *Paulownia coreana* trees (오동나무) told of an older history of human habitation—these tall, broadleaf trees with bell-shaped flowers outlined the borders of former villages, where they were planted by parents every time a daughter was born, to provide the future materials for the daughter's marital household furniture. Other changes were much more current and represented disturbing trends in the land use of the CCZ. New ginseng fields were appearing on the landscape every week, their blue and black-tarped fields like flat bruises on the landscape, while in other areas, tourism infrastructure and facilities were leading to more artificially paved roads and pathways, and original trees were being removed for "Eco-Trails" (생태 탐방로) only to be replaced by new trees. Apple orchards were also being planted—as farmers made bets that climate change would make it possible to cultivate apples in warming climates of the border area. As we drove along the roads of the CCZ, Director Kim would point out areas where horseweed had come in—a sure sign that there had been a recent disturbance.

Given these dramatic changes, it was not hard to sympathize with the dismay felt by the DERI regarding the state's indifference to the actually existing biodiversity in the border area. In their minds, President Lee Myung-bak's PLZ agenda was no different than the "green washing" of his Four Rivers Restoration Project. Although some changes were being made by the Gyeonggi provincial government—for instance, ecological contracts were offered to farmers as economic incentives to leave out rice grains after the autumn harvest for migratory birds—these were considered to be insufficient stopgap measures that ignored the escalating problem of habitat destruction across the western coast and Han River estuary area. Meanwhile, the illegal conversion of forests and grasslands into ginseng fields was ongoing.

On one of my first trips with the DERI in October 2011, as we wended our way back along the narrow roads to exit at the checkpoint, we stopped by Y. S. *dumbeong*—(uncharacteristically) named after one of the group members, Y. S., who had discovered it. We were shocked to find that the entire area, which had been on the side of a small slope, was now covered over with dry soil. The water had been drained out and the pond filled in with dirt. The consensus was that the land was going to become yet another ginseng field. A few of the members were angry and disappointed. Y. S. himself seemed quite resigned. But for Director Kim, there was also a sense of guilt. He wondered whether their research on private property had annoyed the old man (할아버지) who owned it, and thereby led to the *dumbeong*'s destruction. Mr. Kang said he had noticed a couple who seemed to be "outsiders" (외지인) looking around the area and speculated that they purchased the land as an investment. What became immediately clear was the limitations of the DERI's placemaking practices. *Dumbeong* were located on private property, and the DERI was powerless in the face of what they believed to be the narrow and single-minded profit motives of the farmers and landowners. And despite the interest in the ecological value of endangered species for developing ecotourism, neither the local city or provincial governments nor the central government ministries were viewed as having the political will to truly protect nature in the DMZ or CCZ.

One of the students, an avid Apple consumer, on hearing the news and seeing the photos, cried out, "This news is more disturbing than the death of Steve Jobs!" (Jobs had died just the week before.) Discussion turned to the ignorance of the farmers, but Kang, who himself was raised in a farming family in the border region, defended them, saying, "How can you blame them? They have to live too." Jae Hyun exclaimed, "We are trying to tell them how to coexist with nature, but they don't listen to us." Mr. Oh, the marine biologist and restauranteur, joked that the only solution was just to buy up all the land in the area, as no one else was going to protect it. Although it sounded like a flippant comment at the time, within a few weeks, members of the group were attending land auctions and bidding on plots of land with the goal of establishing a small conservation area.

Their first bid was on a small plot, less than a quarter of an acre, not large enough for migratory birds to use comfortably, but perhaps a space to create a *dumbeong*. Although they were unsuccessful in their first bids, they had crafted a solution to the problem of conservation in the face of an indifferent state. They agreed that whatever land was purchased would be collectively owned and not inherited by their children but turned into public land. Bidding on land became a way to imagine a possible future for biodiversity, despite the ongoing ruination of the landscape.

The project of actualizing a commons was ultimately abandoned, but it crystallized a desire among the group to act against the rush of change. Like the stories of endangerment that Timothy Choy describes in postmillennial Hong Kong, the monitoring work of the DERI was suffused with "anticipatory nostalgia"—"an expectation that something of the present will, in the near future, be lost" (2011: 49). But as he suggests, this nostalgia needn't be construed as politically quietist, but rather can "engender politics" by offering a critique of modernist temporal logics and spatial orders (49). As the negative infrastructure of division, these ponds exist in the "meantime of division" (see chapter 1), an anachronistic time from the viewpoint of the post–Cold War or the global economy. This is in contrast to the dominant discourses of peace—conservative peace offensives, liberal peace and prosperity agendas, or progressive dreams of unification—which are all future oriented, whether developmentalist or dispensationalist.

Along with the commitment to data, which was their form of documenting change and loss in the present, the DERI's attempt to conserve a small plot of land in the CCZ was a mode of commoning, privileging actually existing nonhuman life-forms over property relations. A small plot for a *dumbeong* could achieve a more-than-human peace that would be both collective—to the *sikku* and the "life"-supporting habitat—and non-commodified by being "off limits to the logic of market exchange and market valuation" (Harvey 2012: 73). Although the Korea National Trust had been working to establish a DMZ National Trust, the DERI was not interested in the capitalist logic of Ecosystem Services that guided the National Trust's approach (Hwang 2013). In the context of the national division and its Cold War legacies, as well as the Anthropocene and the climate crisis, purchasing land as a more-than-human commons offers a provisional vision of "staying with the trouble" (Haraway 2016), and moving beyond the right-wing/left-wing and communist/capitalist binaries that have afflicted South Korean division politics for nearly a half century.

Conclusion

Before I left the field in 2012, Heo Young gave me a painting of a *nabi chamjari* (나비잠자리) or butterfly dragonfly. Commonly known as "flutterers" in English, *rhyothemis fuliginosa* have short tails and wider wings than most other dragonflies, and they flutter like butterflies, so "butterfly dragonfly" is an apt moniker. The painting itself is a delicate rendition of the creature in flight, centered against a background suggestive of the spring leaves on the maple and birch trees prevalent in the western DMZ region. When she gave me the painting, inscribed with "early summer, Year of the Dragon [2012]," it was a memento of hours spent in the company of good friends, including companion creatures such as the dragonfly, and a record that evoked a series of quotidian encounters out of which interspecies care and knowledge were constituted.

Early in my fieldwork, Heo Young spoke of how people often compliment a photo by saying it looks like a painting and compliment a painting by saying it looks like a photo. She expressed her desire to work in the space in between. I locate the *nabi chamjari* in this ambiguous space of representation and realism, which is analogous to the productive tension in anthropology between interpretive art and empirical science, or between ethnography and fieldwork (Ingold 2018). In contrast to the obsessive photography of the men in the group who sought to capture documentary evidence, Heo Young's work apprehended the affective and experiential situatedness, the pleasure of direct encounter, and the specific habitat of the *nabi chamjari* as singular creature, in "early summer, year of the Dragon," both more and less than an indexical record of a given species' existence. For Heo Young, the dragonfly may be an iconic representative of nature, but it is not a symbol of political transcendence. It is instead a highly localized creature that prefers, for some reason, Half Moon *dumbeong* over the other ponds in the area. Its existence is threatened by any number of immediate factors, such as water pollution from pesticides or herbicides, the decline in microorganisms that constitute its diet, or the disappearance of the pond itself.

Dumbeong, like the DMZ/CCZ itself, are inherently hybrid—at once artificial and natural, conditioned by the militarization of the border area but not limited by it. From one vantage point, they are insignificant "puddles," and from another, precious sites where biodiversity comes into being through the social practices of attention and care that constitute DERI's research. Of course, in the name of planetary resilience and biodiversity, one might prefer the rice paddies and *dumbeong* to revert naturally to woodland.[24] This distinction can seem merely academic, however, when faced with their endangerment, as the future of the CCZ likely portends industrial water management, irrigation channeling, and development, particularly if the two Koreas were to decide to open up the Han River estuary for joint use.[25]

The uncertain future of *dumbeong* has contributed to the amplification of their scientific and cultural value as traditional ecological knowledge (G. Kim et al. 2019), and in the process, they become available for commodification. A study by the Korean Construction Technology Research Institute, for instance, proposed that *dumbeong* could be built as artificial wetlands and educational facilities, as a tourist attraction that would align with the state's interests in sustainable development and ecotourism (C.-h. Ahn et al. 2012). These ponds would be *dumbeong* in name—planted with representative vegetation and engineered water management in order to be presented as exemplifications of a traditional past—but, like the National Institute of Ecology's Ecorium Pond, abstracted from the agricultural ecosystems and social relations that make them valuable.

Recalling Bowker's insight about the importance of "site" to biodiversity science (2000: 744), I suggest that *dumbeong* are habitats whose value is produced in relation to the attentiveness and attunement of humans who care about them—what Marisol de la Cadena calls "ecologized nature" or "nature recalcitrant to universality" (2015). *Dumbeong* are valuable not just for the endangered species or the sentinels of climate change—after all, in South Korea, as elsewhere, most creatures, whether common or rare, are facing endangerment—but for the singularity of creatures such as the (non-)endangered, nonendemic butterfly-dragonfly, whose preference for Half Moon *Dumbeong* is part of a "secret code" (비밀 코드) that has yet to be fully unlocked.

Coda

The *dumbeong*-as-commons ultimately fell short of DERI's expectations, but in its initial conceptualization it exposed the limitations to the existing paradigms for the DMZ area's conservation and the anthropocentrism of state-centric frameworks of peace. In 2017, the DERI began a different commoning project, one that engages farmers and villagers directly. The project involves residents in the village of Ogeum-ri (오금리), located outside the CCZ but on the banks of the Han River estuary, the terminus of the DMZ and where the CCZ likewise disappears. This is the site of a major wetland area and habitat for wintering cranes. The 1953 Armistice Agreement left the Han River estuary open to civilian use, but it has remained off-limits under the jurisdiction of both the ROK and DPRK.[26] In fact, Ogeum-ri and its neighboring villages in the South are not buffered from the North by anything but the estuary, and the distance between them and the villages in North Korea's Kaep'ung County (개풍군) is a mere one kilometer.

With support and funding from the Ministry of Environment and Paju City, the DERI began collaborating with villagers to lay the social and ecological foundations for a future cross-border Ramsar wetlands village that would provide wintering habitats for endangered white-naped cranes (재두루미) and thereby connect people and ecologies across the estuary. This idea is not as farfetched as it might first seem, given the fact that South Korea has been a signatory to the Ramsar Convention on Wetlands since 1997 and has twenty-four wetlands recognized by the convention, and North Korea became a signatory in 2018, at which point two wetlands of international importance were named—the Rason and Mundok Migratory Bird Reserves.

Director Kim reasons that, should white-naped cranes return to their former wintering sites in the Han River estuary and western coast of the Paju CCZ, and in light of the short distance to the villages of Kaep'ung County, the cranes could find their way to the rice paddies on the North Korean side as well. His vision, as he explained it to me, is that "these creatures (생물) can protect each other (서로 보호) as they go back and forth from South to North. In other words, they can become messengers of peace and provide a foothold for exchange and cooperation."

Kim's reference to "exchange and cooperation" draws attention to how this familiar refrain in state-centered unification discourse—which typically invokes economic relations as the basis for peace and prosperity— might also include multispecies relations, which are vital for crane *and* human survival. This project thereby strategizes a different approach to peace, one that is designed to safeguard against unification-as-economic-development and the "accumulation by dispossession" (Harvey 2003) that such development would likely entail. The ecological connectivity of rice paddies and irrigation ponds, as well as humans and birds, would protect both sides of the estuary from future dispossession, with assistance in the form of a Ramsar wetlands designation. In this sense, nature would not be used to overcome the division, but the division itself would be the basis of a shared commons; what art historian Sohl C. Lee, in another context, calls "a precarious state of being in common despite differences" (2015: 294). By weaving together crane habitats and residents' rights to land and residence, this network of ecological relations could link the precarious futures of birds and humans and help them to "protect each other."

In this chapter I focused on *dumbeong* as the negative infrastructure of the division, suggesting that they defamiliarize the dominant chronotopes of the DMZ as the future site of exchange and cooperation, oriented around capitalist development and economic values. In chapter 3, I turn to the networked assemblages of avian flyways, which I frame as alternative infrastructures that intervene into prevailing imaginaries of ethnonational restitution. Migratory birds have become iconic symbols that signify not only nature's ability to transcend geopolitics but also the unification of divided families. In contrast, I show how taking on multiple bird's-eye views can decenter naturalized categories of the Korean nation and genealogical kin.

BIRDS

Migratory cranes and waterbirds migrate annually over national borders without passports or visas, but ironically it turns out that they are not completely independent of national boundaries, as their reliance on the Korean DMZ shows.

Hiroyoshi Higuchi and Jason Minton, "The Importance of the Korean DMZ to Threatened Crane Species in Northeast Asia" (2000)

Starling C7655

The most prominent and only internationally recognized ornithologist in Korea's prewar modern period was Won Hong Gu, born in 1887. He was a high school teacher who first began collecting birds to use in his natural history classes, and he would eventually study natural sciences in Japan and publish lists and articles related to Korean birds beginning in the 1930s. The American principal of the high school where Won was teaching had first helped him contact Shimokoriyama Seiichi, a Japanese ornithologist working in Korea during the Japanese colonial period (1910–45). At the time, ornithological knowledge was led by Japanese residents in Korea, Shimokoriyama and Mori Tamezo, who relied on information provided by Korean scientists and assistants but published their works in Japanese. Won became a key figure in native Korean natural sciences and was the first person to compile bird guides in the Korean language. After liberation and the national division in 1945, he became a professor at Kim Il Sung University and the preeminent natural scientist in North Korea.

His son, Pyong-Oh, was born in 1929 in Kaesŏng, the former capital of premodern Korea that now lies north of the DMZ that separates the two Koreas. The Korean War started shortly after Pyong-Oh had completed his university degree in agricultural sciences, and at his father's insistence, he and his two brothers headed south in 1950, leaving behind their parents and two sisters. With the beginning of the war on June 25, 1950, they became one of the hundreds of thousands of families separated by the division (이산가족; see N. Kim 2017). After the war, Pyong-Oh continued his studies, earning a doctorate from Hokkaido University in Japan, and then he returned to South Korea to serve on the faculty of Kyunghee University until his retirement in 1994. During that time, he was a pioneer in the establishment of the natural sciences in South Korea and was responsible for identifying more than fifty new bird species. The author of some 150 scholarly papers and dozens of birding manuals and general interest books, he also trained a generation of ornithologists in South Korea, all of which earned him the nickname "Dr. Bird" (새 박사).

This story of patrilineal succession may be heartwarming enough, but what makes it mythic is the fact that Pyong-Oh's love of birds, nurtured by his father, became a crucial link that overcame insurmountable political and geographic boundaries. In 1965, Won Pyong-Oh received a letter from the Asia headquarters of BirdLife International in Tokyo, informing him that a purple-backed starling (쇠찌르레기; Daurian starling; *Agropsar sturninus*) that he had banded two years earlier in Seoul had been identified in North Korea. The person who had captured the banded bird was none other than Won Hong Gu, Pyong-Oh's father. At the time, BirdLife International had no office in South Korea. For that reason, the band that the elder Won found was inscribed with the word "JAPAN." Won Hong Gu, however, knew that the species only migrated within the Korean peninsula. Intrigued by the band's inscription, he contacted the Tokyo BirdLife office and learned that the bird had been banded in South Korea by his own son, Pyong-Oh. Due to the near total impossibility of communicating between the two Koreas, neither father nor son had known during the intervening fifteen years whether the other had survived the war. As the story goes, Pyong-Oh's parents treasured the aluminum metal band, imprinted with the code C7655, weeping as they caressed it, missing their distant son.

As this brief account suggests, the history of ornithology in North and South Korea is intimately tied to Japanese colonialism and the national division. In this case, however, banding—a relatively modern technique used to track migratory birds—resembles the more ancient technology of using homing pigeons to post messages, this time for family members who had become painfully excommunicated by Cold War geopolitics. This extraordinary story is symbolically powerful because it simultaneously

denaturalizes human political boundaries and naturalizes kinship (and the nation), embodying the desires of
so many Koreans, such as Dr. Won, for reunification.
As he told the *Dong-A Ilbo* newspaper in 1993, "How
endlessly envious I am of the birds who traverse the
wall of the national division" (분단의 벽을 넘나드는 새가
끝 없이 부럽구나).[1]

Won Hong Gu passed away in 1970, but his son was
not granted permission by the South Korean government to visit the North until 2002, long after both his
parents had passed away. The scientific achievements
of father and son ornithologists and the saga of their
reunion were duly appropriated in both South and North. They were the
subject of a number of children's books in South Korea, and they inspired a
film coproduced by North Korea and Japan in the 1990s. The DPRK, which
has a tradition of issuing natural history–related postage stamps, released
one with a Daurian starling in 1992 that commemorated Dr. Won Hong Gu
and featured a reproduction of the aluminum band accompanied by the
words "The bird flown to Dr. Won Hong Gu" (figure 3.1).[2]

If Starling C7655 literally transcended political boundaries to recon-
nect father and son, in the intervening years, migratory birds have served
merely as metaphoric links uniting North and South. In place of the prosaic

Figure 3.1
The DPRK released a
commemorative stamp
in honor of Dr. Won Hong
Gu in 1992, showing the
starling and the aluminum
band, with the words
"The bird flown to Dr. Won
Hong Gu." His son,
Won Pyong-Oh, was not
granted permission by the
South Korean authorities
to visit North Korea until
2002.

starling, the charismatic and iconic red-crowned crane (RCC) now figures as the talismanic emblem of unfettered freedom and human desires to cross the wall of division.[3] Yet, a closer look at this story of re-sutured kinship reveals that the starling, an individual bird—tagged, banded, and tracked as C7655—rather than transcending geopolitics, was fully enmeshed in a militarized and transnational network of knowledge production. In other words, a key point that is generally missed in the sentimental story of a small bird reconnecting father and son is the preexistence of the flyway as a human–avian infrastructure that came into being out of human love and care for birds and their milieux, as well as post–Korean War US military expansion and the biopolitical projects of Cold War–era state-funded sciences.

The history of Korean ornithology is beyond the scope of this chapter, but it is notable that the first naturalists to record birds in the Korean peninsula were British and American consular officials and missionaries. Of these, the most significant collector of the period was Pierre Louis Jouy (1856–94), who worked for the US Legation and collected more than five hundred specimens for the Smithsonian (formerly the US National Museum), along with pottery and ethnological data.[4] After the division in 1945, Oliver L. Austin, Jr., an American ornithologist who was stationed in South Korea with the US military government, published the first English-language study of South Korean birds (Austin 1948). In the absence of an indigenous birding culture in South Korea, soldiers and officers of the US Army observed and published their findings, and also created networks of amateur birders with other Western expatriates. In his endeavors, Austin relied heavily on Won Hong Gu's information, despite his reservations about Won's lack of methodological rigor and what he critically referred to as Won's "patriotic ambition" (Austin 1948: 21).[5]

Ornithological studies in post–Korean War South Korea continued to be influenced by US military presence. Won Pyong-Oh, after returning from his studies in Japan, became the most senior ornithologist, and he established the first national records of bird populations, largely through the US Army-funded program, Migratory Animals Pathological Survey (MAPS). The earlier generations of birders in Korea had focused on capturing specimens and drawing up lists, but modern ornithology, influenced by the "flyway concept," sought to track the migrations of birds through the technique of banding. Between 1964 and 1970, Won banded 185,650 birds of 135 species, focusing on smaller common migrants such as buntings, swallows, and wagtails. Indeed, the banding of the purple-backed starling C7655 may have been funded by the US military. The recovery of these bands produced data about their migratory routes, mostly between the Koreas, Japan, and Southeast Asia.[6]

The Cold War era witnessed the expansion of scientific networks that, in following flyways, generated communication networks that did not transcend but were able to partially breach ideological boundaries. Dr. Won's ties to the international scientific community included those with Soviet and Polish colleagues, as well as North Koreans, and it was through these links that he was able to intermittently exchange messages with his family in North Korea. He heard of the passing of his father in 1970 from a Japanese scientist, and a North Korean colleague at an international scholarly conference informed him of his mother's death, albeit six years after her actual passing.

Grounding the drama of family reunion in a history of the flyway helps us to understand that birds, although they may seem to be the epitome of freedom, have always already been enmeshed in human geopolitics and biopolitics. For it was not any starling, but a marked bird—enrolled into a transnational surveillance network and its technologies of banding and coding systems—which, in turn, linked a broader network of humans, which included father and son. Without the human labor and relations that constituted the flyway, the technology of the bird band, and the networked, militarized infrastructure of avian research, the chances that Starling C7655 could link father and son would have been even more infinitesimal. In other words, the bird was just one node in a flyway that made it possible for the familial connection to be revealed.

Thus, as compelling as the narrative of the Won family may be, its plot maps a conventional romance, which erases power and history, and relegates Starling C7655 to a supporting role. Ornithologists and conservation scientists understand that birds, despite their aerial advantages, do not enjoy limitless freedom from state power. Instead, they depend on safe harbors in the form of feeding, resting, wintering, and breeding sites that are governed by multiple states and monitored by international organizations. Ongoing habitat destruction in the form of land reclamation and urbanization constitute major threats to their survival. The very worldliness that makes migratory birds so charismatic is what makes them vulnerable in multiple locales, subject to a myriad of hazards and disturbances that affect their flight patterns, habitats, and survivability. As the epigraph by ornithologists Higuchi and Minton underscores, birds are "not completely independent of national boundaries" (2000: 130), especially when it comes to the DMZ. The national division is thereby hardly overcome by birds' migrations. Rather, their ability to make their annual journeys depends on the militarized spaces that secure their remaining habitats from the encroachments of capitalist development. The birds are not unifying the divided nation but are surviving in part due to, and also in spite of, militarized geopolitics.

In this chapter, I draw on and elaborate the conservation concept of migratory bird flyways to adopt another vantage point that doesn't dichotomize air and ground but that focuses on the relations between up there and down here, and between humans and nonhumans, mapping multilayered and enmeshed cartographies of global climate change, capitalism, securitization, and state power. The encounters of ornithologist and conservation biologist Lee Kisup and the endangered black-faced spoonbills (BFSs) that he studies exemplify how biopolitical forms of knowledge production also involve ethical "enactments" that "[blur] the clear cut divide between knowing subject and known object" (Despret 2013: 69). This blurring of subject and object and the alternative imaginaries of bird scientists and bird lovers resonates with Merleau-Ponty's notion of "strange kinship" (*étrange parenté*; strange relatedness) introduced in his *Nature* lectures (2003). Strange kinship decenters the anthropocentrism of the Won family story and "allows for an intimate relation based on shared embodiment without denying differences between lifestyles and ways of being.... This strange kinship is not based on descendants or on generation but on shared embodiment in a shared world, even if the style of body and the style of inhabiting that world are radically different" (Oliver 2009: 222). Strange kinship thereby also permits a line of flight away from the ethnonationalist narrative of authentic genealogical kinship that appropriates birds as metaphors for reunited families.

The Flyway Concept: Beyond Biopolitics

Ornithologist and conservationist Dr. Lee Kisup's study of birds taught him to view the flyway as a human–avian network. His understanding of this network, moreover, affects his larger view of the physical world, which he perceives as a Gaia-like entity. He told me, "I believe that the Earth is like an organism connected by a network. Through the birds, I've come to feel this very strongly." Birds' migrations connect tidal flats and wetlands across the East China and South China Seas, linking the two Koreas, Japan, Hong Kong, China, Taiwan, and Cambodia. For Lee, who began researching cranes in 1983, as more knowledge of the birds' flyways was being generated through banding, bird-watching, and especially satellite tracking, the movements of the birds created what he called "organic" linkages with other bird lovers along the flyway. Lee's vision echoes Stefan Helmreich's notion of gaiasociality, in which "knowledge of the globe, understood as a cybernetic whole...is enlisted as an important node in and context for relations among humans and nonhumans" (2003: 348).

Lee emphasized to me a truism of the bird conservationists' worldview—if one part of the flyway is ruined, it will all be ruined—or, as stated in "Bird's Eye View on Flyways," a 2012 brochure by the Convention on the Conservation of Migratory Species, "For each species, the migration chain is only as strong as its weakest link" (UNEP and CMS 2012: 8). Local conservationists in countries linked by bird migrations must thereby coordinate with their counterparts in those other locations. Although migratory birds adapt to changes in their flyways, the stresses on their annual migrations can be fatal if they are unable to reach their destinations or are unable to access adequate food sources to fuel them along their way. In the calculus of extinction, the loss of a single individual can constitute a severe setback to the survival of the entire global population.

The seasonal migrations of the DMZ's endangered cranes, spoonbills, and vultures are part of the larger East Asian Australasian Flyway, the largest of the world's nine flyways, which is used by 40 percent of the world's migratory birds. First coined by American ornithologist Frederick Lincoln in the 1930s, the flyway concept was, from its origins, a scientific and administrative category, literally mapping biological processes of migration onto social relations of political boundaries and governance (Wilson 2010: 73–74). Conservation scientists Boere and Stroud's widely cited "The Flyway Concept: What It Is and What It Isn't" (2006) defines a flyway as "the totality of the ecological systems that are necessary to enable a migratory [bird] to survive and fulfill its annual cycle" (45). Their general definition of a flyway is: "A flyway is the entire range of a migratory bird species (or groups of related species or distinct populations of a single species) through which it moves on an annual basis from the breeding grounds to non-breeding areas, including intermediate resting and feeding places as well as the area within which the birds migrate" (40). As this definition suggests, the flyway concept is impressively capacious in its scaling from individual birds within a given population to groups of birds within or across species (including their unpredictable variations). It also extends to transnational human activities, which respond to the needs of bird survival. Despite the crude diagrammatic nature of the

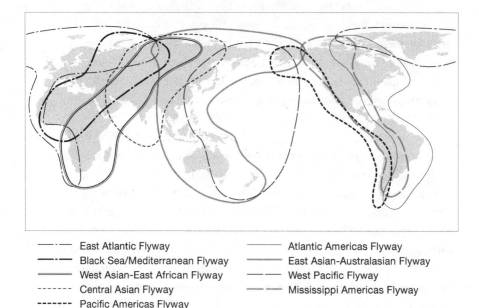

─ · ─ East Atlantic Flyway	───── Atlantic Americas Flyway
─ · ─ Black Sea/Mediterranean Flyway	═════ East Asian-Australasian Flyway
═════ West Asian-East African Flyway	─ ─ ─ West Pacific Flyway
------- Central Asian Flyway	─ ─ ─ Mississippi Americas Flyway
------- Pacific Americas Flyway	

Map 3.1

The world's nine major flyways. Adapted from the East Asian Australasian Flyway Partnership (EAAFP).

conservationists' map of the world's flyways (map 3.1), the flyway concept attempts to encompass evolutionary and idiosyncratic relations that are—in definition and practice—multispecies, multi-scalar, transhistorical, and linked to imperial histories, contemporary geopolitics, and national and international conservation efforts. Flyways might be Borgesian maps that risk becoming the territory, but in the hands of conservationists, they are also part of a range of techniques and knowledge projects that objectify bird behaviors and lifeways in order to manage their populations. We can think of the flyway as mediated and multiple—it is continually emergent out of the patterned activities of breeding, feeding, and migrating birds, which are inextricable from the knowledge techniques humans use to document and interpret these activities.[7]

Conservationists and scientists engage in biopolitical projects of knowledge production and transnational governance to protect rapidly shrinking or degraded bird habitats, or to intervene directly into the lives of individual birds to help ensure their reproductive futures.[8] Yet, both geopolitical and biopolitical frameworks fall short of capturing the complexity and emergent nature of flyways, which are, following John Law

(2004), naturaculturetechnics that enact an other-than-human security. In other words, they are social, natural, cultural, and technical assemblages in and through which conservationists labor to understand, regulate, and control the flows of migratory birds in order to ensure species survival.[9] As products of human and nonhuman intra-actions, they entail various techniques of observation and calculation, which are linked to longer histories of military surveillance and biopolitics. But they are, most importantly, generative of other kinds of relations and imaginaries.

The flyway is composed of multiple "birds'-eye views" (as opposed to the singular "bird's-eye view") that are crucially mediated through visual technologies, which are, in turn, integral to producing knowledge about the birds. Specifically, scientists rely on visual technologies of surveillance, from banding to motion-detection cameras to satellite tracking to produce knowledge about the birds' whereabouts and their well-being, which, as they circulate, generate networks of social relations among humans tied virtually and affectively to their avian friends. "Virtual birds" thereby help to create a "meshwork" of epistemological and affective connection (Ingold 2011) as ornithologists and conservationists strive and struggle to understand the global meaning of bird behaviors through seasonal observations and satellite tracking.

I consider these collective attempts to grasp the complex lives of migratory birds to be a form of "phatic labor" (Elyachar 2010) in which "a social infrastructure of communicative pathways" (460) materially and imaginatively emerges out of the enmeshed activities of humans, birds, and technologies.[10] Much of the work of conservation science involves tracking the numbers of individuals in a population—monitoring their presences and absences. These practices of enumeration then become evidence of a given species' endangered status, which is a key part of the production of its value relative to other (non-endangered) species, and helps to produce the "nonhuman charisma" of specific animals (Lorimer 2007: 912), and, of course, their objectification and commodification.[11] But prior to and apart from the production of charisma is the arduous work of collecting and compiling the data themselves, which I frame as ethical enactments (Despret 2013) and experimental encounters, made possible by the flyway itself.

Flyways could be characterized as infrastructural in that they are used by birds to migrate across distances, but they are also a functional abstraction that scientists use to coordinate across national borders to craft international and global conservation strategies. In other words, the flyway comes into being out of a combination of bird migrations and the observations humans make of their mobile lifeways. And even though birds are often described as "using" a flyway, it is more apt to describe the flyway as the iteration of millions of individual trajectories in coordination with a transnational network of humans who care about and for them. Thus, flyways do more than merely describe the migratory patterns of birds. As my rendering of Starling C7655 underscored, they are also constituted out of specific communicative pathways, technologies, information, and intersubjective imaginaries of humans who maintain channels for the exchange of knowledge and who are, in turn, affected by birds across their distant habitats.

Although the cranes, particularly the RCC, are indisputably the DMZ's primary flagship species, this chapter focuses on the BFS (저어새; *platalea minor*),[12] which, in contrast to migratory cranes, are very well tracked across their flyway, with dozens having been banded since the 1990s. Both RCCs and white-naped cranes, despite their ubiquity in cultural representations from ancient scroll paintings to contemporary tourist brochures, are negatively habituated to humans, and the presence of idling cars or approaching humans frighten them off easily.[13] Capturing cranes for banding or satellite tracking is difficult and stressful for the birds. In South Korea, only those cranes that have been injured and rehabilitated are banded, but most of the ones that my interlocutors and I observed were not, making it impossible to view the birds as anything but representative of their species. BFSs, on the other hand, are documented as individual birds in online databases and social media, where researchers and volunteers share information, map their migrations, and create virtual worlds that link networks of birds, habitats, and people. The birds enable the relationships of sentimental attachments with experts and bird watchers who identify individuals and follow their movements along the flyway.

BFS

In 1966, one year after Starling C7655 reconnected father and son, another avian flyway linked the elder and younger Wons through their shared concern with the BFS. In an English-language report by Won Pyong-Oh in South Korea, he stated that the BFS breeding status was unknown. According to him, "old records" mentioned a breeding area on "Piung-do, an offshore islet in the west coastal area." His attempts to locate the breeding ground were unsuccessful, however, and local residents said that the bird had not been seen for five years (P.-O. Won 1966: 7). In North Korea, that same year, Won Hong Gu wrote an article in the English-language journal,

Korean Nature (published by the Association for Nature Conservation of the DPRK), which detailed the birds' feeding behaviors, appearance, and nests, accompanied by multiple photographs. According to Won Hong Gu, North Korean conservation efforts included protection of the spoonbills' island breeding areas, which was actively supported by concerned local residents. These islands off the western coast, he wrote, "have long been proclaimed sea-birds sanctuary" (H. G. Won 1966: 10) and were guarded by patrol boats during the breeding season.

The elder Won lamented the fact that, in contrast to the knowledge and conservation efforts in the North, little was known of the birds in South Korea, and quoted his son's 1963 report for the International Council for Bird Preservation (ICBP), writing: "A South Korean biologist, Won Byong Oh wrote in the ICBP Bulletin, No. 9, 1963, '...but, as no investigations have been made, there are no accurate reports. A rapid investigation and conservation of declining nesting grounds are needed'" (10). A story in *Korean Nature* reported that when Won Hong Gu first read the ICBP report in 1963, he had suspected but couldn't be certain (given the English romanization of Pyong-Oh's name) that the South Korean author was his son (Jo 1966: 14). By 1966, however, with knowledge of his son's existence and vocation, he concluded his own English-language article with a poignant, yet veiled, message expressing concern for his South Korean colleagues and a desire for connection, in the name of conservation: "This state of affairs in South Korea arouses concerns of the North Korean biologists. We sincerely desire to establish between the North and South Korean scholars for the preservation of wild life [*sic*] and its habitats and for the regular exchange of informations [*sic*] about the rare species of our country" (10).[14]

Won Pyong-Oh and other biologists in South Korea helped the species gain designation as a natural monument from the South Korean government in 1968, but there was little to no scientific knowledge about the entire range of the BFS flyway prior to the 1980s, when the first global census recorded fewer than three hundred individual birds. Scientists began banding BFSs, and Japanese ornithologists began using satellite telemetry in the late 1990s.[15] This work confirmed the anecdotal evidence that the islands off the DMZ were important breeding and summering sites (Ueta et al. 2002). It is now known that 80 percent of the BFS breed in South Korean tidal flat habitats every spring before heading to their wintering sites in Taiwan, Hong Kong, Vietnam, and southeastern China (map 3.2).

By 1995, scientists in these countries were collaborating on a conservation plan under the auspices of BirdLife Asia. Through this transnational

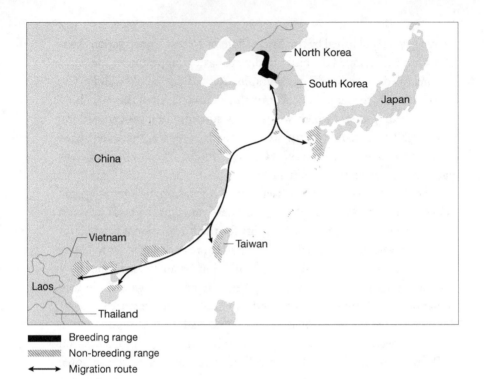

Breeding range
Non-breeding range
⟵⟶ Migration route

Map 3.2
BFS flyway. Adapted from
EAAFP.

network of conservationists working in coordination, the BFS was saved from extinction, with the most current winter census of 2020 documenting a record high of 4,864 BFSs.[16] These annual censuses count birds in all of the countries except for North Korea. Estimates based on existing population numbers of other spoonbill species set the 1900 population of BFSs at ten thousand, and the goal of BFS conservationists has been to bring the total number back to that figure. Yet, the limited carrying capacity of existing breeding and wintering habitats make this goal unlikely, especially in light of climate change, pollution, and the increasing destruction and threats to their habitats. Thus, although the BFS represents one of the great conservation success stories of the recent past, this success is under continuous threat of being short-lived.

I learned about the conservation efforts for BFSs from Dr. Lee Kisup, whom I first met through his work with RCCs. When I went to visit him in his office in downtown Seoul in May 2012, with the cranes having departed in March for their breeding areas in northeastern Russia, Lee was much more preoccupied by the BFS, which had recently arrived at their breeding sites on the remote islands off the coast of the DMZ. Lee received a PhD from Kyunghee University and founded the Korea Crane Network in 2007 and the Korea Waterbird Network in 2010. He eventually quit his teaching position to devote himself full time to bird conservation. Dr. Lee showed me a PowerPoint presentation he had recently given at a meeting for the BFS Working Group, under the auspices of the East Asia Australasian Flyway Partnership, which brought together scientists from across the BFS flyway. The slides showed his efforts to support the reproductive success of the BFS, particularly the joint action plan Dr. Lee had organized with Japanese colleagues in 2010.

The transnational efforts to rescue the BFS coincided with major environmental transformations of East Asia, which witnessed record-breaking rates of economic growth and urban development in the 1980s and 1990s, simultaneous with the fall of the USSR and North Korea's concomitant economic collapse. Over the course of the 1990s, land reclamation on the western coast of South Korea led to the destruction of wetlands and tidal flats, most recently in the name of renewable energy and green urbanization, as exemplified by the futuristic Songdo International City and Business Hub (Halpern 2015; Ko, Schubert, and Hester 2011). The effects of these developments on maritime ecologies and local fishing economies have been profound. Also in the late 1990s, BFSs stopped showing up in their regular breeding areas along the coasts in North Korea. The reason for this sudden disappearance, according to Dr. Lee, must have been a major disturbance. He speculates that this large-scale change occurred during the famine in North Korea, when starving people stole eggs from BFS and other birds' nests to sell on the black market or to consume themselves. Ultimately, dramatic changes in the late–Cold War economies of both Koreas (rapid expansion and rapid decline) contributed to the shift of BFS breeding grounds almost exclusively to the islands of the Yellow Sea.

Strange Kinship

Dr. Lee has been frequenting those western islands to monitor the BFS since 2006 and has brought colleagues from Taiwan and Japan to South Korea to observe the same birds that they monitor during the winter months. He invited me to join him on a monitoring trip in May 2012, which was to be coordinated with Taiwanese colleagues from the BFS network. Unfortunately, they were unable to raise the funds to come to South Korea.

Our team thus consisted of a South Korean environmental activist and journalist, two of Dr. Lee's research assistants, and myself. That morning, we departed from the western port of Incheon on a two-and-a-half-hour ferry ride to Yeonpyeong-do (연평도) in South Korean territory. The island lies just seven and a half miles from the coast of North Korea, directly adjacent to the controversial NLL.[17] Yeonpyeong-do made international news in 2010 when it was battered by DPRK artillery in what the North Korean leadership called a "training exercise" that led to one of the most serious skirmishes between the two Koreas since the 1953 armistice, in which two civilians and two South Korean soldiers died. After disembarking at Lesser Yeonpyeong-do (소연평도), we rented the services of a local fisherman who brought us by motorboat to Guji-do (구지도), a small uninhabited islet ten minutes away.

In premodern times, the islet was central to the fishing economy, a fact that is reflected in its original name, Guŏji-do (구어지도), meaning "place to seek out fish." After the war, because of its strategic location, it was converted to a South Korean military target range for air bombing drills. Sometime in the 1990s, however, it became a de facto preserve when a resident of the main island transported eight black goats there in an act of defiance. From what Dr. Lee told me, this person owned an inn on Yeonpyeong-do and felt that the disturbances from the military exercises detracted from his business. Black goats (흑염소) are also valued for use in traditional Korean medicine. According to Dr. Lee, the island's colonization by a resident population of goats made it impossible for the military to continue using the island for training purposes. The goat stratagem may have been effective for decommissioning the islet, but it created other unexpected ecological outcomes.

When we arrived on Guji-do, the detritus of artillery shells and other evidence of military presence, including a commemorative umbrella for the sixtieth anniversary of the Korean War, littered the shore. We saw the remains of bombing targets in the ground, marked by stones in a circular formation. The goats, which are notorious for consuming any and all vegetation, including tree bark, had multiplied to twenty, and had reduced the island's trees to scrawny stick figures poking out of the ground. Dr. Lee was not sanguine about the future sustainability of the island for the BFS, calling it a "complete mess," ecologically speaking. The goats present no immediate threat to the BFS but are consuming and killing off the organic nesting materials used by the birds. White herons, which used to build nests in the trees of Guji-do, had already disappeared (figure 3.2).

Before departing from Seoul, Dr. Lee gave me precise instructions about what to wear and what to bring with me. The non-negotiable sartorial require-

Figure 3.2
Guji-do, May 2012.
Photograph by the author.

ments were a camouflage or dark-colored waterproof jacket and a black umbrella. The reasons for the umbrella became immediately obvious once we landed—the seagulls were Hitchcockian in their vicious disdain for us—shit-bombing onto and nose-diving into our umbrellas, and violently pecking at our heads during our moments of weakened vigilance. But protection from the gulls didn't explain why the umbrellas had to be black. The reason, I soon found out, had to do with the fact that the goats wore black coats, and we were—to borrow (opportunistically) from Gilles Deleuze and Félix Guattari—"becoming-goat" in our quest to get close to the BFS nests (figures 3.3 and 3.4). Becoming-goat required us to hold the black umbrellas close to our crouched bodies, less like umbrellas than military shields, while making our way in a single line, incrementally—indeed, very, very slowly—in a squatted position, up the hill to where the BFS nests were (figure 3.5). Once there, we took pictures, counted the number of nests, pairs, and chicks. The banding that had been done in coordination with the network of BFS conservationists helped to identify two birds, and we also saw a one-legged female, who had been previously identified by researchers in Taiwan.

Figure 3.3
Black goats grazing on
Guji-do. Photograph by
the author.

The island of Guji-do is a militarized training ground and ecological dystopia—a naturalcultural borderland where BFSs have found a temporary haven in the narrow interstices of capital and militarization. Yet, it is not only the BFS but also Chinese fishermen who have located a space of illicit freedom in these contested waters. North and South Korean fishermen are prohibited from entering the waters between the western islands of South Korea and the North Korean coast. Chinese fishing vessels, however, regularly appear as overfishing has decimated fish populations in Chinese (and other Korean) waters.[18] Dr. Lee feared not only that this activity would negatively affect the birds' food supply, but also that the fishermen might use the remote islands as resting areas and introduce new disturbances in these sanctuaries.

Dr. Lee described to me the differences between RCCs and BFSs as a problem of interspecies intimacy. With the BFS, the ability to get close to them and to observe at close hand their nurturing and feeding practices, especially with their chicks, helped to create anthropomorphic identification as well as networks of shared knowledge and friendship. Yet, what does anthropomorphic connection mean for someone like Dr. Lee, who, in his placid way, described himself as someone who "knew a lot about

Figure 3.4
Ecological researcher "becoming-goat," that is, adapting to the biosemiotics of the island. Photograph by the author.

birds but nothing about people"? For him, the BFS mediates a transnational network of BFS lovers that is an extension of the relations of friendship created with and through the birds.

This network, which has to overcome steep financial and political hurdles to meet in various parts of the region on a regular basis, has compiled an internet database with a detailed directory of banded birds and where they were seen in other parts of the region. Naming the birds and being able to identify them in their migrations was another way to develop a sense of closeness to the birds and friendship among the human network. In contrast, the RCC, with breeding grounds in the Amur region of Russia, were too remote and expensive to access, and the wintering cranes in the DMZ too skittish to get close to. Without the ability to share the same space and create an affective intimacy, RCCs could be icons but not friends.

The BFS, on the other hand, were seemingly much more tolerant of human company, and we strove to be respectful and unobtrusive guests to our island hosts. Did that mean that our strange disguises and poor pantomime of their goat companions were effective? We were certainly more like wolves in sheep's clothing than the Yukaghir hunters of Rane Willerslev's (2007) ethnography who employ practices of "mimetic empathy" to get close to their prey. Perhaps the BFS saw right through us, but we

Figure 3.5
BFS and chicks.
Photograph by the author.

nevertheless took on the guise of goats—performing goat-ness helped us to both view the birds and also imagine the birds seeing us, granting us a bird's-eye view or a "double perspective," to quote Willerslev, a "kind of optical oscillation" in which "the inter-species boundary is affected and some degree of 'union' is experienced" (99). This interspecies union, however, was triangulated—we needed the goats to get close to the spoonbills, and, indeed, we never encountered the goats themselves, only glimpsed them from a far distance (a bird's-eye view, in fact, from the top of the ridge, looking down into a small valley). Becoming-goat to gain a bird's-eye view was how we entered into the environment of the island, through a process of corporeal dehumanization and strange kinship. Well before we were within viewing distance of the BFS nests, we began the process of becoming-goat, and after moving on to other parts of the island, we continued in our painful and tedious goat-like movements, until we finally took a break from the heat and dust to sit in a human space, delimited by a large multicolored umbrella that Dr. Lee planted in the ground like a flag.

If the black umbrellas decentered our humanness, the beach umbrella returned us to our human form and perspective. Under its relative security, having shed our goat-umbrella coats, I experienced a Sloterdijkian moment of realization: the beach umbrella was a sphere that made explicit the Umwelt or extensive environment of guano, blood, dust, dead trees, and the incessant, deafening cries of thousands of seagulls around us and that we had (hopefully) stealthily passed through (Sloterdijk 2011). (Dr. Lee had once slept, or attempted to sleep, on the island overnight, but the birds never stopped their cries.) In the near future, however, Guji-do may become a much more explicitly curated space of human/nonhuman design that will need to be actively managed in order to support the reproductive success of the BFS colonies. As he has done on the artificial eco-islands of Songdo International City (an exemplary case of air-conditioned modernity and technologically designed natureculture), Dr. Lee and his assistants may bring in nesting materials for the birds and may have to figure out ways to prevent the goats from consuming them before the birds learn how to use them. And, as he and his colleagues have done on other uninhabited islets, he may experiment with helping to build the nests themselves, configuring the birds' spaces, "like rooms in an apartment," co-constructing habitats and communicating with his partners in Taiwan, Hong Kong, and Vietnam to figure out where these birds will go as climate change alters their wintering sites and diverts their flight patterns.

Sometime after our trip to Guji-do, Dr. Lee posted time-release images, which had been recorded by motion-detection camera, to the Korea Waterbird Network online café. The camera had been set up next to a BFS nest and was intended to provide visual documentation of the birds' breeding and nurturing practices. Like our goat performances, the camera was a form of stealth surveillance, but more high-tech and remote. The images that he posted, however, were not just of our avian friends, but also revealed the presence of human invaders. In the images, at least three different men are seen taking photos of the birds. Whenever a man appears in the frame, the birds depart from the nests and leave their eggs unattended. Dr. Lee was emphatic in condemning the invasive lack of politesse, titling his post, "This is not photography etiquette. Going too far" (너무합니다).[19]

The men were on the island for at least four and a half hours, alarming the BFS mothers and carelessly striding around taking photos here and there while the exposed chicks might have been attacked by seagulls and even killed. Dr. Lee's concern was unvarnished: "It's so sad to see the mothers look so worried about whether their newly hatched babies will die from being exposed to the sun's rays." He suggested that if chicks were to die, the birds might not return next year. Despite its remoteness, this breeding site was not a true sanctuary, and without protected status from the state, strangers could come at will.

Members of the network, with handles borrowed from nonhuman species (e.g., Birch, Warbler), responded to Dr. Lee's post with messages indexing their shock and distress: "How can we stop this?"; "To be doing this while they're incubating their eggs—that's going too far"; "Extremely selfish! Ignorant...bastards.... My heart is aching." With a vivid memory of the sensory and bodily experience of becoming-goat, I viewed the images of the men's fully human bipedal forms with disgust. They were a stark reminder of our earnest umbrella-clad attempts to alter our bodies to assimilate to the biosemiotics of the island ecology. That day we counted 150 pairs and measured a dozen eggs, moving excruciatingly slowly, taking great care not to disturb the nests, crouching, covering, and squat walking while trying to hear each other over the din of the seagulls' calls and shrieks.

On further reflection, however, the images of these umbrella-less humans made clear to me the genuine ambiguity of our effects on the birds. If our intrusion in the name of science was unavoidable, our dedication to be polite guests required us to attenuate our human form and reduce our semiotic effect on the island biosphere. The rationale was to ensure that the birds were not frightened away from the urgent task of procreation, as well as to make sure that they did not become habituated to humans and thereby become vulnerable to the predatory members of our kind (a motion detection camera in another breeding site documented a fisherman stealing BFS eggs). But are we really that different from the careless photographers? Perhaps all that separates us is our more expansive imaginaries, such as the possibility that the birds could recognize us, umbrella cloaked, as other than human and as categorically different from ruder human intruders. Traci Warkentin, drawing on Val Plumwood's feminist interspecies ethics, describes an "ethical praxis of paying attention" that resonates with the decorporeal methodology Dr. Lee required of us. She writes: "the kind of attentiveness we are concerned with here involves one's whole bodily comportment and a recognition that embodiment is always in relation to social others, both animal and human" (2011: 100).

The conservation work of Dr. Lee is more empirical than experimental, organized around solving migration and reproductive challenges. But it is also underwritten by a theory of avian personhood in which connections to habitat and kin are affective and real. Strange kinship helps me to describe a form of relationality that doesn't seek to valorize nonhuman species as allegories against which to measure human morality or to find a new ground of nature against which to construct alternative myths or models for the social (M. C. Watson 2016). Rather, it brings into focus ambiguous and ambivalent relations of hospitality and ethical praxis involved in the pragmatics of living and surviving together. I foreground the strange kinship among the humans, goats, and spoonbills made possible on Guji-do to suggest the necessity of attending to the specific enactments of interspecies relations; instead of drawing categorical distinctions between human self and nonhuman other, scientific knowledge production required us to refine our etiquette and practice an ethics of attentiveness.

Avian Bio-social-graphies: A Bildungsroman

A crucial, yet expensive, aspect of Dr. Lee's conservation efforts involves understanding in detail the migration patterns of BFSs. In addition to banding and monitoring activities, Dr. Lee has raised money through individual donations and grants from Korean corporations to fund the purchase of satellite transmitters to attach to some of the juveniles that fledged on the rocky islets and uninhabited islands where he and volunteers have monitored BFS nests. In what follows, I ask how militarized flyways are also virtual flyways, mediated by GPS infrastructure and distributed across online platforms.

Although some cultural analysis of satellite imaging and visual regimes of scientific knowledge production might frame the static representations of bird flight patterns as reductive or even violent, in the case of human–BFS flyways, I found that they served as the ground for empathy and critical anthropomorphism. In the spirit of feminist STS scholars, I follow the ways in which military surveillance technology may be put to the service of producing objectifying and totalizing knowledge of avian flyways but may also produce situated knowledges (Haraway 1998) and stage affective relations through visual media that, I posit, is coproduced by birds and humans. In this section, I follow Dr. Lee's tracking of Seonghyeon E12. Seonghyeon was captured and banded as a juvenile and outfitted with a backpack platform transmitter terminal (PTT) satellite telemetry tracking device. In addition, she was given another identifier, which circulates in an irregular fashion across the human network—a nickname derived from the place of its birth, a person associated with the network, or some combination of the two (figure 3.6). For instance, "Gaksi-hiro," or E37, was named after the small islet in the Yellow Sea, Gaksi-am, where it was born in 2011. "Hiro" was derived from Professor Hiroko Koike, a collaborating researcher in Japan who provided the satellite tracking device. Seonghyeon was named after

Figure 3.6
Seonghyeon E12 with
backpack PTT transmitter.
Courtesy of Lee Kisup.

a Korean colleague, Dr. Kim Seonghyeon, who helped to attach its PTT at its birthplace off Yeonpyeong-do.

If not already naturalcultural assemblages, by the time these PTT birds are returned to their nests, they have become natural-cultural-technical ensembles par excellence, biotechnical species that were born into the contact zones of human–avian flyways. I view these birds as life forms that are not only mediated by technological infrastructures and human networks; they also mediate the networks through their migratory movements. In what follows, I contrast the narrative of discovery documented on the social media website where Dr. Lee posted updates about Seonghyeon with the scholarly article that resulted: "New Perspectives on Habitat Selection by the BFS *Platalea minor* Based upon Satellite Telemetry," coauthored by fourteen individuals, including Dr. Lee and scientists from Japan, China, and South Korea (Wood et al. 2013).

Early technical difficulties related to the weight of the devices and their frequency of transmission have been addressed (Ueta, Kurosawa, and Allen 2000), but despite many improvements in the technology, PTT failures still occur frequently. Although the effects of the devices on individual birds' behavior and well-being are somewhat controversial and would constitute a research subject unto itself, the importance of remote sensing through satellite technology for conservation efforts and scientific knowledge is largely considered to outweigh the risks. As the website for Northstar, a PTT manufacturing company, technocratically asserts, its products can "turn tracking and monitoring into knowledge."[20] The PTT devices work with software that decodes the satellite data and produces images that correspond to the coordinates relayed between the PTT and the satellite as the bird moves through space and time. The image itself is not indexical of the bird's precise movements but is an archive of the signals communicated between the device and the satellite.

In the winter of 2010–11, Dr. Lee tracked Seonghyeon's southward migration and posted his reports to the Waterbird Network's Daum café, a members-only social media site. Included were numerous shots of the Google Earth satellite images representing Seonghyeon's flight pattern, based on transmissions received a couple of times a day, every two days. These coordinates were connected as straight lines layered on a Google Earth background, offering what other scholars have critiqued as a "view from nowhere" (Dodge and Perkins 2009), an authoritative, panoptical image that empowers the visual consumer but that disguises the process of image production and its historicity. Certainly, the lines that Seonghyeon seemed to be literally drawing on the globe need to be further scrutinized not just as representations but as a process of what Bruno Latour would call inscription, "the types of transformations through which an entity becomes materialized into a sign, an archive, document, a piece of paper, a trace" (1999: 306). Like the diagrams produced by the soil scientists he accompanied in Brazil, the satellite images are inherently contradictory. Latour writes: "it is not realistic; it does not resemble anything. It does *more* than resemble. It *takes the place of the original situation…*" (67; emphasis in original). Similarly, the images posted by Dr. Lee move beyond the mimetic and can be seen as inscriptions inspired by Seonghyeon's movements.

Keeping this in mind, I offer a close reading of the posts by Dr. Lee, in which the satellite image as inscription, a literal human–avian– technological coproduction, is an abstraction that purifies and simplifies the movements of this individual bird, "taking the place of the original situation." Despite this simplification, I locate in Dr. Lee's visual and textual narrative a tension between the diagrammatic inscription and his biographical representation that draws attention to the inherent gap between the PTT's data points and the worldliness and idiosyncratic nature of Seonghyeon E12.

As mentioned earlier, the shelling of Yeonpyeong-do by North Korean artillery on November 23, 2010 represented the most significant confrontation between the two Koreas since the signing of the armistice in 1953, leading to the evacuation of the island residents to the mainland. On this day, Dr. Lee began his record of Seonghyeon's migration, reminiscing about the day in March 2010 that they had named and tagged Seonghyeon on Yeonpyeong-do, which was shortly after the Cheonan incident, another moment of heightened political tensions when a South Korean submarine was allegedly torpedoed by North Korea.

Dr. Lee's posts crafted a textual and visual narrative of Seonghyeon's winter migration that included satellite tracking technologies, Google Earth, Google Earth's Panoramio photo archive, and images taken by conservationists or bird lovers along the flyway. Receiving two to three coordinates every two days from the PTT, Dr. Lee could track Seonghyeon's travel from late October when she started heading across the Yellow Sea, "traveling 650 kilometers over the wide ocean, a dangerous first flight." She traveled for ten hours straight without rest, ending up in Yancheng, China, leading Dr. Lee to wonder whether there had been a strong tailwind helping her along. Having survived her "maiden voyage," Seonghyeon stayed just one day in Yancheng before heading farther south. As Dr. Lee wrote, "Exceeding the distance she's already flown, she's gone an additional 900 km, to the area of Putian on the coast of Southern China. On her stopover she looked over Shanghai's forest of huge buildings, countless Chinese villages and towns, the muddy waters of the Yangtze, and a huge 60-kilometer-wide lake—a world she never once experienced before" (map 3.3).

From Putian, the satellite transmission showed Seonghyeon moving to Hai'an, in Jiangsu Province. Dr. Lee posted this information to the network in Hong Kong, Taiwan, and China, and although the monitors from the Putian Wild Birds Society were on the lookout, they couldn't locate her. In the end, birdwatchers in China were able to spot her and take a photo, which they sent to Dr. Lee, who sexed Seonghyeon as female, and commented that she "appeared healthy and mature."[21]

Seonghyeon was not finished with her travels. Having been photographed in China on November 6, two days later, she started moving back toward Hong Kong, but Dr. Lee's prediction was proven wrong—she bypassed Hong Kong and Macao and headed southwest. "Why the hell would she do that?" he wondered. When she was seen in Putian, she seemed to be traveling alone. One of her knees appeared to have been hurt from her long journey over the ocean. She seemed not to know where she was going. Dr. Lee speculated that she was unaware that, among the densely com-

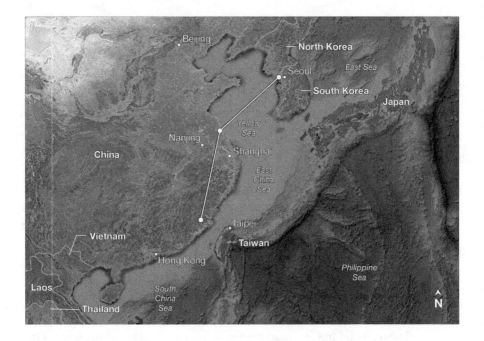

pacted high-rise buildings in Hong Kong and Macao, there are hiding places for BFS "mothers" (어미들).

By November 10, she had logged a thousand kilometers and was heading past the island of Hainan, where there were BFS habitats. She arrived in Vietnam,

Map 3.3
Seonghyeon E12's maiden voyage (re-created from original Google Earth image).

logging two thousand kilometers in three days. But where she ended up, in the Bình Thuận area, was not a wintering site for BFSs but rather a shrimp farm—a difficult place for birds to survive in. Dr. Lee assumed that the area lacked electricity or adequate food for the human inhabitants, and projected his fear that, given the opportunity, people might capture and kill wild birds to eat. Perhaps she got something to eat or was chased away by the locals, but in any case, she moved on. Dr. Lee hoped that she would start heading north again toward an ecologically protected area that BFSs use as a wintering spot. But Seonghyeon kept heading west to a place forty kilometers south of Ho Chi Minh City. Dr. Lee worried that, because of the number of small-scale fishermen in this area, Seonghyeon might get caught up in a fishing net.

He ended this travelogue with an emphatic request to the goddess of the Mekong River to "have mercy" on Seonghyeon and help her to live— she who, at a mere two hundred days old, had already traveled four thousand kilometers. Other South Korean members of the group responded to his post, writing, "A truly long and difficult journey. Surely she won't be flying all by herself?" And "Your heartfelt explanation and E12's difficult journey—you've made my heart stop. I will join in your prayers for the grace of the Mekong." But this dramatic story was not over yet. In February 2011, Dr. Lee received correspondence from expat birdwatchers in Cambodia who had spotted four BFSs in a crane reserve in Takeo Province. According to the satellite, Seonghyeon had been in Cambodia in January, but without active bird monitoring in Cambodia, it was difficult to verify the bird's well-being and existence.

The heart-stopping journey was also a scholarly finding, as it had not been previously known for BFSs to fly as far south as Cambodia. In 2013, a short communication report was printed in *Bird Conservation International*, the publication of BirdLife International, the oldest birdwatchers' and ornithological NGO in the world. Established now as scientific fact, the communication asserts the importance of satellite telemetry to the understanding of BFS habitat selection by presenting evidence of birds having wintered in inland freshwater areas as opposed to coastal areas where birdwatchers often focus their monitoring activities. Especially in light of extensive land reclamation along the BFS flyways, and the strange dip in the BFS population census in 2011, the authors argue that monitoring should not overly emphasize coastal habitats to the neglect of potential inland areas being used by this species. In the article, the "objective" basis of satellite telemetry is presented as generalized data, contrasted with the subjective bias of human monitoring. The satellite-tagged birds are identified only by their PTT serial numbers, and the wintering habitats mapped onto the East Asia region according to zones, defined by a ten-kilometer-square grid system.

This scientific communiqué offers a point of contrast for understanding Dr. Lee's posts as part of the co-construction of the flyway that I described earlier. His collage-like missives of interwoven texts and images foregrounded their inherent instability and referentiality. It is less interesting to me that there is room for interpretation in the satellite inscriptions than that Dr. Lee attempts to fill in the gaps and how he does so. Between a strictly objective approach and an anthropocentric one, Dr. Lee's is a playfully anthropomorphic and fully engaged narration that privileges Seonghyeon's agency and intentions, underscoring a fundamental uncertainty about what she is doing and why. There is certainly a theory of mind at play here, but I focus on how the technobiopolitical assemblages of bird-human-tracking devices produce not only scientific knowledge, as advertised by Northstar, but also situated knowledge that projects humility and

love for an inherently unknowable other. I'm drawn especially to the subjunctive mood of Dr. Lee's posts and what I read as an interspecies poetics of strange kinship in which heterogeneous gazes, shifting scales, and multiple registers disrupt any attempt to create a coherent narrative. This approach is akin to what Kath Weston calls "perspectivalism," which "is no garden-variety anthropomorphism that attributes humanized traits, habits, or sensation to an emphatically non-human creature.... Perspectivalism becomes the very ground that opens up representation to allow some not fully fathomable communication to take place" (2016: 30). As aesthetic accomplishments, these posts are forms of "not fully fathomable communication" that are constitutive of avian migrations and human–avian relations.

Figure 3.7
Gaksi-hiro E37, after being banded and outfitted with PTT backpack. Courtesy of Lee Kisup.

113

Conclusion

Gaksi-hiro, or E37, was banded in early summer 2011 and, as I described earlier, named after the small rocky islet Gaksi-am, off the coast of Gang-hwa-do, South Korea, where he was born, combined with the name Hiroko Koike, a Japanese professor who provided the tracking device (figure 3.7).

Dr. Lee provided a first report on Gaksi-hiro, who was banded and outfitted with a PTT backpack on July 1, 2011. Dr. Lee continued to report on Gaksi-hiro's flight southward to a wintering site in Taiwan, as well as his return trip. After a brief stopover in Incheon, South Korea, on August 24, Gaksi-hiro made a beeline north, traveling 260 kilometers to the shores of Gwak-san County in North Pyongan Province, North Korea. Dr. Lee posted a Google Earth image, registering his surprise: "I have no idea why Gaksi-hiro suddenly moved there in particular. It is Gaksi-hiro's parents' hometown. He matured a bit after heading north [from Taiwan] and stopped over at Gaksi-am, [but] all he did was breed. One has to assume that he then returned to his hometown. Although it is difficult to observe firsthand (via on-the-ground monitoring), the satellite coordinates will continue to transmit, therefore it would be great if from here on out you all would pay close attention."

On his northward journey in 2013, Gaksi-hiro's route baffled Dr. Lee yet again. After one false start, a strong headwind, and foggy conditions, he finally finished his two-thousand-kilometer roundtrip journey back to the Korean peninsula, but this time bypassed his birthplace in South Korea altogether and headed straight to Haeju in North Korea. Dr. Lee's final message read: "For some reason, the crowded lights of South Korea didn't suit him. Or maybe it's because he had previous experience going to North Korea? Even though he has headed to Haeju in North Korea, please welcome Gaksi-hiro E37 back home. Despite the tough weather, he succeeded in his migration. Gaksi-hiro is a hero."

Is the bird's migration driven by avian kinship knowledge, territorial familiarity, or something else? The agency of Gaksi-hiro exceeds any nationalist or narrative frame, and his return to the North renders the political division irrelevant, not overcome. In South Korea, the existence of endangered species in and around the DMZ continues to underwrite the naturalization of kinship, ethnicity, and nation in contemporary narratives of Korean peninsula politics. Dr. Lee's biography of Gaksi-hiro E37 instead denaturalizes these human categories and is premised on a more-than-human logic in which the location and meaning of home is destabilized—we welcome Gaksi-hiro home, even as it is on the other side of the division, for it is not our home but his chosen one (map 3.4).

Multiple stresses on their habitats have brought BFSs to the uninhabited islands off the DMZ, outposts of militarized nature. Birds' flyways may have always been subject to turbulence and disturbance, but the DMZ shows in extremis how the rapaciousness of capitalism, even in the name

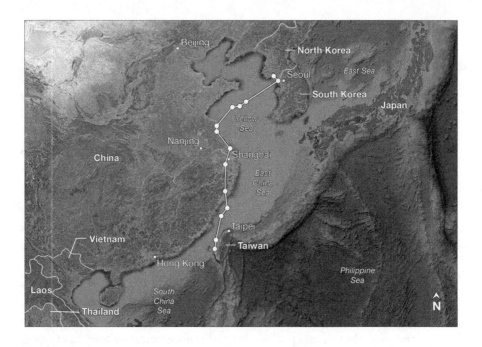

of sustainability, has rendered militarized spaces the most realistic refuges for endangered species of all kinds. For Dr. Lee and other bird lovers, celebrating our avian friends as symbols of freedom, transcendence, and reunification abandons them to a fantasy

Map 3.4
Gaksi-hiro E37's 2011 northerly migration route (re-created from original Google Earth image).

world of pure nature in which nothing will survive for very long. The birds and other nonhumans do not escape the folly of human politics but are truly enmeshed within them. If there is a biopolitics to conservationists like Dr. Lee in his project of optimizing birds' lives across the flyway, it is in the management of a degraded milieu, which exercises a hierarchy of value that privileges the BFS over other more common cohabiting species— seagulls, cormorants, fish, and, of course, the goats. In fact, we observed with horror, yet passively, the viciousness of the gulls who pecked rivals' chicks to death in their competition over the limited space and nesting materials on the island.

Yet, there is another story that Guji-do and other BFS conservation efforts tell—that the migrations of birds open up passageways for exchange and cooperation, not between North and South Korean states and markets, but across the flyway, creating transnational networks of friendship, affinity, and care. I view pantomimes of humans in goat clothing and co-produced satellite biographies as part of the channels that constitute a human–avian collective or "gaiasociality" (Helmreich 2003)—which is crucial for BFS survival. Here, the pragmatically hopeful narrative is not one describing lines of flight transcending the division, but one that homes in on ethical moments in which human vision is decentered through the poetics and pragmatics of interspecies mimicry and dehumanizing choreographies. The goat performances, motion-detection cameras, satellite images, and banding technologies that attempt to capture data of avian behaviors are neither entirely socially constructed nor wholly unmediated reflections of avian lives. These technologically networked relations enact a poetics that decenters human exceptionalism and defamiliarizes the orders by which we typically understand space, belonging, and politics.

In the context of the national division, migratory birds are often framed as symbols of a unified peninsula or post-national world. In a similar vein, avian flyways can be symbolically inspiring because they map a nonhuman geography and decenter an anthropocentric perspective on space and belonging, revealing our political boundaries to be contingent and even absurd. It is profoundly anthropocentric, however, to consider migratory birds to be natural cosmopolitans, for cosmopolitanism itself, as Derrida suggests in his writings on hospitality (Derrida and Dufourmantelle 2000), requires an absolute openness to difference that is difficult if not impossible to achieve. In classic political theory, cosmopolitanism attempts to grapple with the human propensity for violence toward others and the potential for some kind of universal peace based on a notion of shared humanity. Too often, nonhuman others become the basis for what anthropologist Matthew C. Watson (2016) calls "multispecies mythologies," a symptom of modernist nostalgia in an age of extinction and ecological devastation.

In contrast to this anthropocentric vision, this chapter has shown how technologies of bird monitoring—the aforementioned banding, satellite tracking, and motion detection cameras—do not merely abstract the birds into "objective" scientific data, but instead generate the strange kinship of the human–avian relationships that constitute the flyway. These flyways are examples of militarized ecologies and also of biological peace (see Introduction), offering critical openings onto other-than-human perspectives. This is a way of thinking of nonhumans as agents that are shaped by and, in turn, shape specific historical, political, and contingent relationships, rather than merely exemplifying instinctual or evolutionary behaviors (Hathaway 2013). It is also a way of thinking cosmopolitically and also planetarily, with an attention to stratifications of space and scale.

As I have underscored, birds are not free of human, terrestrial concerns. In fact, just as they are affected by human activities, from climate change to pollution to land reclamation, birds also reflect back to us the dimming prospects for ecological recovery. Conservationists consider migratory birds to be ideal indicator species, and they use data on their presence or absence to infer the sustainability of an ecosystem. Recent reports on the population declines of more than half of the world's migratory bird species due to the reduction in their seasonal habitats are therefore intensely worrisome indicators of global ecological degradation and biodiversity loss (Runge et al. 2015). Perhaps more than just decentering human views of planetary space, flyways are, more accurately, our very own cartographies of the Anthropocene.

Coda

In an interview with Dr. Lee, he shared with me an ambivalent yet open-ended post-nature, posthuman and post-national vision that reflected not only his place in a geopolitically stratified world, but also his desire for a future in which freedom could be universalized across species. His statements inverted the romantic assumptions that inform the dominant narratives of iconic cranes and of Starling C7655, in which the supposed freedom and natural cosmopolitanism of birds serve as models for our own multispecies mythologies and "affirmationist alternatives" (M. C. Watson 2016: 169). In contrast, for Dr. Lee, it is the cosmopolitanism of people—the freedom to move and the freedom to desire freedom itself—that must be imaginatively extended beyond the human.

He mentioned to me that he had only ever been to one place in the United States: Denali National Park, many years before, as a college student. There was another student he met on that trip, a white American from the Arizona desert who had traveled a long distance by herself. He was surprised by her independence, as "we [Koreans] rarely go about by ourselves." She told him that she had come to see the animals, the caribou, grizzly bears, and polar bears. "At the time, I really didn't understand [her], because you could see these animals in the zoo. I saw them in Anchorage before arriving in Denali. I saw the polar bears, the caribous, all of them. They were frolicking there too. But when the people saw them [in Denali], they were like, 'Wow!'"

This experience—meeting a young independent woman, who traveled hundreds of miles (like Dr. Lee had) to witness animals "frolicking in the wild"—made a strong impression on Dr. Lee. As he explained it to me, he came to a new understanding about human nature. "Ah, the thing that people want is 'freedom' [using the English word]. They are in awe, witnessing animals frolicking freely. What I realized then is that American consciousness (정신) is one of 'freedom.' I thought, so that's why it's a wondrous thing. Going around the world, not just freedom for Koreans, or for people in general, but a world in which animals can also move about freely ('free'-하게) would be the loveliest world (가장 멋진 세상), wouldn't it?"

Freedom, like peace, is a universal that we may not be able to do without (see Tsing 2005)—even as it has been instrumentalized to justify US empire, militarization, capitalist extraction, and the dehumanization of enemies from the Cold War to the Axis of Evil and the War on Terror to the ongoing war with North Korea. In desiring freedom for our nonhuman friends and in desiring more-than-human peace, do we risk reinscribing a politically naïve hierarchy of humanity, or worse, ignoring the radical unfreedom of people around the world, many of whom are unfree precisely because of US empire and the ideology of universal freedom that it debases? I view Dr. Lee's story as an ethnographic insight—he observed the affective power that freedom held for Americans who were in awe of "wild" animals roaming within the boundaries of a national park. Thus, his conclusion is less of a valorization of American cultural values of freedom and more of an opportunity to reorient freedom away from the prescription of Western individualism and private property as the apogee of cultural progress and toward a descriptive model of freedom of movement and migration as the basis for biological peace. In essence, he theorizes a (de)universalized freedom that can include not just humanity but all forms of life.

In chapter 4, I shift focus from the islands of the Yellow Sea to the prairie heartland of the peninsula's "rice bowl" where late–Cold War discourses of peace stand in discordant relation to local residents' experiences of ongoing violence in toxic (post)war landscapes. I frame landmines in Cheorwon County and other parts of the border area as rogue infrastructures that are deeply entangled with local histories, giving further lie to state discourses of peace and life and suggesting that "making peace with nature" requires a reckoning with the ongoing psychic and material effects of US empire.

LANDMINES

The period 1966–69 is often referred to by military historians as the Second Korean War because of the frequent low-intensity conflicts that took place between the United States/ROK and North Korean forces. North Korean soldiers continuously breached the SBL, and more than four hundred firefights took place during that time, with increasing numbers of casualties and deaths among both soldiers and civilians, especially during 1967 and 1968. According to military historian Daniel Bolger, US forces, under the command of General Charles "Tic" Bonesteel, focused on deterrence rather than conflict, and fortifying the DMZ became a major preoccupation. Bonesteel (who, with Col. Dean Rusk, had been in charge of drawing the dividing line that partitioned Korea on the night of August 14, 1945) asked the Pentagon for $32 million to design an anti-infiltration system that could delay, detect, and neutralize intruders. His experimental "DMZ barrier system," which was expanded to the entire width of the peninsula by July 1967, installed four layers of defense on the southern edge of the DMZ. Based on interviews with retired General Bonesteel, Bolger describes the barrier system in this way:

> The system centered around a chain-link fence, ten feet tall, topped by triple strands of concertina wire and reinforced by interwoven saplings and steel engineer pickets. A narrow, raked-sand path paralleled the fence on the allied side to highlight footprints. Just past the sand strip lay a 120-meter-wide kill zone cleared with plows, chain saws, axes, and chemical defoliants. In that area, mines and tanglefoot wire fronted a line of conventional defensive positions. From there, defenders used a final protective line of interlocking machine guns and on-call mortar and artillery concentrations to dominate the kill zone. Observation towers stood at

intervals along the track to permit clear view of the open areas. Local patrols checked the fence line and covered dead ground between positions. (Bolger 1991: 49–50)

The barrier system reminds us that the DMZ is hardly demilitarized and hardly pristine. Rather, it is a terraformed area that has been "cleared with plows, chain saws, axes, and chemical defoliants," in which mines and barbed wire secure the "kill zone." Patrolling the barrier system and checking for any disturbances or vulnerabilities is one of the primary tasks of the soldiers stationed at the DMZ. This system, which denudes the area to render it dead ground, may be unambiguous in its design. By focusing on the landmines that are central to the DMZ as a barrier and uncompromising border, however, this chapter suggests that it is also generative of multiple and ambiguous effects. In fact, the ecological exceptionalism of the DMZ credits mines themselves for rendering the border space an ecological haven by forbidding human crossing and habitation, to the benefit of its nonhuman biota.

Landmines link multiple exceptionalisms—they, along with the barrier system, materialize the political exceptionalism of the DMZ, they secure its ecological exceptionalism, and they exist and persist in Korea as an exception to international norms in a contemporary humanitarian context where landmines are viewed nearly universally as abhorrent and morally unacceptable. As I will show, the exception made for landmines in Korea is inseparably linked to US empire and has been reproduced for decades under a US policy referred to, fittingly, as the "Korea exception." The Korea exception has permitted every US president since Bill Clinton to use the ongoing war on the Korean peninsula as a justification for maintaining a strategic stockpile of antipersonnel landmines. This, in the face of the highly successful International Campaign to Ban Landmines (ICBL), which, since the historic signing of the 1997 Ottawa Treaty (Mine Ban Treaty), has led to a widely adopted ban on the production and use of antipersonnel mines.

The Korea exception holds specific implications for people who live in the DMZ region of South Korea, for whom landmines are an irrefutable aspect of local histories, landscapes, and livelihoods. This chapter tracks landmines and their material and affective traces in the villages of the DMZ region as a way to interrogate US empire as an imperial formation (Stoler and McGranahan 2007). This is especially important, as in the ambiguous spatiotemporalities of the DMZ as PLZ, landmines and their victims too often disappear into the landscape, replaced with military kitsch or state-sanctioned peace and life narratives that metaphorically decommission landmines as elements of a distant past.

This postcolonial critique is compelled by the stories and discourses I heard among local residents and anti-mine activists, which tended to emphasize the disenfranchisement and victimization of locals, whose lives were deeply scarred by mines and violent landscapes on the front lines of an unending war. Other stories that emerged in my conversations, however, suggested alternative ways in which landmines and minefields, as technical and material things, coexist with humans. Many residents experienced mines as heinous and deadly weapons, to be sure, but mines and minefields also appeared in some narratives in ways best grasped through an infrastructural lens—one that can account for their unpredictable spatiotemporality, volatile materiality, and heterogeneous natural-cultural-technical entanglements.

In what follows, I discuss the history of mines in South Korea, tracing them back to the Korean War and US military presence, as well as the imperial relations that they mediate, especially with respect to the Korea exception. I then attend to the performative intra-actions of humans and landmines but focus less on the normative intentions of mine layers and more on the persistence of mines in postwar landscapes and the unanticipated effects, affects, and relations that they generate. I develop the framework of "rogue infrastructures" to foreground the spatiotemporal contingency of mines. The roguishness of mines is related to their status as "matter out of place" (Douglas 2002 [1966]: 44) and their ability to deprive humans of agency, but also—and more significantly for my argument—to their unintended affordances and ecologically embedded ontologies. Rogue infrastructure attempts to capture the multiplicity of mines in their intra-actions with humans as "area denial weapons" (in US military parlance), indiscriminate and anti-humanitarian political agents, military property, useless waste, and valuable (un)natural resources. As I explore, mines may be implicitly connected to sovereign power and imperial geopolitics, but they can also exceed expected technological and political determinations.

Extensions of War

...Japan became a signatory [to the 1997 Mine Ban Treaty]. And if you sign the treaty, you have to destroy the mines. Japan was ordered to destroy them, and I heard it took them 15 days to destroy however many tons of mines and TNT. But in our country, not only are the mines not destroyed, they continue being buried. And this has to do with what we were talking about before. Our fellow villagers were just going about their business, and three people died—on a road that they frequented every day. There—right in the place where they eat and fetch water. That day, three people are going along, two people get killed, and one of them is too scared to say anything. As it turned out, one of the two was able to crawl away a bit. So, the first one died on the spot—the one who stepped on the mine. The [woman] behind him was hit with shrapnel and was able to crawl away, and crawl away, and then died. What could the husband do, knowing this? If only he had been faster, perhaps—we'll never know—she might have lived. But since [he was too scared] he hid himself and didn't get help, and she died. The husband ended up killing himself. He committed suicide, and their children—where could they go? They were sent for adoption overseas. What can you say about all this? What you can say is, however you look at it, these are all war victims. As I said before, this is an extension of the war (전쟁의 연장선).

Mayor Lee recounted this story to me and three other local residents as we chatted around a picnic table on the deck of the CheongJeon-ri community center, Red-Crowned Crane Peace Hall, named for the endangered avian species whose migration routes connect the two Koreas. The crane, which symbolizes long life, has become iconic of the DMZ's nature, and the hall's christening in 2009 marked an attempt by the village to invest in the economic promises of ecotourism in the DMZ region. In fact, my visit had coincided with an ecotourism training program spearheaded by a professor at the provincial university who was seeking to integrate local communities into a project that would link the Border Area to a future UNESCO-designated Geopark. He came with support from the provincial and central governments to bring "sustainable development" to the region. And in keeping with global mandates that local or indigenous people be included as stakeholders in biodiversity conservation projects, engaging participation of "local residents" (지역주민) was crucial for him.[1] The professor framed locals as important assets to the region's cultural diversity and enrolled them as tour guides who could objectify signature activities or practices as "local culture" (지역문화) while also educating tourists about geological features of the landscape.

Given this immediate context, I began the interview by asking about villagers' views of these various ecotourism development projects. Their attitudes were mixed, as I had expected, with Mayor Lee expressing skepticism of "PhDs and experts" coming with "their research materials to tell us to keep in mind the 'originality' of our village," and Mrs. Kim enthusiastically echoing the rhetoric of "contentification" (컨텐츠화) common in neoliberalized iterations of rural development. Yet, the conversation continually circled back to landmines and weaponized landscapes, which, as suggested in the opening narrative, were framed as material instantiations of unequal geopolitical relations, US empire, and unending war. In this and other conversations in CheongJeon-ri, I came to understand that for these residents, state and NGO framings of the DMZ as a zone of biodiversity and a source of ecotourism income coexisted uneasily with their personal and collective histories of restriction, marginalization, and death. After reminding me that the United States used Agent Orange not only in Vietnam but also in the Korean DMZ, a farming couple I spoke with concluded, "So if you ask the local people, they'll say, 'What nature?'" and "Everything's been ruined, frankly. America has ruined everything."

Since the fortification of the southern half of the DMZ by the US Army in 1967, landmines have been a central element in South Korea's border security. Yet, during my fieldwork, landmines, if they appeared at all, were in the margins of the frame, a persistent problem that was only briefly mentioned as a "stumbling block" (걸림돌) by policy makers, in their Arcadian models for the peaceful utilization of the zone. As it would take an estimated 489 years to clear the one million or more landmines from the DMZ region, no one could deny that they presented a primary challenge to converting it into a peace park or biosphere reserve. Yet, almost no one outside of a few NGOs spoke of the dangers of landmines in areas south of the DMZ, where, by South Korean government estimates, there are 1,100 "planned" minefields (기획 지뢰지대) and 208 "unconfirmed" ones (미확인 지뢰지대), with the latter comprising approximately thirty-seven square miles. The planned minefields are those documented by the South Korean military, and the unconfirmed ones refer primarily to fields laid by US armed forces, but for which records do not exist. In these unconfirmed minefields, mine removal expert and researcher Kim Ki-ho estimates that as many as 200,000 mines may be buried. Despite these sobering numbers, policy makers and bureaucrats uniformly neglected the problem of landmines and their victims, even as eco-friendly tourism ventures bring more and more civilians into close proximity to unconfirmed minefields (map 4.1).

If landmines themselves were hard to discern in discussions of the DMZ, their warning signs—bright red, inverted triangles, threaded with barbed wire—were ubiquitous in government documents, media reports, touristic pamphlets, and marketing posters. Those red signs are an integral part

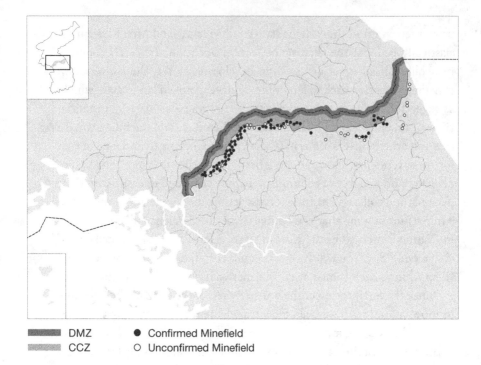

DMZ   ● Confirmed Minefield
CCZ   ○ Unconfirmed Minefield

Map 4.1

Confirmed and unconfirmed minefields in the CCZ/Border Area. As the CCL has moved northward, more minefields now exist in civilian areas. Adapted from Green Korea United (2013a).

of the visual iconography of the DMZ as a "forbidden zone," and are increasingly coupled with images of nature—wildflowers, deer, otters, birds—advertising the DMZ as PLZ, and its unlikely juxtaposition of wildlife and militarization. These images reassert the story of nature's resilience and indifference to human politics and militarized violence. Yet, in their ubiquity, landmine signs have become iconic of themselves, rather than indexical of the presence of mines, fetishized for the remote and unimaginable dangers they represent, but losing reference to actual mines, and especially their human victims.

As described in previous chapters, the ambiguous and contradictory temporalities of the meantime of division—those of war/postwar, conflict/post-conflict, and ongoing war/future peace—are nowhere more present than in the DMZ region. Landmines highlight the heterotopic nature of the DMZ and bring these multiple temporalities into simultaneous focus, along with the perduring effects of the Cold War on purportedly post–Cold War environments. When it comes to landmines, Rob Nixon's notion of "afterdeaths" is apropos. As he writes, "in such societies, where landmines continue to inflict belated maimings and what I call afterdeaths, the *post* in post–Cold War has never fully arrived. Instead, whole provinces inhabit a twilight realm in which everyday life remains semi-militarized and in which the earth itself must be treated with permanent suspicion, as armed and dangerous" (Nixon 2007: 169). For the United States and South Korea, mines are not considered to be military waste as they would be in post-conflict zones. Rather, they are viewed as crucial to the buffer area's function in "maintaining the peace." Therefore, figuring the DMZ as a PLZ requires grappling with the actuality of landmines in civilian areas, their existence, their deadly agency, and discourses about them.

There are obvious physical risks involved in conducting an ethnography that takes landmines and their material existence seriously. In my own research, I avoided mines and minefields at all costs, but the suggestion of them was all around. The telltale red triangles and barbed wire indicated that certain areas were off-limits, and large placards near unconfirmed minefields, erected by local military battalions, warned passersby not to trespass and reminded them that any injuries or accidents would be at the person's own risk. Despite or because of their ubiquity, as I became accustomed to the scenery, these signs rapidly receded into the background, reduced to visual static that had become as unremarkable to me as they were to my DERI colleagues, who, when I asked them about mines, would say, "Oh, yes, there are so many around here," without further elaboration.

It was in this visual and discursive context that the villagers' stories resonated for me with unnerving presence. Mayor Lee's narrative in particular brought together the most intimate and distant scales, from infrastructure (roads, water) to kinship (orphaned children sent away for transnational adoption) to state power (in the form of indifference) to international geopolitics (the 1997 Mine Ban Treaty), and ultimately linked to the unending war and US empire. In this account, the border area is a space of exception in which the national division and Cold War politics rendered mine victims a kind of bare life (Agamben 1998), recognized by the state neither as war victims nor as citizens deserving of compensation. Whereas misery and tragedy constituted the affective core of most mine stories I heard from villagers—especially when they were directly solicited—in other instances, mines appeared at unanticipated moments, pointing toward a more complex relationship between mines and residents, suggesting to me how the value of mines could be more heterogeneous and multivalent than their dominant associations with inhumane wars of attrition might allow.

In one instance, after a presentation of my research for local people in Cheorwon County, during the Q and A, I asked my audience what they thought of observers who claimed that CCZ residents were not natives to the area and therefore didn't feel a moral obligation to preserve their environments. Mr. Hong, who had lived in CheongJeon-ri since childhood, responded by schooling me in the particular habitus of border area people. He said, "There's a saying: If you run, it'll take five minutes; if you walk, it'll take ten." This saying, he implied, determined who was a true local, as only those who had lived for many years in the border area could comprehend it. These were people who knew what it was like to live in a weaponized landscape, where, as Mr. Hong put it, "mines continue to go and lie in wait" (계속 매복하러 들어가요). He went on to explain that when the swampy wetlands of Cheorwon freeze over in the winter, the landmines become "useless objects," since their trigger mechanisms won't be able to detect human footsteps. With the frozen ground holding them in place, it doesn't matter if one runs or walks through a minefield to cover the same distance. This conversation took place in March 2015, after the spring thaw, when the mines would be coming out of hibernation, so to speak. For this reason, Mr. Hong offered to accompany me across a frozen minefield the following winter, personally guaranteeing my safety.

I never had the desire to take him up on his offer, but through this and other conversations, I began to think of mines as ecologically embedded actants whose agencies in specific relation to human actors can generate unexpected values, relations, and affects. Rather than presupposing the suspension of human agency that is common in scholarly and humanitarian approaches to landmines, I consider mines to be "enacted in practice" (Mol 2002). The framework of rogue infrastructure, as I will explain, attempts to capture the volatile materiality of mines and their heterogeneous naturalculturaltechnical entanglements among the humans they exist alongside. I hold that an infrastructural approach to landmines can productively complicate both humanitarian approaches that frame them as toxic remnants of war and postcolonial critiques that frame them as traces of imperial power and ongoing violence.

The Korea Exception

The ICBL has been one of the most successful civil society movements in recent history, transforming landmines into a global humanitarian issue and leading to the historic signing of the Mine Ban Treaty in 1997. The United States' reluctance to become a signatory, despite its stated commitment to humanitarian mine action, has, since 1997, been premised on the Korea exception, which rationalizes the United States' stockpiling of mines as necessary in the event of another war on the Korean peninsula (US Department of State 2014). Although the United States reports that it no longer stockpiles "dumb" mines on American soil, it continues to store remote self-neutralizing or self-detonating "smart" antipersonnel mines in South Korea.[2]

This position is premised on the false assumption that mines exist only within the DMZ, and not in civilian areas, and has been morally buttressed by the United States' commitment to humanitarian mine action in developing nations. Yet, border residents view the Korea exception as tacitly underwriting the South Korean state's long-standing indifference to civilian mine victims, whose rights to compensation were only legislated in late 2014.[3] Comprehensive government statistics on landmine casualties do not exist, but estimates by the South Korean NGO Peace Sharing Association (PSA) count a thousand civilian casualties and two to three thousand military casualties. Over the past two decades, South Korean activists and NGOs associated with the PSA have brought increasing attention to landmine victims, who have, as they argue, "suffered in silence" for too long. In a 2011 survey—the first of its kind—it was found that three-quarters of the 228 respondents who were survivors of mine accidents did not report their accidents to the government because (1) they didn't know how to seek compensation, (2) they feared retribution from the local military battalion, or (3) they were led to believe that landmine accidents were their own responsibility.[4]

From the perspective of military strategists in South Korea and the United States, mines in South Korea are not postwar military waste as they are in a place like Bosnia, but rather active parts of the national security strategy, even as their anti-humanitarian image has forced both governments to deny or dissimulate when asked about the laying and/or stockpiling of landmines.[5] Whereas some observers question the necessity of landmines as a deterrent, given the revolution in military affairs in which tanks themselves are being retired as dinosaurs of a previous generation's military arsenal, in the case of the two Koreas, landmines are still considered to be the most effective deterrent and crucial for maintaining peace. In response to the Mine Ban Treaty in 1997, the position of the South Korean security state was quoted in a *New York Times* op-ed by Nicholas Kristof: "'Many people talk about the humanitarian aspects of landmines,' said Lieut. Gen. Park Yong Ok, the Deputy Defense Minister and a fervent defender of the mines. 'Deterrence of war is more humanitarian than anything. If we fail to deter war, a tremendous number of civilians will be killed. And the use of landmines is a very effective way of deterring war.'"[6] The Orwellian attempt to harmonize humanitarianism with landmines is no longer part of state rhetoric, but the truism that landmines constitute an essential part of national defense strategy has only recently been questioned.[7]

With the softening of tensions between the two Koreas during years of the Sunshine Policy (1998–2008), the South Korean Joint Chiefs of Staff began a process of mine clearance, especially in areas flooded by heavy rain and in certain areas deemed militarily appropriate in the CCZ, and today spends approximately US$1 million annually on mine removal. Following the 2018 inter-Korean summits, the Korean War battleground of Arrowhead Hill (화살머리고지) was excavated to retrieve the remains of soldiers missing in action. Originally planned as a joint Korean project that required the demining of the entire area, the operation ultimately moved forward without North Korean participation. Yet, even as soldiers are clearing minefields for these peace projects, which include the building of tourist sites and the reconnection of prewar infrastructures, the environmental NGO Green Korea United found in its 2020 analysis of the Ministry of National Defense records that, during the nearly twenty years since the government announced the beginning of the demining process, none of the thirty-six minefields in so-called rear areas (civilian areas outside the frontline/forward areas along the DMZ) had been cleared.[8] In the border area in particular, many minefields are unmarked or poorly maintained, presenting an ongoing threat to civilians and soldiers, and in clear violation of the law on the Use and Regulation of Landmines and Certain Conventional Weapons (Green Korea United 2010). The Korea exception holds particularly strong associations for residents in Cheorwon County, where military weapons have been a defining feature for some villages.

Approaching Landmines

The identification of landmines with US imperial power among residents of CheongJeon-ri resonates with Ann Stoler and David Bond's exhortation to identify imperial formations by "tracing them through the durabilities of duress in the subsoil of affective landscapes" (2006: 95). Landmines materially embody and are embedded in histories of power and domination, suggesting how "imperial formations persist in their material debris, in ruined landscapes and through the social ruination of people's lives" (95).

Analyzing landmines in South Korea is therefore not simply about accounting for the environmental effects of war, but also requires a recognition of landmine-infested territories as metonymically and metaphorically linked to US empire and what Rob Nixon (2011) compellingly critiques as US empire's unspectacular, slow violence.

Figure 4.1
Kim Kiho, with M14 mine (floating in plastic cup) and M16 mine. March 2015. Photograph by the author.

Yet, the anthropology of mines, I contend, must also attend to their indisputable materiality. As naturalcultural elements of living landscapes, whether scattered randomly or laid deliberately, mines create indelible effects on the humans and nonhumans that inhabit these spaces, securing and proliferating geographic and social borders. They are spatiotemporal, socio-environmental, material–affective, lively and deadly, and can be "smart" or "dumb." M14 antipersonnel landmines, for instance, are smaller than a hockey puck, made out of lightweight plastic, and are easily dislodged during floods or heavy rains (figure 4.1). They can remain active for decades, and as their outer shells decay after a long period, they can be difficult to distinguish from fallen leaves.

Despite a wide engagement with militarization in anthropology (e.g., Gusterson 2007; Lutz 2007), until recently, few scholars have focused on mines and their materiality.[9] One exception is David Henig, who, based on research in mine-infested areas of post-conflict Bosnia, calls for anthropologists to attend to military waste, including landmines and other explosive remnants of war (ERW). He suggests that "an anthropology of military waste can shed light, not just on the ways that mines and military debris pose a hazard of explosion and other dangers, but also on the emotional distress that the waste provokes in people who dwell alongside it" (Henig 2012: 23; see also Henig 2019). In a similar vein, Yael Navaro-Yashin's ethnography of life in Northern Cyprus (2012) analyzes the ruins of war through the lenses of abjection and melancholia, asking how war's detritus and debris become affectively charged, and Christina Schwenkel describes ERW in Vietnam as "ambiguous, abject matter out of place" (2013: 137).

I depart from these melancholic and abject framings by attending to the posthuman performativity of mines as actants in human–nonhuman networks that I call rogue infrastructures, in which the material–affective relations of mine–human assemblages prove to be unpredictable and even counterintuitive. Humanitarian and postcolonial analyses that trace histories of mines as "imperial debris" or sources of distress are certainly not to be discounted (Stoler and Bond 2006). As already suggested, villagers who live among mines see their own experiences in this light, linking everyday anxieties and mine deaths to US empire and unending war. Yet, theoretically and politically, this is only part of the story and, as I will argue, reduces the politics of mines to one in which mines act as proxies of state violence to which local residents are passively subjected.

This attempt to theorize the agency of mines was, in some respects, anticipated by Alfred Gell in *Art and Agency* (1998). There, he famously used the example of Pol Pot's soldier laying mines to illustrate his theory of "distributed personhood," in which the "primary agency" of the soldier was distributed to the "secondary agent" of the mine. For Gell, the antipersonnel mine presents a particularly suitable analogy because, although it may seem to be a "mere lethal mechanical device" that "could not help exploding," it is in fact what makes Pol Pot's soldier a "malign" agent (20–21). Gell's model of agency, however relational and recursive, still depends on a linear and hierarchical connection between "primary agents" and "secondary agents," in which "social agency manifests and realizes itself, via the proliferation of fragments of 'primary' intentional agents in their 'secondary' artifactual forms" (21). In this framing, moreover, the political and moral implications of mines are presupposed in that they are extensions of the evil intentions of Pol Pot's soldiers. If one shifts focus from the nexus of soldier–mine to that of civilian–mine, and considers the variable of time, other relations and agencies that are left out of Gell's approach become analytically salient. Mines' long yet unpredictable life spans introduce an uncertain spatiotemporality and historicity, in which their distributed agency can be redistributed over time (Latour 1999).[10]

My broader analytical approach draws on Karen Barad's "relational ontology" (2003) that theorizes agency as always intra-active. Rather than agency being distributed through objects that mediate a self-knowing subject's intentions, subject and object come into being through their concrete performative relations. To think of landmines through a relational ontology means refuting the notion that either mine or human are ontologically pre-given. Rather, landmines, which were emplaced as an articulation of sovereign power, become, over time, unpredictable and deterritorialized through their ecological entanglements and evolving relations with humans and nonhumans.

Understanding landmines infrastructurally highlights how they are irreducibly technical, cultural, economic, and political things that may have, at one time, distributed the cruel intentions of soldiers and sovereign powers but that consequently enter into other relations, (re)configure naturalcultural spaces, and tender novel affordances and circulations. In the following pages, I suggest how mines, which may continue to distribute the immoral agency of Gell's original soldiers, are anti-humanitarian to be sure, but they can also be outwitted. In rogue infrastructures, I locate the unexpected agencies and affects of human–mine assemblages, among humans who harvest and disable them, dismantle and circulate them, and in the process, generate psychic freedom, however provisional, from the spatial incarceration and thanatopolitical inevitability of minefields.

Landmines as Rogue Infrastructure

Anthropological scholarship on infrastructure has tended to focus on urban or cybernetic systems and less frequently on military infrastructures, despite the military roots of the term (Petroski 2009). A central premise of these studies is that infrastructures constitute and reflect fundamentally modern projects, entailing the construction and maintenance of systems and exemplifying human mastery over nature, with attendant aesthetics of modernity, progress, and futurity (Larkin 2013). If we take this to be true, then landmines might easily be seen as anti-infrastructural in their intended normative function as explosive devices that are categorized as "area denial weapons" in US military terminology. They are often laid to destroy or prevent access to critical infrastructure, to disrupt, block, or divert flows of people, resources, supplies, or commodities. In post-conflict settings, mines and the suspicion of their existence continue to restrict human mobility and land use and impede or prevent the repair or maintenance of basic infrastructure, in what Unruh, Heynen, and Hossler call a "switch from an intentional to an unintentional remaking of nature" (2003: 858).

In this way, mines foreclose, especially for people living among them, the economic, social, affective, and aesthetic possibilities afforded by infrastructure. Landmines' long life spans can affect the health, livelihoods, and economic development of post-conflict societies for generations. Moreover, the political economy of mine contamination and mine removal depressingly reinforces global patterns of environmental racism and inequality, starkly illustrating the uneven distribution of not only economic resources to clear mines but also the disproportionate physical and psychic burdens shouldered by the most politically, economically, or racially marginalized groups (Nixon 2011).[11]

A view of mines as merely anti-infrastructural, however, would fail to account for the unintended effects of mines, especially as mines and minefields persist and change over time in specific ecologies, generating novel configurations among humans and nonhumans. Following Larkin's definition of infrastructure as "matter that enable the movement of other matter" (2013: 329), I emphasize not only how landmines may disable systems, but also how they, like other infrastructures, "produce environments" (Carse 2014) and come to enable the movement of other matter.

My invocation of roguishness highlights mines' aberrant and unpredictable behaviors, which can seem arbitrary and volatile (see also Dawdy 2008). I focus less on their illegitimacy in relation to normative or sanctioned operations and more on their inherent instability and indiscriminateness, what renders them abhorrent in humanitarian terms and also potentially undermining of sovereign legitimacy. Roguishness in my usage also draws significance from the notion of rogue states that became integral to the ideological consolidation of US power in its post–Cold War imperial formation. The "rogue" moniker vilified states that were viewed as nonconformist and operated to exclude and delegitimize sovereign powers in order to reassert the norm of US hegemony, even as, under its own terms, the United States and its allies must be viewed as the first rogue states (Derrida 2005: 102). Moreover, identifying such rogues justified the proliferation of militarization in the name of global security. Rogue states are also importantly associated with "blowback," in cases such as Afghanistan and Iraq, where covert operations and the arming of Cold War allies, with the shifting of political priorities, ultimately leads to those very arms being used against their former benefactor (Johnson 2001).

Landmines in South Korea can be seen as rogue in precisely these terms—laid by the United States during the Cold War, and subsequently abandoned, mines are disavowed by the United States, even as they continue to stockpile them for future use on the Korean peninsula. Uncontrollable, indiscriminate, and anti-humanitarian, mines are also proving to be environmental "blowback," in the form of weaponized nature that repels human passage and occupation, and that undermines the moral legitimacy of the state's monopoly on violence. The insecure and uncertain environments of the border area exemplify for residents the limits of South Korean state sovereignty and the rogue power of US empire, but they also exceed political and ideological designs. In the more-than-human natures of the DMZ, wild boars may be at the top of the food chain (next to the apocryphal Siberian tiger), but landmines in fact supersede them, while simultaneously rendering the environment safe for nonhuman flourishing. In rogue infrastructures, I locate unforeseen agencies and affects of human–mine intra-actions, among humans who may avoid, harvest, disable, dismantle, and circulate them, and mines that can lie in wait, freeze, corrode, move, explode, or self-neutralize.

Rogue infrastructures contribute to a broader literature on militarized environments but move beyond the empirical question of how war and militaries affect nature to ask how military infrastructure, including waste and weapons, are natural, cultural, and technical things that become constitutive elements of ecosystems. This question is increasingly relevant as militaries around the world are identifying decommissioned sites as ecologically valuable spaces of "wilderness" (Masco 2004) and embracing "military environmentalism" in their attempts to remediate heavily polluted areas—oftentimes by celebrating ecological features of decommissioned sites and downplaying their toxicity (see the epilogue).

These examples recall what Joseph Masco (2004: 523) calls "mutant ecologies" and are sites where environmental despoliation, accumulation by dispossession (Harvey 2003), and global security converge. If, following Masco, mutant ecologies are "cold war survivals" of contaminated nature in the nuclear age, rogue infrastructures, instead of reconfiguring biological matter at the level of the molecular or the species, are part of the material transformation of landscapes that become infrastructural over time. They become significant naturalcultural elements whose multiple affordances divert and recompose human–nonhuman worlds. As my conversations with the residents of CheongJeon-ri revealed, landmines in their persistent, if hidden, existence offered a different kind of ambient noise or background hum than that of conventional infrastructures. Theirs is a subterranean, explosive, and risky parallel infrastructure that is constitutive of the peculiar hetertopia of the DMZ.

Landmines in the DMZ and Beyond

In post-conflict settings, landmines not only restrict land use, but also, due to the cost of demining procedures (between $300 and $1,000 per mine), which is often viewed as prohibitive, lead to thousands of deaths and casualties every year (Nixon 2007: 163).[12] Since 1997, 164 countries have become party to the Mine Ban Treaty, spearheaded by the ICBL.[13] Today, antipersonnel landmines are widely seen as a humanitarian issue, given the fact that 70–85 percent of mine casualties are civilians in countries no longer at war. As stated on the ICBL website, "Landmines don't obey peace agreements or ceasefires."[14] South Korea has the dubious distinction of being the country with the highest concentration of landmines in the world.[15] According to South Korean government figures, 970,000 mines are in the southern part of the DMZ, and another 38,000 mines in other parts of the Border Area. South Korean NGOs, however, assert that there are an estimated 600,000 mines in the CCZ and border areas. Based on defectors' testimonies, it is believed that North Korea has also buried at least as many landmines on their side as South Korea has.[16]

Mines were first used by US and UN forces during the Korean War. According to an account from a lieutenant in the US Corps of Engineers, 120,000 mines were sent to Korea, but "only 20,000 were recorded or on hand. The remaining 100,000 were either abandoned or buried unrecorded!" (Starobin, quoted in Westover 1987: 23). Antipersonnel mines included the M14 "toe-popper" and the M16 "Bouncing Betty" fragmentation mine. M6 anti-tank mines were also laid widely. North Korean and Chinese troops did not initially use mine technology but began to deploy mines captured from the other side against US and UN forces. Eventually, Soviet-made wooden box "Schu" mines became part of their arsenal. Large numbers of US casualties were attributable to mine incidents. Lt. Sam D. Starobin of the 65th Engineer Combat Battalion stated: "Failure to record minefields was a serious problem in Korea. It is not until you return to a mined area that you appreciate accurate minefield reports. We should lay mines indiscriminately only if we never intend to return and do not value the friendship of the population. Yet we had repeated instances of units laying minefields which they did not record. Under the pressure of hasty withdrawal, mine-laying sometimes degenerated to pitching armed mines from the back of a moving truck" (Westover 1987: 24).

What this testimony does not indicate is that the indiscriminate laying of minefields was not just due to "the pressure of hasty withdrawal" but was also part of approved US military strategy. According to the 1952 army training guide, *Landmine Warfare*, "nuisance minefields" are those in which "all types of mines, booby traps, dirty trick devices, and firing devices are used. The desired effects of demoralization, confusion, and fear are quickly gained by such use of mines.... Nuisance minefields may be laid to standard patterns or may be scattered. Scattered mining is preferable because of added difficulty in removal by the enemy" (Smith 1972: n.p.).

According to expert deminer Kim Ki-ho, when US forces were drawn down in the 1970s, they left behind as many as 200,000 mines, the locations, types, and numbers of which were never shared with the South Korean military (Korean Landmine Removal Research Center 2008). And in response to the Cuban Missile Crisis in 1960 and the attack on the South Korean presidential mansion by North Korean spies in 1968, mines were laid in the southern half of the DMZ and in areas throughout the CCZ. According to Major Daniel Bolger, as the quality and training of US troops declined in the 1960s, hundreds of toe-poppers (M14) were laid "without regard for regulation marking procedures" (1991: 107).

The South Korean military laid additional minefields in advance of the 1986 Asian Games and the 1988 Seoul Olympic Games, in the name of national security, reinforcing sensitive military bases and other strategic sites, including Umyeon Mountain (우면산) in southern Seoul.[17] Landmines are frequently dislodged in mudslides and flooding during the summer rainy season, and both South Korean and North Korean mines have led to civilian deaths in the border areas as well as the islands off the west coast. The Status of Forces Agreement (SOFA or Mutual Defense Treaty) between the United States and South Korea shields the United States from accountability for any number of violations, including environmental pollution and landmine casualties due to US laid mines.

The Materiality of Mines

As suggested by the testimony of Mayor Lee, for people living in the border region, mines and mine accidents are a continual reminder of the unending war. In these weaponized landscapes, the uncertainty of where mines are, their ability to lie in wait and ambush their victims, and their volatility as explosives produce psychic effects that render them effective area denial weapons. Mines are, however, also technical objects, composed of physical materials that have specific qualities, characteristics, and values. Not only can they become useless objects when Siberian winds bring a deep freeze to the central plateau of Cheorwon, but their mechanisms can also erode, rust, or become defective, depending on variables such as time, weather, soil composition, and exposure to water.

Expert deminer Kim Ki-ho showed me M3, M2, and M16 antipersonnel fragmentation mines, which are encased in steel and feature pressure pin triggers at the end of a fuse rod, which is about the diameter of a thick marker (figure 4.1). When triggered by a tripwire or by the pressure pins, the M16 "Bouncing Betty" is designed to launch about one meter into the air and explode shrapnel to a radius of thirty meters. If the steel fuse rod has been weakened by rust and corrosion, however, it's easy to sever it from the body containing the explosives, effectively disabling the mine. In the late 1960s, US forces laid approximately 310,000 mines of this kind in the DMZ area. Kim Ki-ho estimates that only 20 percent of these mines have a life span of more than twelve years. He explained that despite his preliminary findings regarding the probable deterioration of steel fragmentation mines, South Korean military authorities are loath to approve more extensive research because of the implications: either they would have to replace the defective mines, or they would have to remove them completely. Thus, the ignorance of mines' locations and *technical* efficacy—even as it undermines the legitimacy of the state in the eyes of anti-landmine activists and local residents—is a crucial aspect of mines' *tactical* efficacy for the state, which uses mines and their fearful consequences to limit human mobility and agency.

The M14 antipersonnel mine, also known as the "toe-popper," is a very different technology. At four centimeters in diameter with plastic housing, it contains a tiny amount of metal, making it difficult to detect with a metal detector (though later models include a washer that allows for easier detection). If it is buried more than a few inches under the ground, it is unlikely to be triggered by a human footstep. Yet, it is buoyant in water, and therefore can travel within the many wetlands, streams, and irrigation channels of the border areas. These are the mines that Kim Ki-ho finds hidden in the reedy banks of rice paddies, and they are the most widely distributed mines in the DMZ and surrounding areas. The plastic casing grants the mine a life span of up to a hundred years and weighing only three ounces (whereas steel mines weigh one pound or more), they are more mobile, especially during the Korean monsoon season (장마), which brings torrential rains, run off, and mudslides to the peninsula in July and August. In August 1998 alone, seven incidents of mines having been accidentally carried away by floods were reported at both US and South Korean military sites (KCBL 1999). Mine accidents are thereby also more frequent during the summer months, sometimes involving M14 mines but also North Korean "Schu" mines that are encased in wood and are easily carried downstream across rivers and streams that transect the DMZ.

In addition to the estimated 300,000 M14 landmines, anti-tank mines are also widely distributed in the DMZ area, including older steel-encased mines (M15 and M6) and the newer plastic M19. With their large size (thirty-three centimeters in diameter) and weight of four to six pounds, they are relatively easy to detect and to disable, but antipersonnel mines are strategically planted around them to deter their removal. Because the M14 can be difficult to locate with a metal detector, the safest and most effective way to clear them is to use a specialized tractor that overturns the top layers of the earth, which either explodes the mines or exposes them for easy removal. This process is obviously extremely destructive environmentally and would only be possible on flat and relatively clear ground. Much of the terrain in the DMZ area, especially on the eastern side, is mountainous and forested, and these are the areas from which mines are often swept away in mudslides during the summer rainy season.

Weaponized Landscapes in the CCZ

Cheorwon County is located in Gangwon Province, where the vast majority of mine accidents and deaths have taken place in areas close to the thirty-eighth parallel. During the latter half of the Korean War, after the Chinese People's Army entered the war, the most brutal wars for position were waged in places such as Baekmagoji (White Horse Hill), leaving behind tons of spent artillery, landmines, and other military waste. Following the signing of the armistice, the CCZ was designated as a restricted military space by the Eighth US Army in February 1954 to house the heavy artillery and armed troops disallowed in the DMZ proper. Oversight of the CCZ was handed over to the ROK forces in 1958, and since that time, the majority of the 600,000 South Korean troops and the roughly 50,000 US troops (now 28,500) have been housed in the CCZ, along with military facilities and training grounds. Between 1959 and 1973, the South Korean government moved civilians into the CCZ for both economic and ideological purposes, allowing some former residents to return to extant villages and assigning others to reclaim land in new settlements. These propaganda villages were established under the rubrics of "CCL north-facing villages" (민통선 북방마을), "strategic villages" (전략마을), and "reunification villages" (통일촌; Kim Ch'ang-hwan 2011; Seo 2018).

CheongJeon-ri, established in 1967 by 150 former soldiers, was one of 111 such CCZ villages intended to counteract propaganda villages in the North and to reestablish agricultural production particularly in the central area of the peninsula, Korea's historic rice bowl. These first settlers were lured with promises of land and secure livelihoods and were subject to a strict screening process to ensure their patriotism and ideological commitments. That the farms established in the CCZ took the form of Israeli kibbutz-style collectives is a fact that is celebrated in official narratives, although residents in CheongJeon-ri explained that it was necessitated by the fact that the land was controlled by the state and because few of the settlers had any agricultural experience. At a time when South Korea was less economically developed than its northern nemesis, these farms were meant to be models of South Korean prosperity and wealth for the North Korean workers in the socialist farms that were visible across the division.

In CheongJeon-ri, military training exercises and war game operations took place around and oftentimes in farmers' rice paddies. Residents endured relentless loudspeaker propaganda broadcasts between North and South, as well as mandatory curfews and lights out at dusk. The village was not electrified until 1975, and any change to the buildings or infrastructure of the village required explicit permission from the military authorities under the Military Installments Protection Law. Most significantly, residents signed memoranda of understanding (MOUs) with the local battalions indicating that any injuries or deaths would be the sole responsibility of the victim. Those who complained or defied this order were at risk of being expelled from the village.

Once the war-ravaged territory had been securely reclaimed, the state reneged on its promise to reward the sacrifices of the first settlers with land ownership, in light of complicated land disputes that arose in the 1980s between locals and title holders who came back to claim their property. Today, local residents own less than 30 percent of the land in CheongJeon-ri, meaning that the majority are tenant farmers who have been unable to benefit from the boom in real estate prices in the Border Area especially during the optimistic Sunshine Policy decade of the late Cold War (1998–2008) when reunification seemed to be on the horizon. In conversations with long-term residents, the "huge sacrifices" they had made were explicitly linked to this betrayal on the part of the state and its refusal to compensate landmine victims. As Mayor Bae, who moved to CheongJeon-ri with his parents as a fifth grader in 1968, explained to me, "When we came in, they gave us these conditions—even if you are to die, don't say a single word—and we signed the MOUs. If a landmine accident occurred, we agreed not to ask about government responsibility. That's what we signed. But if you think about it, we locals were totally ignorant and scared of the military. Therefore, even if someone died from a landmine, we'd promised not to say a word, and no claims were filed."

With the end of the authoritarian regimes in the 1990s and the village's release from the CCZ in 2000, residents no longer felt obligated to keep silent about mine accidents and deaths especially because the promise of land ownership had been broken by the state. They sought monetary compensation for themselves and their deceased relatives, but the state determined that the statute of limitations for filing a claim had passed, leaving already impoverished survivors without legal recourse. This troubling history has fueled the oppositional yet ambivalent politics of residents in CheongJeon-ri, who are at once staunchly patriotic anti-Communists, proud of the role they played in South Korea's agricultural revival and nation building, but also deeply resentful of the state and its broken promises.

As this brief account attempts to convey, in the South Korean border area, especially during the Cold War, territorial security was privileged over human security in a decidedly illiberal space. The infrastructure of division is organized around containment and is composed of checkpoints, roadblocks, tank barricades, dams, reservoirs, defunct rail lines, barbed wire, and landmines, as well as well-guarded military service roads, barracks, and training grounds. Residents of CCZ villages like CheongJeon-ri were held captive to disciplinary, militarized modes of sovereign power that rendered them internal primitives who were excluded from the nation's rapid and highly celebrated capitalist successes. Since the 1980s, many of the checkpoints have moved northward, shrinking the CCZ by half and freeing the villages from the most onerous militarized restrictions. CheongJeon-ri is now administratively included in the civilian Border Area. Yet, minefields and military infrastructures continue to be salient features of the landscape.

From Reclaiming Land to Harvesting Mines

That mines were integral elements of the socio-ecological landscape of CheongJeon-ri was undeniable for the four residents I spoke with in March 2012, each of whom had lost a close family member to landmines. For Mrs. Kim, it was her father-in-law in 1998. He had gone to pay respects at his own father's tomb. According to her, he would collect firewood along the same route every year but didn't know that the previous autumn the local military battalion had laid more mines. After his death, Mrs. Kim said that they had to search for his bodily remains, locating "one foot, one leg hanging off a tree. But that's all we could find…And three hours later it started raining, and it rained until his funeral." They reasoned that an explosive powerful enough to scatter his remains across the landscape meant that it couldn't have been a regular antipersonnel mine or even a North Korean wooden box mine that might have been dislodged in the summer rainy season, but a high-explosive anti-tank mine that killed him. Carrying a load of firewood must have given him enough weight to set it off.

Mayor Lee then added that his father, one of the first 150 settlers of the village, had died from a landmine in 1970, when Lee was eight years old, right before his youngest sibling's 100th-day birthday celebration. Mrs. Kim and the mayors recounted tragic stories of kinship loss, cracking jokes about their traumas in a way that suggested that landmine casualties and deaths were a part of their everyday lives, and naturalized elements of landscapes that organized their situated knowledges of place. As Lee told Mrs. Kim regarding her father-in-law, "Oh, you should have asked me—I would have been able to find all of his body parts!" In fact, in the first decade, before people learned where the landmines were concentrated, it was common for one or two people to die every year. The reason for this was that after each death, women who collected wild herbs and mountain vegetables for the funerary banquets also perished from landmines while foraging.

Even as black humor was a source of momentary levity, as our conversation continued, deep resentments surfaced. For Lee, the sudden death of his father left his mother a widow with two children and no government support or compensation. Instead, soldiers showed up at their house to interrogate his mother about her husband's whereabouts and activities at the time of his death. The indifference of the state was still a sore spot for Lee: "They didn't send us anything, not even a bottle of rice wine for the funeral." More than financial compensation, Lee insisted that mine victims deserved state recognition as honorable war heroes of an enduring war. As he said, the government will send support to Angola for humanitarian mine relief, even as it ignores the unknown numbers of landmine victims in its own country.

These discourses fit neatly into a biopolitical framework in which the South Korean state renders a population disposable in the name of national security, which is underwritten by US Cold War exceptionalism. For these villagers, the United States' complicity in mine deaths in South Korea is not merely traceable to the actual mines that originated in US factories and were laid by US soldiers, but is also ideologically linked to the Korea exception and the South Korean state's subordination to US empire. Yet, as our conversation continued, reminiscences of everyday life in weaponized landscapes offered discursive renderings of how material relations between humans and mines exceeded a strictly thanatopolitical interpretation.

Settlers first arrived in 1967 to reclaim the land by clearing mines as military waste and establish collective farms, at which point military authorities recategorized landmines as military property, the removal of which was subject to criminal charges. Then, as now, when residents discover mines, they are required to report them to the local military battalion, which cordons off the area with barbed wire and mine warning signs. As these "unconfirmed minefields" (미확인 지뢰밭) proliferated across the DMZ region, they became infrastructural over time, since, due to the army's limitations of equipment, manpower, and expertise, they remain uncleared wastelands and, by law, off-limits. Yet, the ability of mines to deter human trespass is also viewed as a form of social control, surveillance, and dispossession, to which some villagers are resistant, especially as they are loath to let perfectly good land remain uncultivated. According to a news report, in one village, local residents are considered to be "fools" (바보) if they report mines to the local military battalion because it means that the unconfirmed minefield will remain unproductive for an indeterminate amount of time.[18] Villagers sometimes breach the boundaries of these fields in order to cultivate them, entering into a tug-of-war with soldiers who reinforce the barbed wire or attempt to fine the farmers for trespassing.

These fields might then be considered the negative space of the border region, where mines or the suspicion of them organize space, restrict movement, and police land use. Some unconfirmed minefields have become literal wastelands, where residents or visitors dump trash and junk, creating what one NGO calls a "ticking time bomb," with tons of discarded consumer goods, including refrigerators, car engines, and other detritus, at risk of creating a massive shrapnel explosion were the mines underground to be set off (Green Korea United 2010). Thus, although landmines are precisely designed for human triggers, once emplaced, their ontological instability creates opportunities for the reterritorialization and deterritorialization of space.

Landmines as rogue infrastructure not only affect the spatial organization of the border area villages, but also create other infrastructural relations. These effects were especially evident during the early years of the settlement in CheongJeon-ri. According to residents, the idealism of President Park Chung-hee's Israeli kibbutz-style farms was not enough to overcome the challenges of establishing regular crop production. In the absence of government support and on the brink of starvation, most people struggled financially and supplemented their income by collecting *sinjju*, which is a residual loan word from the Japanese colonial era that came to refer to brass artillery shells, as well as any kind of military waste, including steel, barbed wire, or the metal parts and explosive compounds of landmines, to sell on the black market.[19] As in other postwar nations, military waste and landmine pollution became economic resources in the form of scrap metal. The former mayor, Mr. Bae, described what it was like working in collective farm units in the late 1960s and early 1970s:

> We had to work in teams of five people, always. When clearing mines, five people; when eating meals, five people. Put together in these teams, that's how we would go around. The reason was that four people could pick up and transport the fifth person if someone died. That's how it was. But, think about it—we had cultivated the land, but there were no big rains. One only had to look at the sky. The rice wasn't coming up. People had to put their thinking caps on (사람들이 머리를 딴 데로 굴린 거야). President Park [Chung-hee] came up with the project modeled on Israeli kibbutz-style collective farms, and we tried it. But they should have given us food; there was nothing to eat. So, then, [we decided,] let's sell scrap metal, meaning steel, artillery shells, *sinjju*. *Sinjju* is what goes into making artillery shells. Spent cartridges. If you sold those things, you could bring in a lot more than from farming. And if you cleared mines, there was explosives inside, and *sinjju*. If you took it all apart, then you could go somewhere and sell it and that was more than you could get from farming. So, farming took a back seat.... Then

again, there were lots of accidents. Usually in the winter, no one would die, as the earth was solidly frozen, and the mines wouldn't move. But usually when it thawed, and the earth had melted, people moved the ground. At this point, it would be like, "Ah, who's died now?" This was how things were in the beginning. One or two people a year left us. So that was how it was in the beginning.

The first settlers earned a sense of militarized citizenship by engaging in state sanctioned land reclamation through clearing mines, but after a few years, lacking other modes of subsistence, residents resorted to mining for mines, reclaiming land and harvesting military waste for their exchange value. *Sinjju* and scrap metal served as currency and commodities in poor communities, and especially around the border areas in the postwar period, when people traded brass artillery for alcohol or rice, or turned artillery shells into cigarette ashtrays and other household containers. Scrap metal of all kinds was also currency for children who bartered their findings with traveling peddlers, in exchange for taffy (엿). Thus, in conditions of extreme poverty and resource scarcity, especially during the South Korean developmentalist period, the political ecology of the border area was one in which former battlefields became (un)natural resources for gleaning discarded remnants of war. Harvested metals, especially steel, were melted down and eventually molded into the steel bars and i-beams that reinforced the concrete high-rise buildings that emblematized the rapid urbanization of 1960s and 1970s South Korea.

Mines connected people and economies not only through commodity exchange, but also through a process of reclaiming land that had been enclosed by the state. Mines appeared in residents' narratives as heterogeneous actants that could be, sometimes simultaneously, military waste, military property, or natural resources. The dynamic entanglements of mines and humans and their intra-action was most strikingly evoked by Lee in the following narrative. In contrast to humanitarian accounts that foreground victims and their lack of agency, here, minefields constitute the literal ground for an expanded sense of personhood, spatial control, economic agency, and psychic deterritorialization. Lee described the moment that he first trespassed into an active minefield:

> I was sharpening a scythe nearby, and suddenly I heard an explosion. Two men had gone into the minefield, and I thought, "Aah, they stepped on a mine." I went out to see, and one was down, and the other was thrown behind him. With those two people injured like that, suddenly I'm walking

in the minefield. I went in just like that, and I ask myself, "Am I ok?" I looked up just like that, and "Yeah, I'm ok." The person who had been thrown backwards is up and walking. [I ask him,] "Are you ok?" [He says,] "Yeah, I'm ok." At that moment, my overwhelming fear turned into ecstatic joy (환희), and I helped the one who had been injured out of the field. It was plastic—he had a plastic prosthetic leg. So, I gave him $30 to get a new leg, and I cleared the remaining hundred meters of the field.

From that moment, he continued to harvest mines not only to render fields safe for agricultural use but also to sell for cash. The irony of his turning to clearing landmines after having lost his father to a landmine accident was not lost on Lee, who described his condition as "pathetic" (한심한). But, as the eldest son and head of his household, conditions of extreme poverty led him and many others to clearing mines and collecting scrap metal to survive.

In this context, I suggest that Lee's transformative moment, in which his "overwhelming fear turned to ecstatic joy," casts his "pathetic" narrative in a different light. Rather than considering mine removal to be an abject activity to which poor people are "reduced," Lee's testimony describes a moment of expansiveness, opening up to other modes of existence, suggesting how an "armed and dangerous" landscape (Nixon 2007: 169) can not only be disarmed, but also can be disarming—transforming a fear of death and trespass into ecstatic joy and spatial liberation. A framework of abjection might view the mine as "matter out of place," a transgressive object that psychically transforms the subject, by dissolving boundaries between self and other. In contrast, rather than the mine as an ontologically pre-given object, it was the intra-action of mine and human—Lee's entering the minefield, "just like that," without consequence, the mines *not* detonating—that constituted this moment of joyful liberation. This was an instance of transformation in which the enactments between Lee and mines became reconfigured and multiple, generating new political and economic possibilities.

Many of the mines that Lee cleared were M14 plastic mines, which had no exchange value, and were considered by residents to be especially insidious, given the difficulty of detecting them. New infrastructural affordances and human–mine intra-actions emerged in the 1980s, with the state's promotion of industrialized farming. Lee described how, with the arrival of a high-capacity backhoe, which could dig up one cubic meter of earth at a time, he considered burying the plastic mines he had cleared. With the backhoe, it would be easy to bury the mines to a depth of two meters, where their ability to ambush their human targets would be mitigated. But given the unpredictability of mines and their long life spans, Lee couldn't be certain that they wouldn't eventually cause problems. He decided to report the mines to the local battalion, despite the fact that he might be cited for "destruction of military property." As he spoke, he didn't disguise his disdain for the soldiers who arrived, outfitted in specialized equipment, in contrast to his simple farm tools and well-honed wits: "These fifteen guys show up, well-built soldiers. They are in full military gear, wearing metal helmets. Then they start trying to intimidate me, asking me where I got these mines from."

As Lee continued his story, it became clear that demining, for him, was an extension of the nation-building project, which he framed as an act of patriotic dedication. Yet, this expression of nationalism was criminalized by the state. That he was ultimately acquitted and even received a formal apology from the local military battalion was a vindication of his efforts, but, as he put it, rather than an apology, he should have been given an award. Mayor Lee, like the mines that I frame as rogue, embodied roguishness in his disregard for legal sanction and his insistence on the legitimacy of his own actions. As he put it, "I followed the proper procedures... who are they to tell me to follow the rules?" The violence of mines and the South Korean state's failure to protect its own citizens under its subordination to US empire delegitimized the state in his mind, and thereby justified his own violation of the law.

By learning how to live with mines, not simply as lethal agents, Lee earned a sense of personhood that was connected to the ecologically embedded enactments of mines' multiplicity as economic (mines as scrap), political (mines as military property), and moral (mines as indiscriminate weapons). Lee's roguish exhilaration and vindication are therefore difficult to reconcile with a model of subaltern resistance to the state or the transgressive potential of abject matter. In fact, Lee considered clearing mines to *normalize* his status as a citizen and patriot, whose labor contributed to the nation rather than threatened its security. From being criminalized to commended by the military, receiving due recognition in the eyes of the state was also a confirmation of his moral personhood, masculinity, and economic agency. The normalization of this militarized citizenship also became, in the course of Lee's testimony, closely tied to a vision of the United States as a rogue power, articulated in a forceful critique of Bill Clinton's ignorance of the existence of US mines in areas outside of the DMZ.[20] Part of the affective charge in Lee's story of mine removal had certainly to do with the rush of having a near-death experience, but this is a death that is ultimately framed by the Korea exception and the residual thanatopolitics that lies at the heart of US imperial relations with South Korea.

The United States' position rests on a conjunction of humanitarian mine action and the Korea exception that, in effect, disavows the existence of South Korean mine victims, tacitly underwriting the South Korean state's anti-humanitarian stance toward mine victims, and underscoring Stoler and Bond's assertion that "modern empires thrive on such plasticities and reproduce their resilience through the production of exceptions" (2006: 95). Yet, even as actually existing landmines may disappear from view under the shadow of the Korea exception, as I suggest in the Coda, they now reappear in the economically liberalized landscapes of the DMZ region where the branding of the DMZ continues apace.

Conclusion

South Korean journalist and DMZ chronicler Hahm Kwang Bok (2007) offers a posthuman depiction of landmines in the DMZ, calling them "living creatures, intelligent, higher forms of life" (161). If landmines think at all, however, they do so in a binary way as automated switches that respond to a certain degree of pressure, indifferent to the identity of the body producing the weight. Less like cyborgs than von Uexküll's tick, the landmine can lie in wait for years for the right trigger to set off its mechanism, which, when it is working properly, ignites an explosive that has been precisely measured to blow off human toes, feet, or legs. The mine's agency is attuned to its victim's actions (stepping on it), and its effects are amplified by a victim's sudden evacuation of agency, that is, his or her inability to evade the instantaneousness of the mine's explosion.

In contrast to a post-humanist approach that might consider mines to be inherently vibrant, intelligent, or alive, I offer an infrastructural and performative anthropology of landmines that attends to their multiple effects and affordances, yet always in relation to human interlocutors. By framing landmines infrastructurally, I also seek to avoid the implicit technological determinism of postcolonial or humanitarian critiques that presuppose the human–mine relation to be a unidirectional mediation of human agency. Rogue infrastructure represents my attempt to capture the emergent ontologies of human–mine assemblages, without evacuating questions of power and moral responsibility. This infrastructural anthropology of landmines acknowledges the social-ecological ruination of militarized natures in the context of US empire, while also accounting for how their unexpected affordances engender human–nonhuman agencies that constitute everyday modes of survival in weaponized landscapes.

When I met Mr. Lee, he was mayor of district one of CheongJeon-ri, a position of prestige that he earned despite, or perhaps because of, his so-called criminal activity. His elected leadership suggests not only the shifting politics of the border area, from "propaganda villages" to normalized ones, but also a liberalization of citizenship for residents in the late–Cold War era. In the face of this trend, Mr. Lee insisted that more than monetary compensation, mine victims deserved recognition as war heroes, with merits of honor bestowed by the state for their sacrifices at the front lines of an unending war. Indeed, as mine stories proliferated within conversations purportedly about the DMZ's nature, I began to understand how the volatile, risky, and sometimes transcendent relations of mines and humans was not just about identifying the unethical and anti-humanitarian nature of mines as indiscriminate weapons of war, but also about acknowledging the complex political and historical subjectivities of people in heterotopic spaces that are civilian and military, "postwar" and ongoing war, demilitarized and hyper-militarized, who know when to run and when to walk across unconfirmed minefields.

Coda: Landmines as Gold Mines

As I discussed in chapter 2, political and economic developments have transformed the border region from a static space of Cold War–era walls to a site of potentially global flows, in anticipation of a unified peninsula. Even if the flows northward across the DMZ are not yet realizable, the branding of peace and life has generated new circulations of capital between Seoul and the economically depressed border villages. Developments in Cheorwon in particular entail the building of new tourist infrastructures and the reconnection of old infrastructures, designed to bring more metropolitan Koreans (and international tourists) to the border, as well as to improve rail and road links between Gangwon Province and the megalopolis of Seoul. These new linkages are bringing more civilians into proximity with the military infrastructures of the CCZ and DMZ, which are integral parts of national security, but also framed as touristic spectacles, whether it is the guard posts visible in the distance of the DMZ, the young soldiers manning checkpoints along the CCZ, or underground tunnels built by North Korean soldiers to cross under the DMZ. Mines and minefields, which may be more difficult to package as tourist attractions, have nevertheless been infrastructurally foundational to the border area and its militarized naturecultures.

In the western part of the CCZ, close to the Joint Security Area, where North and South Korean soldiers face off across the actual MDL, DMZ-related security tourism has been supplemented with ecotourism and the branding of local culture. In commemoration of the sixtieth anniversary of the Armistice Treaty, Tongil-chon (Unification Village), located within the CCZ, unveiled its updated image as Unification Brand Village (통일촌 브랜드 마을) at the July 2013 Branding Event. Following speeches by local government leaders and military officials, the Tongil-chon Village Museum was opened to visitors. Developed in conjunction with an ethnographic researcher at the Gyeonggi Province Cultural Institute and the "Tongil-chon Brand Village Development of DMZ Global Brand Business" [sic], it also received funding from the municipal and provincial governments as well as the Ministry of Security and Public Administration. In keeping with developments in the South Korean tourism industry, a key methodology employed in the museum was that of "storytelling" (스토리텔링), in this case, the crafting of collective narratives based on oral histories of the villagers themselves, accompanied by artifacts from their personal effects, as well as video interviews with the aging residents in their sixties and seventies who compose the majority of the eighty households who have lived there since its founding in 1973.

A placard featured quotes from villagers who described the entire area around their homes as an "unidentified minefield," especially following the reinforcement of forward positions after the 1968 attack on the presidential mansion. Although the original Korean states, "Even today, minefields and farmland coexist in the village surroundings," the English-language translation is ambiguous: "Mines and farmland existed together around this village until the present." This indistinct use of the past tense in the English translation reflects a broader indistinction in representations of landmines and mine victims, especially in the past–present spatiotemporality of the museum, located in the very village that may be surrounded by unidentified minefields (figure 4.2).

Actual landmines and *sinjju* were displayed as part of the material culture of the village, but victims were noticeably absent in the museum's master narrative and in the accompanying text, "Research Report on Unification Village: Unification Village People, Stories of their Lives" (Gyeonggi Province Cultural Foundation 2013). The oral histories of the elderly villagers were

consistently told in the past tense, conforming to a narrative of progress and development: "It was scary. It was impossible to live. People died from stepping on mines as they worked. Hurt their legs. Back then, this was an impossible place to live. Things have gotten much bet-

Figure 4.2
Mines on display at the Tongil-chon Village Museum. July 2013. Photograph by the author.

ter" (Gyeonggi Province Cultural Foundation 2013: 108). Not surprisingly, the most recent mine accident from May 2012 was not mentioned, nor were the ongoing conflicts between locals and the South Korean military over rights to farm unidentified minefields and the dispossession of farmland by the US military when it unilaterally expanded a firing range in the western CCZ.

The landmines included in the exhibition were presented as if they were historical relics of the past (they were US military-issue mines, not South Korean ones) and displayed innocuously in glass vitrines surrounded by slogans of future unification and peace. These displays recalled other ones I had seen, which exist at the entrance of the checkpoints one must pass through to gain entry into the CCZ. At these checkpoints, landmines are framed not as relics but as *samples*, intended to act as informational warnings for visitors. Nevertheless, in the dozen times I have passed through

149

Figure 4.3
"The DMZ is a gold mine of nature." From South Korean promotional video about the DMZ. IUCN World Conservation Congress. May 2012. Photograph by the author.

CCZ checkpoints, the soldiers allowing us passage have never pointed out or explained the landmines to me or my traveling companions. Thus, even the samples had a relic-like quality, but unlike the mines in the museum, they were displayed in the open air, neglected and unremarkable. They existed as part of the military's mandate to provide risk education but, like other aspects of their stated programs, have been spottily implemented (International Campaign to Ban Landmines 2013).

Between the Korea exception and the folklorization of border village cultures, landmines as imperial debris and their persistent potentiality may be disappearing from view, but the branding of the DMZ demands more iconography, and mine signs have thus proliferated in DMZ-related promotional materials. The telltale red sign appeared as the final image in a 2012 state-produced video about the DMZ's ecological renaissance, with a message inscribed on it: "The DMZ is the gold mine of nature" (figure 4.3). The Korean word *pogo* (보고; repository or treasure trove) was translated as "gold mine," creating a pun out of "landmine" and "gold mine" that renders momentarily apprehensible the violence that neoliberal captures of "natural capital" depend on. This slippery and perverse sign suggests that in a moment when the state is seeking sources of surplus value in the DMZ, its landmines are being symbolically neutralized and abstracted from deadly ordnances into natural resources that the state may freely exploit and diversely commoditize.

Development of the border area has followed typical neoliberal patterns in South Korea, which, since the shift to local self-governance in the 1990s, have led to the buildup of tourism and branding of local cultures across the nation. The DMZ Geopark and the Unification Brand Village are just two examples of such attempts to conform to the demands of global capital. In addition, border area agricultural products are marketed with the DMZ name, creating associations between rice and other produce with the DMZ's purportedly pristine air and water. Indeed, when I was conducting fieldwork in the border areas in 2012, as the United States and South Korea negotiated their free trade agreement, there was more insecurity regarding South Korea's economic subordination and fears among farmers about the domestic rice market than there was regarding North Korea's aggressions toward the South.

The narrative of the DMZ's natural restoration is a utopian one that represents the present as if it were the distant past. Landmines are presented as artifacts of a dark history overcome, even as they continue to inhabit landscapes of ruination in zones of indeterminacy. That the mine sign, which functions to index the existence of actual mines, can be mobilized to brand the DMZ as a PLZ intimates that the interpenetrating processes of militarization and naturalization at the border may have reached a new level of convergence with capital. Landmines mediate and embody the multiple registers and scales of US empire as military and economic hegemon, but the affective engagements and incommensurable narratives of border denizens such as Mayor Lee exceed the folkorized versions of branded villages and state-funded storytelling. In so doing, they underscore the indeterminacy of landmines as naturalcultural elements of the DMZ's militarized ecology and their ongoing relationship to peace and life. Landmines, in their ambiguous and frightening spatial and temporal materiality, are proving to be at once "stumbling blocks" and "content" that may yet bring the relations of imperial power into critical visibility.

Epilogue
De/militarized Ecologies

The infrastructural relations of flyways, landmines, and ponds that have appeared in this book exist both because of and in relation to the political division and its material infrastructures. They offer examples of valuing biodiversity in militarized landscapes in ways that neither celebrate the toxicity of militarization nor reinforce an epistemology of purity that looks to nature as a salve for human violence. In the case of South Korea and the national division, they suggest that making peace with nature is also about *making peace with division*, and, thus, redefining unification politics to include what Ursula Heise calls "a human commitment to value biological otherness" (2010: 72). This commitment is akin to the biological peace that Director Kim Seung Ho has made central to his work. Moreover, making peace with division is, as these chapters suggest, about coming to terms with the infrastructures and chronopolitics of division as conditioned by both militarization and capitalist relations. The rogue infrastructures of chapter 4 may press on the limits of humanitarian ethical norms, but the point is not to privilege landmines and other heinous weapons in the name of biodiversity but rather to acknowledge both human creativity and nonhuman affordances in the production of value, even in the face of thanatopolitical violence.

This book has analyzed the DMZ's ecological exceptionalism as a cultural response to the DMZ's biodiversity and the ongoing state of division—a double bind which has, in turn, opened up unexpected and ambiguous worldings in the meantime of division. Dominant discourses of the DMZ's nature tend to rely upon a notion of natural sovereignty or pure nature. These discourses reinforce an anthropocentric metaphysic that finds inspiration in a moral tale of redemptive nature, healing the scars of division. In contrast, the previous chapters have suggested how the DMZ's biodiversity can defamiliarize the temporalities of division and of what constitutes the political. Biological peace gestures toward other possibilities by decentering or at least displacing a human notion of peace as (only) geopolitics. This may be one step toward Michel Serres's natural contract, in which peace is not simply defined in human terms to pacify nature, and nature is not merely mobilized to naturalize political ideologies. What may be needed is an approach to nature that does not expect it to directly address "the division system" (Paik 2011 [1995]) but that is attuned to what Isabelle Stengers calls Gaia-the-intruder, acknowledging that nature, in its ability to overwhelm and disrupt all categories, exceeds our ability to master it (Stengers 2014: 5).

The Korean DMZ is one of many other spaces around the world that scholars and journalists have identified for their seemingly ironic juxtapositions of war and nature. Environmental historians in particular have found the DMZ to be exemplary of militarized landscapes, where processes of militarization have not just been destructive but have also been protective of landscapes and ecologies (see Davis 2007; Pearson, Coates, and Cole 2010; and Woodward 2014; and see Coates 2014 and Thomas 2009 on the DMZ in particular). Environmental historian Edmund Russell noted of colleagues in his own field that "[they] have delighted in the ironic, counter-intuitive notion that military bases have served as nature preserves. We have rarely asked whether the similarities should be predictable rather than surprising, but we should start doing so more often." These "predictable" similarities are related, Russell argues, to the fact that both bases and preserves build and project state power over "people, spaces, and nature" (2010: 232–33).

Militaries are, in fact, highly effective at territorializing space, limiting civilian activities, and constraining capitalist development. Conservation biologist Michael J. Lawrence and his coauthors note in their survey of war and biodiversity that military activities were "found to have overwhelmingly negative effects on ecosystem structure and function," but that "military activity was beneficial under specific conditions, such as when an exclusion zone was generated" (Lawrence et al. 2015: 443). Indeed, the US Department of Defense (DOD) has been particularly attuned to how to use exclusion zones and environmental exception to evade responsibility for remediating military pollution, and at other times to expand territorial control in the name of national security and military readiness (Lachman, Wong, and Reseter 2007). The relationship between militaries and environmental protection can entail the cynical appropriation of ecological protection as a form of greenwashing (Woodward 2014), as well as unintended consequences such as "green buffer areas" that emerge between military bases and civilian areas, which then become havens for endangered and other forms of wildlife.

The DOD works with the US Fish and Wildlife Service through their Integrated Natural Resource Management Plans to address these kinds of entanglements. According to Harold Balbach, a senior research scientist for the US Army Engineer Research and Development Center, the DOD controls more than twenty-five million acres in the United States, and military installations often "represent some of the largest contiguous tracts of relatively undeveloped lands in otherwise fragmented habitat."[1] Many of these military bases also create unintended green zones, where civilian encroachment in the form of suburban housing tracts and shopping malls meet the boundaries of military bases and training grounds (Lachman, Wong, and Reseter 2007). To mitigate environmental pollution, as well as sound and light pollution, military bases are surrounded by buffer areas where endangered species now make their habitats. The Pentagon is required by the Endangered Species Act to hire ecologists who can monitor these areas to ensure that military activities are not infringing upon these species' survival. These collaborations between ecologists, educators, and the DOD are viewed as beneficial ways to build public trust with surrounding communities. Military–environment hybrids such as these also exist at some of the more than four hundred closed or decommissioned bases that have been converted through the M2W (military to wildlife) program in the post–Cold War era (Havlick 2007; Masco 2004). In a process similar to that which scholars have documented in critical studies of national parks, nature is symbolically and materially deployed in these sites of toxicity and military pollution to depoliticize them of the power asymmetries that created their boundaries in the first instance (Wapner 2010; Dowie 2011).

In other places, military–environment hybrids not only mask but also reproduce colonial relations of dispossession and imperial sovereignty. The island of Vieques and Diego Garcia are two instances in which environmental protection has been used as a post facto justification for continued exclusion of local residents. In the case of Vieques, Puerto Rico, DOD representatives testified in Congress that bases were akin to national parks, and therefore "national assets" that needed to be protected from the encroachment of civilians (McCaffrey 2009: 234; see also Davis, Hayes-Conroy, and Jones 2007). Likewise, on the archipelagic island of Diego Garcia in the Indian Ocean, US diplomatic cables made public by WikiLeaks in 2010 revealed that plans to turn areas around the joint US–UK naval base into a marine protected area were intentionally designed to prevent the return of the island residents who had been in a protracted legal battle to regain their territorial rights. Journalist Virgil Hawkins summarized the approach in 2012 in this way: "For the UK, this clever 'solution' looked good from any angle: not only would the possibility of return be taken off the table, but US military activities could continue, and 'points' for environmental concern could also be scored" (see also Vine 2009).[2] These examples suggest that environmental protection is often the handmaiden to national security.

Placed within this broader planetary scene, the DMZ now appears as one example of other de/militarized landscapes—whether they are decommissioned bases or sites of active military activity. Moreover, taking into account the seemingly inexorable expansion of militarization and securitized spaces around the world, including more than one thousand bases controlled and maintained by the United States alone (Klein 2014), forces one to acknowledge the proliferation of seemingly ironic spaces like the DMZ where war and protected nature converge. In fact, the DMZ holds a particularly significant place in the history of Cold War US military expansion. Until 1950, most nations around the world, particularly those in Europe, were resistant to allowing the use of their territory by US armed forces. According to a RAND study of the US Global Defense Posture, "after the Korean War, the fear of communism impelled weakened Asian and European nations not only to align with the United States but also to allow Washington to indefinitely position U.S. troops and their families in large MOBs [military operating bases]" (Pettyjohn 2012: 99). Similarly, historian Bruce Cumings asserts that the Korean War, not World War II, "occasioned the enormous foreign military base structure and the domestic military-industrial complex to service it." This complex, Cumings emphasizes, "has come to define the sinews of American global power ever since" (2011: 210).

The year 1950 not only marked the beginning of the Korean War and the attendant expansion of US bases but is also the year that geological scientists point to as the beginning of the Great Acceleration. This is the point at which industrial production and mass consumption began their exponential rise, eventually leading to the planetary-scale changes associated with the climate crisis and what is widely referred to as a new geological epoch, the Anthropocene, which names *Homo sapiens* as the most consequential force affecting the Earth's geophysical evolution (Crutzen and Stoermer 2000). Linking these two histories—of militarization and industrialization—can serve as a reminder that the hot wars of the Cold War were fought for political and economic interests, which wedded the necessity of containing the Communist threat with the goal of securing markets to extend the reach of US-led global capitalism.[3]

A study of de/militarized ecologies could serve to intervene into Euro- and US-centric periodizations of the Cold War and in so doing center interconnected histories, afterlives, and naturecultures of militarization— from the total war effort imposed by Japan on its Pacific colonies to the hot wars of the Cold War's so-called long peace. De/militarized ecologies such as the DMZ are therefore not ironic but instead are sites where the building and projection of state power over "people, spaces, and nature" (Russell 2010: 232–33) come up against the privatization and securitization of space under capital. Is it any wonder, then, that nonhuman life forms should find provisional refuge within these two world-ordering spatial regimes of capi- talism and US empire? In light of the increasingly coordinated relation- ship between conservation and militarization in a range of postcolonial nation-states (Lunstrum 2014), de/militarized ecologies, which can serve as a mirror image to that of fortress conservation, should be seen as more than the unintended by-products of war and empire. They instead call for greater scrutiny of the violent, impure, and unpredictable entanglements of war and ecologies.

The writing of this book was completed during the early months of the novel coronavirus pandemic of 2020, in which public health mandates for social distancing created unexpected planetary effects—temporary cease- fires, clear skies in the most polluted cities, and reports of wild animals taking over spaces evacuated by humans. The transnational flows of global capital and concomitant fossil-fuel consumption reduced to a trickle. As the oil market threatened collapse, pundits remarked that the "return to normal" would be the only thing that would save "the economy," while cli- mate activists asked how to use this crisis as a chance to reboot our think- ing and priorities. Global tourism and airline industries were predicted to suffer and possibly never recover, and many major tourist sites were bliss- fully empty, according to the few tourists who could travel to them. With this sudden reduction in human mobility and a heightened attentiveness to the activities of other forms of life, social media and news media reveled in reports of endangered turtles hatching on the beaches of Brazil; hungry monkeys, urban commensal species, rioting in the empty plazas of Bang- kok; and elephants, coyotes, goats, and other herd animals taking back the streets in cities and towns all over the world.[4] It was as if the thought experiment in journalist Alan Weisman's bestselling 2007 book, *The World without Us,* had come to pass. It is telling that Weisman discussed places such as Cyprus, Chernobyl, and the Korean DMZ, as they are all examples of de/militarized ecologies where restricted human activity allowed for the privileging of nonhuman-oriented growth.

It's too soon to say whether wildlife cameos in areas associated with human consumption actually point to new adaptations by these creatures. The fact that narratives of "nature's return" emerged as inspiring tales and heartwarming spectacles, however, indexed a brief moment in which the givenness of capitalist growth and overconsumption as inherently good and universally desirable was suddenly denaturalized. If we cease to see places like the DMZ as exceptional, we may start to reframe our thinking to understand how industrialization and militarization not only have endangered webs of life for us and other living creatures but, in tandem with modernist thinking, have externalized nature to such an extent that, in moments like these, we frame it as coming back, when it has always been there.

Notes

Introduction

1 "5,929 Species, 101 Endangered, Inhabit the DMZ," press release, National Institute of Ecology, June 14, 2018, http://www.me.go.kr/home/web/board/read.do?boardMasterId=1&boardId=874030&menuId=286; accessed July 9, 2019.

2 Suk-Young Kim frames the DMZ as paradoxical because it is both a site of "man-made conflict and an environment of natural wildlife" (S.-Y. Kim 2011: 397), and historian Lisa Brady (2008) characterizes as ironic the fact that the Korean War and the national division have created the possibility for the flourishing of nonhuman biodiversity.

3 For the full text of the agreement, see Conference on Disarmament, "Agreement on Reconciliation, Non-aggression and Exchanges and Cooperation between North and South," March 25, 1992, https://peacemaker.un.org/sites/peacemaker.un.org/files/KR%20KP_911213_Agreement%20on%20reconciliation%20non%20aggression%20and%20exchangespdf.pdf; accessed October 11, 2021.

4 President Roh Tae-woo (1987–93) was the first of several South Korean presidents with bold plans for the DMZ. He followed up his 1988 plan for an International Peace City in the DMZ with a detailed plan for a peace zone in 1989. His successor, Kim Young-sam (1993–98), proposed a DMZ nature park in 1994, followed by Kim Dae-jung's (1998–2003) consideration of a DMZ peace park in 2001, Roh Moo-hyun's (2003–8) designation of the Border Area as the PLZ in 2006 and proposal for a marine peace park in the Yellow Sea in 2007, Lee Myung-bak's (2008–13) 2011 proposal for a UNESCO Biosphere Reserve, and Park Geun-hye's (2013–16) plans for an international peace park in 2013. The recycling of the idea over the past thirty years has been remarkably consistent, so much so that it is both ironic and unsurprising that the international peace zone presented by President Moon Jae-in (2016–21) in his September 2019 speech to the UN General Assembly was notably similar to Roh Tae-woo's 1989 peace zone.

5 See the South Korean Natural Environment Conservation Act of January 2016, Act No. 13885.

6 In 2019, important steps toward this goal were achieved, with the entry of the Gangwon Eco-Peace Biosphere Reserve and the Yeoncheon Imjin River Biosphere Reserve into the UNESCO Man and the Biosphere Programme (MAB).

Although the designations do not guarantee successful implementation of conservation and sustainable development objectives, they provide significant international recognition of the biodiversity of the CCZ region. Whether and how the DMZ proper will be protected, however, remains an open question. At least for the near future, it seems certain that the economies of the border areas will be increasingly tied to the expansion of tourism, much of it linked directly to the DMZ's rare ecologies.

7 Eunjeong Kim (2017), in the context of disability rights in South Korea, critiques what she calls "curative violence," which imposes a normative form to the cured body. She interrogates the violence that "cure" imposes through the erasure of difference and the imposition of a teleological and eugenic temporality.

8 On double binds and creativity, see Cattelino (2010: 253).

9 According to a July 25, 2018, report by the South Korean news station JTBC, in spring 2019, there were sixty guard posts on the southern side, with thirty soldiers manning each one, for a minimum total of 1,800 troops. On the northern side, there are 160 guard posts with around ten thousand soldiers stationed. In addition, both North and South are armed with machine guns and rocket launchers and other heavy artillery (http://news.jtbc.joins.com/article/article.aspx?news_id=NB11670803; accessed August 20, 2018).

10 Jang-Hie Lee writes, "The DMZ is not an international public domain, but an area where imperium resides in the UNCMAC and dominium resides in both South and North Korea" (2001: 143).

11 For a critical historical and contemporary analysis of the KATUSA system, see Seungsook Moon (2010), who describes conscripted KATUSAs as a "cheap and reliable human resource that has stood in the place of American GIs, who are expensive in both the economic and political sense" (237). Moon also describes the shifting class and educational status of KATUSA soldiers, especially with the implementation by the South Korean military of a competitive test in 1982 (246) and how any privileges the KATUSA soldiers receive from serving in the US Army are offset by the entrenched racism and institutionalized inequities to which they are subject.

12 See D. Shin (2017) on the DPRK's consistent call for a peace treaty to replace what the DPRK characterizes as the "outdated and obsolete" Armistice Agreement.

13 Other globally circulating discourses connect nature and peace through bodies such as the UN Environment Programme, which promotes environmental peacebuilding. These projects tend to be inherently statist and internationalist, with the goals of peacebuilding defined within conventional political terms.

14 On peace as a process, see Arturo Escobar's *Territories of Difference* (2008). He theorizes "peace-as-justice," which, he writes, "should be seen as always in process, something that can be approached only asymptotically but can never really be reached" (17).

15 Park's critique of the post–Cold War is worth citing: "If the Cold War is to be understood not just as a military rivalry between superpowers but also as an

American project of establishing a capitalist hegemony, then the post–Cold War does not negate the Cold War order but reconfigures a global capitalist order marked by porous borders and neoliberal democracy" (6).

16 The terminology used by scholars to refer to nonhuman creatures has proliferated in multispecies ethnography and environmental humanities. In many instances, the terms "nonhuman," "more-than-human," "other-than-human," and "multispecies" appear interchangeably. Although some writers eschew the term "nonhuman" because it implicitly reproduces human exceptionalism and anthropocentrism (see Pugliese 2020: 3–4 for a recent discussion), I am less inclined to do this because my ethnographic analysis centers the knowledge practices of my human interlocutors. I use "more-than-human" and "other-than-human" to characterize different worldings and performative relations, which emerge out of the ethical enactments that I analyze as key to understanding the lifeways and forms of nonhuman others. I reserve "multispecies" for describing relations that operate at the level of species (such as flyways) or when citing other scholars who use the term in ways that I find useful. But I am generally wary of the taxonomic assumptions embedded in species thinking.

17 As Suk-Young Kim notes in her analysis of Imjingak Peace Park near the western CCZ, trains are curiously ubiquitous "icons of mobility and stagnation" (2014: 148) in South Korean division politics and tourism. Train car relics and reconnected rail lines have become emblematic of the division and complex desires for unification, which now include both histories of trauma and playfully nostalgic kitsch (148 ff.).

18 Kang Chin-kyu (강진규) reported in *NK Kyŏngje* on February 7, 2019, that 2.8 billion Korean won (US $2.4 million) had been invested between 2011 and 2018. A revised budget of 1.3 billion won, covering 225 projects, was passed in 2019. Of those, 108 projects (totaling three trillion won) were earmarked for ecological and peace tourism, and twenty-one projects (totaling 512 trillion won) were targeted for enhancing and building transportation networks around the DMZ area (https://www.nkeconomy.com/news/articleView.html?idxno=1028; accessed February 10, 2019).

19 On "dark tourism," see Lennon and Foley (2000) and Schwenkel (2006).

20 Margaret Talev reported on June 28, 2019, for *Bloomberg News* that "Donald Trump spoke admiringly of the Korean Peninsula's demilitarized zone…making an implicit comparison with his own struggles to meet his top campaign promise and construct a wall on the US southern border.… 'We may go to the DMZ, or the border, as they call it,' he told reporters at the Group of 20 summit in Osaka, Japan. 'That, by the way—when you talk about a wall, when you talk about a border, that's what you call a border. Nobody goes through that border. Just about nobody. That's called a real border'" (https://www.bloomberg.com /news/articles/2019-06-29/trump-calls-korean-dmz-a-real-border-compared -with-his-wall; accessed September 22, 2019).

1   Within a year or two, the Navis were replaced by smartphone map apps such as Naver and Google Earth, which offered more data points than the dashboard GPS.

2   A critical discourse of neoliberalism has been prevalent among progressives in South Korea, and it was particularly widespread during the Lee Myung-bak and Park Geun-hye administrations. The neoliberalization of the state became a common refrain and rebuke in the aftermath of the tragic Sewol Ferry disaster on April 16, 2014, which killed more than two hundred students when it capsized off the southern coast of South Korea.

3   The film was produced by the South Korean National Film Production Center for the Ministry of Culture and Information (http://theme.archives .go.kr/viewer/common/archWebViewer.do?bsid=200200104256&dsid =0000000000001&gubun=search; accessed August 23, 2019).

4   Article 12 states, "To implement and guarantee non-aggression, the two sides shall set up a South–North Joint Military Commission within three (3) months of the coming into force of this Agreement. In the said Commission, the two sides shall discuss and carry out steps to build military confidence and control of major movements of military units and major military exercises, the peaceful utilization of the Demilitarized Zone, exchanges of military personnel and information, phased reductions in armaments including the elimination of weapons of mass destruction and attack capabilities, and verifications thereof." See also Son (2011: 110–11).

5   See also Danielle Chubb (2013) on the rise of the New Right and the pivotal issue of North Korean human rights.

6   Namhee Lee (2019) identifies a conflict between an older Korean War generation and a younger generation of former democratization activists as an explanation for the rise of the New Right. But she also sees it as "part of a triumphal discourse that gave primacy to economic development over redistributive justice, that prioritized gaining personal wealth over a collective future, and most seriously, that involved a willful ordering of the disappearance of North Korea, whose divergent trajectory for South Korea symbolized the North's failure as a civilization, which then justified its anticipated demise" (21).

7   For Dr. Jung, however, the border describes the political reality of the two nations, which are recognized as separate nations by the UN. As he put it to me in an email in early 2021: "My point is that peace between the two Koreas begins with acknowledging this reality. The border between the two Koreas is a border different from other countries, such as the border with China, so I say that the border between the two Koreas is an 'inner border' in a strict sense" (pers. commun., February 13, 2021).

8   For more on the history of *Space* as a node of cultural production, see Katherine Lee (2018) and Delissen (2001).

9   Much more could be written about the Korean Commission for the Conservation of Nature and Natural Resources (한국자연자원보존위원회; KCCNNR) and

the Smithsonian Institution study, but it is beyond the scope of this chapter. See Eleana Kim (n.d.) for a detailed description and analysis of that transpacific collaboration. Led by zoologist Kang Yung Sun, the KCCNNR collaborated with the Smithsonian, with seed money from the US Air Force Office of Scientific Research, to conduct a preliminary study on the ecosystems in the DMZ area. Violent clashes between the two Koreas and the 1968 security crisis led to the premature end of the project, which the investigators had originally planned as a longitudinal study lasting twenty-five years or longer. The KCCNNR continued to study the biota of the CCZ intermittently, certain parts of which were designated as the nation's first "natural preservation zones" (천연 보호 구 역). Even though scholars of South Korean environmental movements have largely dismissed the work of the KCCNNR during the 1960s and 1970s because of their close ties to the authoritarian state, KCCNNR scientists played an important role in setting what little conservation agenda there was under the industrialization-at-all-costs military dictatorship of Park Chung-hee.

10 This vision for an inter-Korean protected area was one of several proposed in the 1970s, including one by the International Union for the Conservation of Nature and Natural Resources (IUCN), which, with the UN Environment Programme, proposed a peace park to both the North and South Korean governments in 1979 (Miura and Bak 2011: 498). Similar proposals have continuously evolved since then into plans for transboundary biosphere reserves, Northeast Asia ecological corridors, and the like, which share the goal of privileging natural boundaries over political borders, in the name of conservation and international cooperation (K. C. Kim 1995, 1997).

11 In issue 4 of *Space*, published in spring 1980, a summary of the ecological surveys by Kang was published, along with a transcript of a conversation among four of the scientists—Won Pyong-Oh, Oh Kye-ch'il, Lee Yŏng-ro, and Ch'oe Ki-ch'ŏl—who had participated in the Smithsonian and 1972 studies.

12 As Lee Bann wrote in the preface to his massive archive of Front DMZ, "If South and North Korea really wants [sic] peace in this land, they must competitively present active methods to conserve the nature of DMZ. This will undoubtedly become the ferment of national consciousness to make the basis for the future of our national community. It will also help to give birth to 'Han Peninsula Declaration,' which will inflate the speed of unification and save the world" (1996: 20).

13 REAL DMZ was the first art project to be located in the Border Area. Since 2012, it has linked its project to local tourism efforts, and has been warmly welcomed by county and provincial officials, even as much of the artwork, including the site-specific work, reflects the values and interests of global art aesthetics.

14 Until its closure in 2016, the industrial complex operated as a unique site where North Korean workers provided the labor force for the manufacturing of products for 123 South Korean companies. A few years earlier, the Diamond Mountain resort, a joint venture with South Korean chaebol Hyundai, opened to South Korean tourists in 1998. The fatal shooting of a South Korean tourist

by North Korean guards in 2008 led to the end of the joint venture and cross-border travel. In the ten years that it was open to tourists from South Korea, more than two million visited the resort.

15 Miura and Bak (2011) note that the number of international conferences increased threefold between the decade of the 1990s and the 2000s, from fourteen to forty-three. Kim Chae-Han (2011) likewise observes the increasing number of DMZ research and policy studies that were supported by government institutes starting in the mid-2000s, when organizations that included the word "DMZ" in their names also began to proliferate.

16 To qualify as part of the Border Area, the region had to satisfy three of five conditions related to economic development indexes: a certain percentage decline in population within the past five years, percentage of road pavement, percentage of water supply, ratio of employment in manufacturing industry, and ratio of territory included in the MIPD.

17 The invocation of *nodaji*/"no touch!" by the environmentalists connotes a complex, polyvocal set of relations, rooted in a history of foreign resource exploitation. *Nodaji* (translated as "gold" or "bonanza") originated in a Japanese or Korean transliteration of the English words "no touch." Don Clark (2003) describes how foreign concessions at the turn of the twentieth century brought American engineers of the Oriental Consolidated Mining Company to northwestern Korea. They attempted to discipline Korean miners and prevent them from pilfering the mined gold by labeling the bullion boxes with the words "No touch." Clark writes, "In fact, the frequently shouted words 'No touchee!' were so well known at Unsan [gold mining country] that they soon became part of the language" (231).

18 This trend has only become more extensive, and now includes numerous television documentaries, most notably "DMZ: The Wild" (2017) featuring the actor Lee Min Ho.

19 When the application was rejected, blame was focused on the county of Cheorwon, which had refused to be included in the plan due to local opposition to the restrictions on development that would be imposed by the designation. But another major factor was the North Korean representative on the commission, who reportedly wrote a letter to the other members asserting that the biosphere reserve would be a violation of the Armistice Agreement. Thus, despite the best efforts of President Lee Myung-bak to act as if North Korea was irrelevant to the DMZ and its representation of "peace," inter-Korean enmity as well as domestic conflict demonstrated the continuing salience of the double bind.

20 According to Sang-wook Kim (2006), GIS Landsat data revealed that between 1987 and 2002, forests in the western DMZ were converted to barren lands or farmland in the North and to farmland and urban areas in the South.

21 The vibrant and complex history of environmental movements in South Korea is beyond the scope of this chapter. The peace and life discourse is most closely associated with the "ecological alternative movement of peace and life"

(Ku 2009), which emerged in the late 1980s, when former democratization movement activists began turning away from ideological struggle to consider more elemental relationships between humans and the earth—a shift from *ttang* (land) to *hŭk* (earth/soil) (Abelmann 1996). This shift was influenced by the relocation of some of these activists from urban centers to the countryside to pursue a simpler way of life (귀농). They formed communes and became farmers, sometimes because their activism had prevented them from finishing their university education, sometimes because their bodies and minds were so beaten down by the struggle that they needed to retreat to a space of healing. Kim Chi-ha, a dissident poet and activist from the 1980s, was a key figure during this time. He emerged from a long period of imprisonment with a new paradigm—the life-movement (생명사상)—informed by indigenous metaphysics, or *Tonghak* philosophy. Kim's writings on "life" (생명) became the basis for the Hansallim manifesto and cooperative movement. Hansallim, which can be translated as "life giving," has become a major food cooperative and community building network that has itself become mainstream.

22 "Introduction to the DMZ Peace Life Valley," YouTube video, July 17, 2016, https://www.youtube.com/watch?v=fhKHfEJrc_s; accessed September 15, 2020.

23 Kim Hyun Mee describes the discourses of "multicultural society" and "multicultural families" as privileging married migrants over labor migrants, and as reflective of "Korean society's contradictory desires to become 'global' and remain ethno-centric simultaneously" (2012). See also M. Kim (2018).

24 On the myth of racial purity in South Korea, see Gage (2007).

25 The DMZ as a militarized borderland has long been an "agent of change" in the social composition of South Korea. The post–Korean War period resulted in "mixed-blood" children, who were born to Korean women, some of whom served US troops as sex workers in the camp towns along the border. These children inaugurated what would become the world's longest and largest transnational adoption program (E. J. Kim 2010). The social changes in the Border Area also included multiculturalism in the militarized camp towns, where migrant Filipina and Russian women began to replace Korean sex workers in the 2000s (Gage 2013).

26 In September 2019, huge commemorative events were planned in South Korea to celebrate the one-year anniversary of the Pyongyang Joint Declaration. Organized by government agencies and ministries, these events included the "DMZ: Peace Economy" conference and the Gyeonggi Province three-day megaevent, "Let's DMZ" (with the Korean tagline, "By meeting at the division (단절), we'll overcome the ordeal (시련을 너머)—Let's meet at the DMZ of Peace!"). The publicity materials on the Gyeonggi Province website advertised the DMZ Forum, which included "Live DMZ," "DMZ Festa," and "Art DMZ," encompassing art exhibitions, performances, and cultural events, including the DMZ Film Festival, DMZ Marathon, DMZ concerts, and ecological tours.

27 For full text in English of the Pyongyang Declaration, see *Korea Times*, September 19, 2018, https://www.koreatimes.co.kr/www/nation/2018/09/103_255848 .html accessed October 17, 2021.

28 Kim Han-joo, "S. Korea Aims to Attract 23 Million International Visitors by 2022," Yonhap News Agency, April 2, 2019, https://m-en.yna.co.kr/view /AEN20190402006100320?section=news; accessed April 11, 2019.

2. Ponds

1 *Dumbeong* (둠벙; *tumbŏng*) has become the word used in scholarly writing and reports about these small irrigation ponds, in both Korean and English, since around 2007. According to a Korea Broadcasting Service environmental special report on *dumbeong* produced in 2004, in other regional dialects in South Korea, they are referred to as *t'umbŏng* (툼벙) or *tŏmbŏng* (덤벙) (Korean Broadcasting Service 2004).

2 According to a study by the National Institute of Agricultural Sciences (M. Kim et al. 2016), between 1960 and 2004, 65 percent of the 9,600 square kilometers used for rice cultivation had been consolidated, resulting in "a loss of natural channels and traditional irrigation ponds...one of the factors in the decline of biodiversity" (150–51).

3 According to the Gyeonggi Research Institute, in the Paju DMZ area, only 26.3 percent of the total land is government owned. In contrast, 35.3 percent is private, 37.4 percent is unknown, and 1.1 percent is public. Policy experts frequently mention land ownership as presenting an inevitable challenge that will have to be debated should the two Koreas achieve a peace agreement.

4 The summit between President Roh Moo-hyun and Kim Jong Il introduced the peace and prosperity language (평화와 번영), which was resurrected by Moon Jae-in's peace initiatives.

5 A South Korean anthropologist friend told me that her father, who was born and raised in Paju, had never heard of *dumbeong*, although he walked the paths between rice paddies (*non'gil*) everyday as a youth. The Ecorium Pond appears on the NIE website (http://www.nie.re.kr/modedg/contentsView.do?ucont_id =CTX001040&menu_nix=3Czingu2&&mu_lang=ENG#place-23; accessed December 28, 2019).

6 According to environmental studies in Japan and elsewhere, an abandoned rice-paddy pond would revert to woodland within ten years, without the need for managed conversion, as long as the surrounding native riparian ecosystems are healthy (C.-s. Lee, You, and Robinson 2002: 312).

7 The charismatic megafauna typically called forth to represent the DMZ's rare biodiversity are the critically endangered red-crowned cranes (두루미; *Grus japonensis*), the apocryphal (but likely extinct) Siberian tiger (호랑이; *Panthera tigris*), and the cute but strange Amur goral (산양; *Naemorhedus caudatus*). In May 2019, the South Korean media exploded with reports of an Asiatic black bear cub (반달가슴곰; *Ursus thibetanus*) discovered by motion-detection cameras in the eastern mountainous areas of the DMZ. This footage of a healthy eight-to nine-month-old bear suggested that there were at least two or three others

in its family also in the area. Until this video evidence, the species had been believed to be nearly extinct in the wild. These large birds and mammals of the DMZ represent just a fraction of the total known species, the majority of which are amphibious insects and plants, identified in the CCZ.

8 Accessible data on military facilities is thin, as well as comprehensive data on fires in the CCZ. Over the past several years, US military facilities have been abandoned in light of base transfers to Camp Humphreys, south of Seoul. As Park outlines, military facilities include dormitories, guard posts, and training grounds and shooting ranges. These facilities are distributed across the entire area. They introduce polluting elements such as waste and wastewater, and they produce detrimental effects such as fires, logging, land clearance, and noise pollution connected to equipment, vehicles, and shooting (E.-J. Park 2011: 104).

9 Kim was also instrumental in the environmental impact assessment for the rebuilding of the Gyeongui railroad tracks following the 2000 inter-Korean summit that led to the opening of the Kaeseong Industrial Complex and the Diamond Mountain Resort.

10 Park Eun-Jin's 2011 study of CCZ ecologies describes how "…traditional organic farming in the CCZ contributes to biodiversity by increasing landscape diversity and connectivity among habitats. Major factors destroying the landscape and habitat structures in the CCZ are military facilities and activities, artificial canalization of streams and waterways, farmland and ginseng field expansion, and road expansion and pavement, etc." (i).

11 Paju City began to promote "Paju Kaesŏng ginseng" (E. J. Kim 2019) in 2005, and until a 2012 law that restricted the establishment of new fields, ginseng cultivation was proliferating rapidly. Ginseng must be shade grown, and the fields were unmistakable, like pixelated black and blue bruises smattered across the beautiful scenery of rice paddies and low hills. They also disrupted the connectivities across otherwise well-connected patches.

12 For more on Paju Book City, see Marshall (2016).

13 According to the LG website (https://www.lg.com/global/business/air-solution/casestudy/factory/lg-display-korea; accessed September 10, 2020).

14 Today, international tourists can take a security tour to the DMZ, which ends with a trip to the outlet mall, for US$35 (http://www.eg-shuttle.com/en/index.php?mc=c&md=01&seq=1; accessed September 10, 2020).

15 As engineer and historian Henry Petroski writes, infrastructure "is believed to have its origin in military usage in France…. Military usage, in which infrastructure connotes the bases and camps needed to maintain, support and deploy troops, was further reinforced in the 1940s following the development of NATO, and this also introduced the word into American English" (2009: 370).

16 In 1972, the section of Highway 1 (the Gyeongbu Expressway) between Seoul and the CCZ, was renamed Tongil-ro.

17 For more on the history of CCZ North-facing villages (민통선 북방 마을; 민북마을), see chapter 4.

18 Nearly 30 percent of the CCZ in Gyeonggi Province is agricultural, with the majority of land used for rice paddies. Another 30 percent is forests, 13 percent military facilities, and the remainder a mix of human settlements, forests, grasslands, rivers, and streams. Thirty-two percent of the land is used for agricultural production. Forests constitute 38.6 percent of the land cover, and the rest is grasslands, wetlands, and industrial areas (E.-J. Park 2012: 29). The author notes that "land cover of this area has gradually changed with increased development since 1990. In this region, total forest area decreased from 67.7% in 1990 to 53.9% in 2009, whereas agricultural land increased from 22.5% to 28.1%. The decrease rate of forest in the CCZ is three times higher than that in the whole area of Gyeonggi Province, and the increase of agricultural land also contrasts sharply with its decrease from 31.7% to 27% in the province during the same period. It appears that the farmlands had changed into wetlands or forests with no cultivation for some time, but then they reverted back with the resumption of farming. In addition, the areas of the CCZ account for 16% in Paju and 20% in Yeoncheon, whereas 58% of the new cultivation in Paju City and 66% in Yeoncheon County started in the CCZ in 2010."

19 Interview, September 30, 2011.

20 Some names of the DERI members are pseudonyms.

21 He goes on to state, "However, for many involved in biodiversity science, the totalization that is sought is a predictive, lawlike knowledge that will allow for an understanding of the wellsprings of biodiversity" (Bowker 2000: 745).

22 Interview, September 30, 2011.

23 Field notes, October 24, 2011.

24 In the context of limited conservation areas, climate crisis and mass extinction present difficult trade-offs. Inside the central DMZ, former wetlands have converted to woodlands, yet this seemingly positive restoration is reducing the resting and feeding habitats for endangered cranes.

25 The South Korean Ministry of Environment officially designated roughly sixty square kilometers of the wetlands in the Han River estuary as a protected area in 2006, making it off-limits to development and human trespassing. Despite this important move, ecological scientists and environmentalists continue to be concerned about the health of the western CCZ, particularly given the shared interests of the ROK and DPRK governments in allowing civilian ships to use the Han River estuary. In addition, the problem of landmines continues to present dangers to civilians. As reported by Hwang Tae-il (황대일) for the *Yonhap News* on October 19, 2021, plans to develop ecotourism sites in the Janghang wetland area were suspended after two civilians were injured by mines in 2020 and 2021. Mines present an ongoing danger due to frequent flooding events during the summer rainy season (see chapter 4).

26 As reported by Chŏng Rae-won (정래원) in the *Yonhap News* on November 1, 2020, a pilot ecological survey of the Han River estuary took place between November and December 2018 with ten scientists from North and South cooperat-

ing for over one month. Although the study was conceived as a joint project, since inter-Korean relations had deteriorated, the next phase of research began in November 2020 with only South Korean scientists participating (https://www.yna.co.kr/view/AKR20201101022700504; accessed October 20, 2021).

3. Birds

Parts of chapter 3 first appeared in *Social Research: An International Quarterly* 84, no. 1 (Spring 2017): 203–20.

1 Reported by Mun Ch'ŏl (문철) on April 3, 1993, in an article titled "분단의 벽을 넘다는 새가 끝없이 부럽구나" ["How Endlessly Envious I Am of the Birds Who Traverse the Wall of the National Division"], 동아일보 [*Dong-A Ilbo*], 31.

2 The North Korean–Japanese coproduction *Bird* was screened at the Tokyo International Film Festival in 1996, and a North and South Korean coproduction resulted in a short animation film, also called *Bird*, in 2006. The children's book *When I See Birds, I Also Want to Fly* was published in South Korea in 2006.

3 In 2013, the RCC was voted by South Korean citizens to be the symbol of the DMZ in a competition to promote the DMZ's nature by the South Korean Ministry of Environment, beating out a dozen other rare and endangered species including the white-naped crane, the Asian black bear (반달가슴곰), the Siberian flying squirrel (하늘다람쥐), the Eurasian otter, the spotted seal (점박이물범), the Siberian musk deer (사향노루), the Eurasian black vulture (독수리), the Amur goral, and the native plants, 닻꽃 (*Halenia coniculata* (L.) Cornaz), 날개하늘나리 (*Lilium dauricum* Ker Gawl.), and the Seoul frog (금개구리).

4 For more information on Jouy and his role in natural history and early American anthropology of Korea, see Robert M. Oppenheim, *An Asian Frontier* (2016).

5 For more detailed information about early collectors and their papers, see Gore and Won (1971). For an overview of Korean natural science during the colonial era, see Moon (2012). Austin (1948) provides a brief professional biography of Won Hong Gu, and offers this assessment:

> One more interesting oriental personality has left his mark on Korean ornithology. Among the sixty million Koreans, only one of them has made any attempt to do serious bird work, to contribute to the knowledge of the avifauna of his country and to publish his findings. This is Hong Koo Won. (The Korean pronunciation of his name is Won, Hong Koo, which by the Japanese reading of the characters is Gen, Kohkiu. On his own specimen labels he writes it Konkyu Gen.) Won's work is very difficult to evaluate for, despite its obvious wealth of material, it is frequently maddening in its omissions, its ambiguity and its questionable veracity. But one must remember that Won was severely handicapped by the social system in which he lived, by the Japanese policy of keeping all Koreans in subordinate positions. When one considers the difficulties he overcame, the lack of instruction, assistance, encouragement and funds, one is forced to admire

his ambition and perseverance and to acknowledge his accomplishments as outstanding among his people. (20–21)

6　The MAPS program had both basic scientific and epidemiological agendas— namely, to track avian-borne diseases in order to defend human populations against them. But as Michael L. Lewis notes, "studying the transmission of biological pathogens by birds for defensive purposes is only a hair's breadth from turning that information to an offensive purpose" (2004: 97). Lewis writes not about MAPS but in relation to the Pacific Ocean Biological Survey (POBS), which was a scandalous Pentagon biological warfare project disguised as a bird-banding study. Nevertheless, the idea of weaponizing animal physiology and ecology to spread disease was already familiar in the Korean context, considering China's and North Korea's claims that the United States had used germ warfare in 1951 and 1952 during the Korean War. Although there is no evidence that Won's bird research was used directly for defensive or hostile military purposes, POBS, which ran between 1962 and 1969, was contemporaneous with his MAPS-funded research, and one cannot assume its status as neutral scientific data, particularly in the Korean context.

7　The concept is currently supported by the ecosystem approach advocated by the Convention on Biological Diversity, which aims to be an open and flexible framework to "refer to any functioning unit at any scale" (45). As with other species, conservation efforts increasingly require coordination across local and international nongovernmental and governmental organizations and the states that regulate the environments on which nonhuman animals depend. Toward this end, the Global Interflyway Network was formalized in 2011 to connect conservation projects across the world's major flyways that transect the northern and southern hemispheres (Global Interflyway Network 2012).

8　For some scholars of biodiversity and endangered species, biopolitics offers a useful framework for analyzing relations of power and agency, whether applying a strong reading in which vulnerable nonhumans in captivity are subjected to the sovereign power of their human caretakers (Chrulew 2011), or a dialectical reading in which nonhuman life continually exceeds capture by human logics of biopower (Youatt 2015). In the relations of conservationists and birds that I examine, sovereign power over nonhuman animals is organized around explicit interventions that seek to create flourishing life, not in the "wild" but in naturalcultural borderlands where maintaining connectivities to kin and habitat is a primary goal. The monitoring activities and technologies of surveillance hardly constitute a totalizing gaze, even in the case of satellite tracking (see, e.g., Whitney 2014). Rather, situated encounters produce partial knowledge and fragmented views.

　　Instead of the panopticon, therefore, a more apt framing for understanding the management of flyways is that of nature as infrastructure, or what Foucault (2009) in his lectures at the Collège de France called "milieu." For Foucault, security operates at the level of the population and requires the sovereign to "exercise power at the point of connection where nature, in the sense of physical elements, interferes with nature in the sense of the human species" (23). If conservationists are like the sovereign in Foucault's formulation, governing a population by acting on its milieu, such governance requires a biopolitical attention to the nature of the (nonhuman) species, "insofar as it has a body and a soul, a physical and a moral existence" (23).

A cosmology in which nonhuman animals can have a soul or a moral existence was not part of my interlocutors' explicit epistemological or metaphysical assumptions, but the conservationist ethos that guided their work framed the birds as having evolutionary needs and biological instincts that were inherently moral (in contrast to the immoral practices of humans and governments that failed to protect them or actively harmed them). One of my interlocutors in particular, as a Christian, was ambivalent about animism, as a pagan belief system, but also thought of it as indigenously Korean.

9 I offer the flyways as a metaphor and model for thinking about human–avian relationships in ways that go beyond what Thom van Dooren calls "flight ways" (2014). For van Dooren, flight ways capture the emergent becoming of birds as individuals whose collective lives constitute a species as a transhistorical unfolding. Yet, his book, even when it includes a critical analysis of conservationists' work, does not consider how human–avian relationships are also part of the coevolutionary process that he considers to be vital to understanding birds or other nonhuman species as forms of life (vs. life forms, i.e., individual beings as opposed to specimens that represent a species).

10 Julia Elyachar (2010), in her study of economic networks in Cairo, draws on Roman Jakobson's notion of the phatic function in his theory of communicative functions (the inspiration of which was Malinowski's "phatic communication"). Phatic labor refers to the work of creating channels of communication, which Elyachar renders infrastructural—those channels allow for the circulation of language, as well as "reputation, information, and emotion" (457), constituting a "social infrastructure of communicative pathways" (460).

11 Bridget Guarasci (2017) critiques birds as "value technologies" on a global scale. She writes of the IUCN Red List of Threatened Species as "a species of capital" and akin to "imperial conquest": "IUCN's biodiversity initiative is a grand unifying plan that harnesses distinct ecologies to a UN mandate of global governance much like other conservation movements that preceded it and which are today more overtly recognized as forms of imperial conquest" (16).

12 The Korean name thankfully doesn't invoke troubling connotations with racist histories. As with many of the native naming conventions for birds in Korea, *chŏŏsae* (저어새) comes from observations of the behavior of the birds rather than their appearance. *Chŏŏsae* could be translated as the stirring/whipping bird, describing how the bird forages for food: by stirring shallow waters and then catching fish in its spoon-shaped bill.

13 There is a resident population in Hokkaido, Japan, which is highly habituated to humans and other animals, including cows. These cranes reportedly regularly attack the cows by pecking their eyes.

14 Lee Kisup, in an October 31, 2013, update about spoonbill Gaksi-hiro, expressed markedly similar sentiments, writing: "He connects not only South Korea and Japan, but also Taiwan (his wintering area), China (a stopover), and scholars in North Korea who spend the summer together so they can exchange information. I hope that the conflict between the two Koreas will be well resolved, so that South and North Korean scholars can study and protect spoonbills together in the future."

15 On the broader history of Argos and PTT technology, see Benson (2012).

16 The 2020 BFS census announced by the Hong Kong Bird Watching Society documented a 9 percent increase from 2019, but also indicated that numbers were decreasing in some locations, specifically Hong Kong and China. Numbers of BFSs in South Korea, which had dipped in 2017, were continuing on an upward trend (https://www.hkbws.org.hk/cms/en/hkbws/work/endangered-species/bfs-en/bfscensus2020; accessed October 23, 2021).

17 The NLL refers to a US-imposed maritime boundary that was never formalized by the 1953 Armistice Agreement. Five islands on the western coast were designated as South Korean territory, but the maritime borders have been disputed by North Korea, which recognizes the distance of three nautical miles, as opposed to the norm of twelve nautical miles asserted by South Korea and the UN Command.

18 In July 2020, CNN described the NGO Global Fishing Watch's reports of so-called ghost ships, the abandoned boats of North Korean fishers who died from being pushed from North Korean waters into more distant Russian and Japanese waters by illegal Chinese fishing vessels (https://www.cnn.com/2020/07/23/asia/north-korea-ghost-ships-intl-hnk/index.html; accessed December 20, 2020).

19 See Haraway on politesse, which she writes entails "articulating bodies to other bodies with care so that significant others might flourish" (2008: 92).

20 https://www.northstarst.com/; accessed December 1, 2015.

21 As juveniles, BFSs are difficult to sex. Once they are mature, the females and males are distinguishable from their relative size, with males slightly larger than females.

4. Landmines

Earlier versions of chapter 4 first appeared in *Cultural Anthropology* 31, no. 2 (2016): 162–87; and *Ethnographies of U.S. Empire*, edited by Carole McGranahan and John F. Collins (Duke University Press, 2018).

1 On the emergence and politicization of the category of local people, see chapter 1.

2 According to the 2020 update of the ICBL's "Landmine and Cluster Munition Monitor," the United States' War Reserve Stocks for Allies, Korea (WRSA-K) included 480,267 M14 and 83,319 M16 antipersonnel mines in 2013, but as of October 2015, they "could not determine whether the US indeed maintained non-self-destructing antipersonnel mines in South Korea" (http://www.the

-monitor.org/en-gb/reports/2021/korea,-republic-of/mine-ban-policy.aspx; accessed September 20, 2021).

3   After eleven years of lobbying by NGOs and National Assembly member Han Ki-ho, the first legislation to support mine victims passed the South Korean National Assembly in December 2014. As the process of filing for claims began in early 2015, histories of trauma are being officially recorded, entering into the public sphere, and drawing further attention to the landmine issue. The maiming of two ROK soldiers in August 2015 by what South Korean investigators determined to be a North Korean wooden box mine (despite DPRK denials) also brought media attention to inadequate medical coverage and monetary compensation for ROK soldiers injured by mines. A study, "지뢰피해자 보상금 지급 분석보고서" ["Analysis of Compensation Payments to Landmine Victims Report"], released on February 15, 2021, by the NGO Peace Sharing Association (평화나눔회), reported that there were 486 civilian victims compensated between 2015 and 2020. These victims represent just half of the estimated total who would qualify. With an average compensation payment of 42 million won (US$35,131), the amount disbursed totaled just 20.41 trillion won (US$17.1 million), instead of the one-hundred-trillion won amount (US$83.6 million) initially estimated by the National Defense Ministry (p. 4, http://www.psakorea .org/board/index.html?id=report&no=92; accessed October 12, 2021).

4   These details were reported by Yi Cha-hŭi (이자희) on May 26, 2013, for *Ohmynews* in an article entitled "남한 지뢰제거에 489년 걸려...무섭습니다. 녹색 순례 4 일차...미확인 지뢰지대" ["489 Years to Clear the Landmines in South Korea... Frightening. Fourth Leg of the Green Pilgrimage...Unidentified Minefields"] (http://www.ohmynews.com/NWS_Web/View/at_pg.aspx?CNTN_CD =A0001869277; accessed September 10, 2020).

5   See the 2013 "Landmine and Cluster Munition Monitor, Country Profile: Korea, Republic of," published by the ICBL (http://www.the-monitor.org/en-gb/reports /2013/Korea,-Republic-of; accessed March 12, 2020).

6   Nicholas Kristof, "South Korea Extols Some Benefits of Landmines," *New York Times*, September 3, 1997.

7   According to the 2021 ICBL country report for South Korea, in the aftermath of the 2018 summits between Kim Jong Un and Moon Jae-in, the South Korean government for the first time sent an observer to the meeting of States Parties to the Mine Ban Treaty in July 2020. Yet, the ROK's stated position continues to be that which it provided in November 2019 at the UN General Assembly vote regarding the universalization of the Mine Ban Treaty—namely, that while it "supports the objectives and purposes of the Ottawa Convention...due to the security situation on the Korean peninsula, we are currently not a party to the convention" (http://www.the-monitor.org/en-gb/reports/2021/korea,-republic -of/; accessed October 18, 2021).

8   This information was reported by Pak Kyŏng-man (박경만) in the *Hankyoreh* newspaper on July 30, 2021, in an article titled "녹색연합 '국방부 227억 쓰고도 후 방 지뢰지대 한곳도 해제 못해'" ["Green Korea United: After 22.7 Trillion Won, the

Ministry of Defense Hasn't Cleared a Single Minefield in Rear Areas"] (https://www.hani.co.kr/arti/area/capital/1005897.html; accessed October 23, 2021).

9 Unruh, Heynen, and Hossler (2003) provide a useful literature review of work in other disciplines, which tends to focus on humanitarian mine removal. See Bolton (2015) for an analysis of mines in the context of the revolution in military affairs. For recent work in anthropology, see DeAngelo (2018) and Zani (2019).

10 The multiplicity of mines and their heterogeneous agencies that I am interested in are better captured by Latour's (1999) model of "distributed agency" than Gell's "distributed personhood." The former does not presuppose moral responsibility among any particular actant in the network, whereas Gell turns to an extreme example of violence to illustrate how mines are "moral entities" whose secondary agency, literally scattering violence across the landscape, "turned [Pol Pot's soldiers] from mere men into devils with extraordinary powers" (1998: 21).

11 According to the UN, mines can cost as little as $3 to produce and an estimated $300–$1,000 to remove.

12 Although there can be no exact accounting of mines buried around the world, humanitarian mine clearance efforts have led to a reduction of the ICBL's 1997 estimate of a hundred million.

13 The Mine Ban Treaty (or Ottawa Treaty) refers to the 1997 Convention on the Prohibition of the Use, Stockpiling, Production and Transfer of Anti-Personnel Mines and on their Destruction.

14 See International Campaign to Ban Landmines, "Arguments for the Ban," http://www.icbl.org/en-gb/problem/arguments-for-the-ban.aspx (accessed March 4, 2021).

15 Although this fact is difficult to determine conclusively, it is widely cited. For one example, see Yoo Yŏng-ho's (유영호) reporting in T'ongil News, "끝나지 않은 전쟁 <대인지뢰>" ["Unending War: Anti-personnel Landmines"], January 31, 2008 (https://www.tongilnews.com/news/articleView.html?idxno=76541; accessed September 15, 2021).

16 This fact appears in a February 4, 2013, article by Kim Ki-ho (김기호), "생태계 보고 DMZ, 기후 변화 대비 친환경 지뢰 제거로 자연생태 관광자원으로 개발 해야" ["The DMZ, an Ecosystem Treasure: We Must Develop Ecotourism by Removing Landmines in an Eco-friendly Way to Counter Climate Change"], Civil Society Times [시민사회 신문] (http://ingopress.ingopress.com/2064; accessed February 15, 2013).

17 As reported in Yonhap News by Kwon Suk-hŭi (권숙희) on March 9, 2014, in "통일이 오기 전에 풀어야 과제들" ["Before Unification Comes, Tasks to Be Solved"] (https://www.yna.co.kr/view/AKR20140309020500060; accessed March 5, 2016).

18 See the series of articles in Kyŏngin Daily from 2014, including the report by 윤재준, 최재훈, 권준우 [Yun Chae-chun, Ch'ae Chae-hun, and Kwon Chun-u], "침묵의 지뢰, 3: 허술한 관리." ["Landmines of Silence, No. 3: Careless Management"] (http://www.kyeongin.com/main/view.php?key=913474; accessed March 5, 2016).

19 During the Japanese occupation of Korea, *sinjju* was collected from Korean colonial subjects, especially in the early 1940s, when brass bowls or cutlery were actively confiscated during the total war mobilization drives (Hurh 2011). These domestic objects were melted down and molded into munitions. After World War II and the Korean War, *sinjju* referred to any kind of metal alloy or scrap metal, though brass was still highly valuable.

20 Mayor Lee recalled that at a press conference in Japan, President Bill Clinton had claimed that there were no mines in South Korea. After a Japanese anti-mine activist corrected him, Clinton replied that he would need to examine the issue more closely. I was unable to verify this exchange, but in an official statement regarding the United States' decision not to sign the 1997 Mine Ban Treaty, Clinton attempted to explain the justification for the Korea exception: "Anybody who's ever been to the DMZ and who has ever driven from Seoul to the DMZ and seen how short it is and has seen a million—you know, the numbers of troops there, and you see our people up there in those outposts and how few they are—and again I say, these mines are put along the DMZ in clearly marked areas to make sure that no children will walk across them. There is no place like it in the world" (Public Papers of the Presidents of the United States 1997: 1185). Clinton's statements were most likely based on the claims made by the South Korean state, which, until 1998, attempted to obscure the existence of landmines in the CCZ and the fact of civilian deaths and casualties. See also Cho (2012: 8).

Epilogue

1 This statement appeared in the abstract for a 2009 panel organized by Harold Balbach of the US Army Corps of Engineers and Scott Roberts of Mississippi State University for the annual meeting of the Ecological Society of America. Entitled "Ecological Research on Defense and other Federal Lands," the panel brought together military and academic researchers who discussed management plans for at-risk species and invasive species. See https://eco.confex.com/eco/2009/techprogram/S3937.HTM (accessed January 16, 2022).

2 Virgil Hawkins, "Diego Garcia's Shameful History Continues," *New Internationalist*, June 7, 2012 (https://newint.org/blog/2012/06/07/chagos-islands-shameful-history; accessed September 1, 2019).

3 Literary scholar Elizabeth DeLoughery asserts that "one of the most obvious worldwide ecological threats—the reach of the U.S. military"—has yet to be fully reckoned with in existing examinations of the Anthropocene (2014: 323; but see Bonneuil, Fressoz, and Fernbach 2016). Along these lines, an examination of de/militarized ecologies could contribute to decolonial and transpacific approaches to the Asia-Pacific (Shigematsu and Camacho 2010) and to a larger intellectual project of provincializing the Anthropocene or "putting [it] in place" (Hecht 2018: 112; Nixon 2014). David Eng, for instance, writes in relation to the slow violence of uranium mining and the radioactive colonialism that

links the atomic bomb to the First Nations of Sahtu Dene in Canada that these histories draw "disconnected groups across the trans-Pacific into unexpected alignment" (2014: n.p.).

4 The *South China Morning Post* compiled a montage of images and videos from social media and news reports around the world, with the title, "Wildlife Roam Streets Emptied by Coronavirus," which appeared online on April 7, 2020 (https:// www.scmp.com/video/world/3078961/wildlife-comes-out-play-while-humans -stay-locked-away-cities-amid-coronavirus; accessed September 24, 2020).

References

Abelmann, Nancy. 1996. *Echoes of the Past, Epics of Dissent: A South Korean Social Movement*. Berkeley: University of California Press.

Agamben, Giorgio. 1998. *Homo Sacer: Sovereign Power and Bare Life*. Translated by D. Heller-Roazen. Stanford, CA: Stanford University Press.

Agamben, Giorgio. 2005. *State of Exception*. Translated by K. Attell. Chicago: University of Chicago Press.

Ahn, Ch'ang-hyŏk, Joo Chin-ch'ŏl, Kwŏn Chae-hyŏng, Song Ho-myŏn [안창혁, 주진철, 권재형, 송호면]. 2012. 둠벙 (소형 저류지) 연구와 생태적 활용방안 [Dumbeong (Small-Scale Reservoir) Research and Plan for Ecological Use]. 물과 미래 [*Water and Future*] 45 (6): 91–97.

Ahn, Ji Hong, Chi Hong Lim, Song Hie Jung, and Chang Seok Lee [안지홍, 임지홍, 정성희, 이창석]. 2017. "습지 복원을 위해 하나의 대조지소로 선정된 둠벙의 식생" ["Vegetation of Doombeong Selected as a Reference Site for Restoring Wetland"]. 한국습지학회지 [Korean Journal of Wetlands Research] 19 (2): 193–201.

Anand, Nikhil, Akhil Gupta, and Hannah Appel, eds. 2018. *The Promise of Infrastructure*. Durham, NC: Duke University Press.

Austin, Oliver L. Jr. 1948. "The Birds of Korea." *Bulletin of the Museum of Comparative Zoölogy* 101 (1): 1–302.

Baik, Crystal Mun-hye, and Jane Jin Kaisen. 2018. "Korea and Demilitarized Peace." *Periscope: Social Text Online*. Accessed January 14, 2019. https://socialtextjournal.org/periscope_article/11908-2/.

Barad, Karen. 2003. "Posthumanist Performativity: Toward an Understanding of How Matter Comes to Matter." *Signs* 28 (3): 801–31.

Barad, Karen. 2007. *Meeting the Universe Halfway: Quantum Physics and the Entanglement of Matter and Meaning*. Durham, NC: Duke University Press.

Bateson, Gregory. 2000 [1972]. *Steps to an Ecology of Mind: Collected Essays in Anthropology, Psychiatry, Evolution, and Epistemology*. Chicago: University of Chicago Press.

Benson, Etienne. 2012. "One Infrastructure, Many Global Visions: The Commercialization and Diversification of Argos, A Satellite-Based Environmental Surveillance System." *Social Studies of Science* 42 (6): 843–68.

Boere, Gerard C., and David A. Stroud. 2006. "The Flyway Concept: What It Is and What It Isn't." In *Waterbirds around the World*, edited by G. C. Boere, C. A. Galbraith, and D. A. Stroud, 40–47. Edinburgh: Stationery Office.

Bolger, Daniel P. 1991. *Scenes from an Unfinished War: Low-Intensity Conflict in Korea, 1966–1969.* Leavenworth Papers 19. Fort Leavenworth, KS: Combat Studies Institute.

Bolton, Michael. 2015. "From Minefields to Minespace: An Archaeology of the Changing Architecture of Autonomous Killing in US Army Field Manuals on Landmines, Booby Traps and IEDs." *Political Geography* 46: 41–53.

Bonneuil, Christophe, Jean-Baptiste Fressoz, and David Fernbach. 2016. *The Shock of the Anthropocene: The Earth, History and Us.* London: Verso.

Bowker, Geoffrey C. 2000. "Mapping Biodiversity." *International Journal of Geographical Information Science* 14 (8): 739–54.

Brady, Lisa M. 2008. "Life in the DMZ: Turning a Diplomatic Failure into an Environmental Success." *Diplomatic History* 32 (4): 585–611.

Brockington, Dan, Rosaleen Duffy, and Jim Igoe. 2010. *Nature Unbound: Conservation, Capitalism and the Future of Protected Areas.* London: Earthscan.

Brown, Wendy. 2010. *Walled States, Waning Sovereignty.* New York: Zone Books.

Büscher, Bram, Wolfram Dressler, and Robert Fletcher. 2014. *Nature, Inc.: Environmental Conservation in the Neoliberal Age.* Tucson: University of Arizona Press.

Carse, Ashley. 2014. *Beyond the Big Ditch: Politics, Ecology, and Infrastructure at the Panama Canal.* Cambridge, MA: MIT Press.

Cattelino, Jessica. 2010. "The Double Bind of American Indian Need-Based Sovereignty." *Cultural Anthropology* 25 (2): 235–62.

Chang, Heejun, Sunhak Bae, and Kyunghyun Park. 2019. "Dreams and Migration in South Korea's Border Region: Landscape Change and Environmental Impacts." *Annals of the American Association of Geographers* 109 (2): 476–91.

Cho, Jae Kook. 2012. "Legacy of U.S. Military Intervention: Landmine Issue in South Korea," Doshisha International Conference on Humanitarian Interventions in the 21st Century, Doshisha University, Kyoto, Japan.

Choy, Timothy. 2011. *Ecologies of Comparison.* Durham, NC: Duke University Press.

Chrulew, Matthew. 2011. "Managing Love and Death at the Zoo: The Biopolitics of Endangered Species Preservation." *Australian Humanities Review* 50: 137–57.

Chubb, Danielle L. 2013. *Contentious Activism and Inter-Korean Relations.* New York: Columbia University Press.

Chung, Hyun-yong, Cheol-Min Yeom, Jae Hyun Kim, Shinyeong Park, Yae-Won Lee, Gina Pyo, and Seung Ho Kim. 2020. "Species Diversity and Community Characteristics of Benthic Macroinvertebrates from Irrigation Ponds in the Western CCZ Area, Korea." *Korean Journal of Ecology and Environment* 53 (2): 173–84.

Clark, Don. 2003. *Living Dangerously in Korea: The Western Experience: 1900–1950.* Norwalk, CT: EastBridge.

Coates, Peter. 2014. "Borderland, No-Man's Land, Nature's Wonderland: Troubled Humanity and Untroubled Earth." *Environment and History* 20: 499–516.

Collins, Samuel Gerald. 2013. "Train to Pyongyang: Imagination, Utopia, Korean Unification." *Utopian Studies* 24 (1): 119–43.

Crutzen, Paul J., and Eugene F. Stoermer. 2000. "The 'Anthropocene.'" *Global Change Newsletter* 41 (May): 17–18.

Cumings, Bruce. 2011. *The Korean War: A History.* New York: Modern Library.

Davis, Jeffrey Sasha. 2007. "Introduction: Military Natures: Militarism and the Environment." *GeoJournal* 69 (3): 131–34.

Davis, Jeffrey Sasha, Jessica S. Hayes-Conroy, and Victoria M. Jones. 2007. "Military Pollution and Natural Purity: Seeing Nature and Knowing Contamination in Vieques, Puerto Rico." *GeoJournal* 69 (3): 165–79.

Dawdy, Shannon Lee. 2008. *Building the Devil's Empire: French Colonial New Orleans.* Chicago: University of Chicago Press.

DeAngelo, Darcie. 2018. "Demilitarizing Disarmament with Mine Detection Rats." *Culture and Organization* 24: 285–302.

de la Cadena, Marisol. 2015. "Uncommoning Nature." *e-flux journal* 65 (May–August). Accessed January 22, 2019. http://supercommunity.e-flux.com/texts/uncommoning -nature/.

Delissen, Alain. 2001. "The Aesthetic Pasts of *Space* (1960–1990)." *Korean Studies* 25 (2): 243–60.

DeLoughery, Elizabeth. 2014. "Postcolonialism." In *The Oxford Handbook of Ecocriticism*, edited by G. Garrard, 320–40. Oxford: Oxford University Press.

Derrida, Jacques. 1976. *Of Grammatology.* Translated by G. Spivak. Baltimore: Johns Hopkins University Press.

Derrida, Jacques. 2005. *Rogues: Two Essays on Reason.* Stanford, CA: Stanford University Press.

Derrida, Jacques, and Anne Dufourmantelle. 2000. *Of Hospitality.* Stanford, CA: Stanford University Press.

Despret, Vinciane. 2013. "Responding Bodies and Partial Affinities in Human–Animal Worlds." *Theory, Culture and Society* 30 (7–8): 51–76.

DMZ Ecology Research Institute [DMZ 생태연구소]. 2009. 둠벙, 자연하천: DMZ 생태 비밀 의 코드를 열다 [*Dumbeong, Natural Streams: Cracking the Secret Code of the DMZ's Ecology*]. Paju, South Korea: DMZ 생태연구소 [DMZ Ecology Research Institute].

Dodge, Martin, and Chris Perkins. 2009. "The 'View from Nowhere'? Spatial Politics and Cultural Significance of High-Resolution Satellite Imagery." *Geoforum* 40 (4): 497–501.

Douglas, Mary. 2002 [1966]. *Purity and Danger: An Analysis of Concepts of Pollution and Taboo.* New York: Routledge Classics.

Dowie, Mark. 2011. *Conservation Refugees: The Hundred-Year Conflict between Global Conservation and Native Peoples.* Cambridge, MA: MIT Press.

Elyachar, Julia. 2010. "Phatic Labor, Infrastructure, and the Question of Empowerment in Cairo." *American Ethnologist* 37 (3): 452–64.

Eng, David. 2014. "Reparations and the Human." *Profession.* Modern Language Association. Accessed September 2, 2020. https://profession.mla.org/reparations-and-the -human/.

Escobar, Arturo. 2008. *Territories of Difference: Place, Movement, Life, Redes.* Durham, NC: Duke University Press.

Foucault, Michel. 2009. *Security, Territory, Population: Lectures at the Collège de France, 1977–1978.* Translated by G. Burchell. London: St. Martin's Press.

Gage, Sue-Je Lee. 2007. "Pure Mixed Blood: The Multiple Identities of Amerasians in South Korea." PhD diss., University of Indiana.

Gage, Sue-Je Lee. 2013. "'We're Never Off Duty': Empire and the Economies of Race and Gender in the U.S. Military Camptowns of Korea." *Cross-Currents: East Asian History and Culture Review* 6 (March).

Galtung, John. 1967. "Theories of Peace: A Synthetic Approach to Peace Thinking." Oslo: International Peace Research Institute. Accessed March 14, 2021. https://www.transcend.org/files/Galtung_Book_unpub_Theories_of_Peace _-_A_Synthetic_Approach_to_Peace_Thinking_1967.pdf.

Geertz, Clifford. 1972. "The Wet and the Dry: Traditional Irrigation in Bali and Morocco." *Human Ecology* 1 (1): 23–39.

Gelézeau, Valérie. 2013. "Life on the Lines: People and Places of the Korean Border." In *De-bordering Korea: Tangible and Intangible Legacies of the Sunshine Policy*, edited by Valérie Gelézeau, Koen De Ceuster, and Alain Delissen, 13–33. London: Routledge.

Gell, Alfred. 1998. *Art and Agency: An Anthropological Theory*. Oxford: Clarendon Press.

Global Interflyway Network. 2012. "Waterbird Flyway Initiatives: Outcomes of the 2011 Global Waterbird Flyways Workshop to Promote Exchange of Good Practice and Lessons Learnt." Seosan City, Republic of Korea, October 17–20, 2011, edited by Chang Yong Choi, Nicola Crockford, Nick Davidson, Vicky Jones, Taej Mundkur, Crawford Prentice, and David Stroud. AEWA Technical Series No. 40, Bonn, Germany; CMS Technical Series No. 25, Bonn, Germany; EAAFP Technical Report No. 1, Incheon, Republic of Korea; Ramsar Technical Report No. 8, Gland, Switzerland.

Gore, M. E. J., and Pyong-Oh Won. 1971. *The Birds of Korea: A Guide to the Birds of the Republic of Korea*. Seoul, South Korea: Royal Asiatic Society, Korea Branch, in conjunction with Taewon Publishing Company.

Green Korea United [녹색연합]. 2010. 접경지역 47개 지뢰지대 실태조사 [Fact-Finding Report on Forty-Seven Mine Fields in the Border Area]. Seoul: Green Korea United.

Green Korea United [녹색연합]. 2013a. 녹색 순례 4일차, 미확인 지뢰지대 [Day Four of Green Pilgrimage: Unconfirmed Mine Zones]. Accessed March 15, 2021. http://www.greenkorea.org/participation/green-pilgrimage/%eb%85%b9%ec%83%89%ec%88%9c%eb%a1%80-2013/31976/.

Green Korea United [녹색연합]. 2013b. 2013년 DMZ 면적 조사 보고서 [2013 Report on the Total Area of the DMZ]. Accessed January 20, 2021. http://www.greenkorea.org/activity/peace-and-ecology/dmz/33470/.

Grinker, Roy Richard. 1995. "The 'Real Enemy' of the Nation: Exhibiting North Korea at the Demilitarized Zone." *Museum Anthropology* 19 (2): 31–40.

Grinker, Roy Richard. 1998. *Korea and Its Futures: Unification and the Unfinished War*. New York: St. Martin's Press.

Guarasci, Bridget. 2017. "Birding under Fire: Learning Ornithology in Wartime Iraq." Paper presented at the Militarized Ecologies Workshop, University of California, Irvine, May 19.

Gusterson, Hugh. 2007. "Anthropology and Militarism." *Annual Review of Anthropology* 36: 155–75.

Guyer, Jane I. 2007. "Prophesy and the Near Future: Thoughts on Macroeconomic, Evangelical, and Punctuated Time." *American Ethnologist* 34 (3): 409–21.

Gyeonggi Province Cultural Foundation [경기문화재단]. 2013. 통일촌마을조사보고서: 통일촌 사람들, 그 삶의 이야기 [*Research Report on Unification Village: Unification Village People, Stories of Their Lives*]. Suwon: Gyeonggi Province Cultural Foundation.

Gyeonggi Research Institute [경기연구원]. 2019. DMZ 도로는 굽은 흙 길로 [The DMZ's Roads as Winding Dirt Paths]. 이슈&진단, 382. August 21. Prepared by Lee Yang Ju, Northern Research Center.

Hage, Ghassan. 2012. "Critical Anthropological Thought and the Radical Political Imaginary Today." *Critique of Anthropology* 32 (3): 285–308.

Hahm, Kwang Bok [함광복]. 2007. 할아버지, 연어를 따라오면 한국입니다. 30년 간의 DMZ 기행. [*Grandfather, If You Follow the Salmon, There Will Be Korea: 30 Years of Traveling the DMZ*]. Seoul: 도서 출판 [Eastward Publishing].

Halpern, Orit. 2015. *Beautiful Data: A History of Vision and Reason since 1945.* Durham, NC: Duke University Press.

Haraway, Donna J. 1998. "Situated Knowledges: The Science Question in Feminism and the Privilege of Partial Perspective." *Feminist Studies* 14 (3): 575–99.

Haraway, Donna J. 2008. *When Species Meet.* Minneapolis: University of Minnesota Press.

Haraway, Donna J. 2016. *Staying with the Trouble: Making Kin in the Chthulucene.* Durham, NC: Duke University Press.

Harvey, David. 2003. *The New Imperialism.* Oxford: Oxford University Press.

Harvey, David. 2012. *Rebel Cities: From the Right to the City to the Urban Revolution.* London: Verso.

Hathaway, Michael J. 2013. *Environmental Winds: Making the Global in Southwest China.* Berkeley: University of California Press.

Havlick, David. 2007. "Logics of Change for Military-to-Wildlife Conversions in the United States." *GeoJournal* 69 (3): 151–64.

Hecht, Gabrielle. 2018. "Interscalar Vehicles for an African Anthropocene: On Waste, Temporality, and Violence." *Cultural Anthropology* 33 (1): 109–41.

Heise, Ursula K. 2010. "Lost Dogs, Last Birds, and Listed Species: Cultures of Extinction." *Configurations* 18 (1): 49–72.

Helmreich, Stefan. 2003. "Trees and Seas of Information: Alien Kinship and the Biopolitics of Gene Transfer in Marine Biology and Biotechnology." *American Ethnologist* 30 (3): 340–58.

Henig, David. 2012. "Iron in the Soil: Living with Military Waste in Bosnia-Herzegovina." *Anthropology Today* 28 (1): 21–23.

Henig, David. 2019. "Living on the Frontline: Indeterminacy, Value, and Military Waste in Postwar Bosnia-Herzegovina." *Anthropological Quarterly* 92 (1): 85–110.

Higuchi, Hiroyoshi, and Jason Minton. 2000. "The Importance of the Korean DMZ to Threatened Crane Species in Northeast Asia." *Global Environmental Research* 4 (2): 123–32.

Hong Kai [홍가이]. 1996. "발기문" ["Manifesto"]. In 비무장지대: 과거 현재 미래 [*Front DMZ: Past, Present, and Future*], 이반 편집 [edited by Lee Bann], 22–23. Seoul: 비무장 지대 예술문화운동협의회 부설 비무장지대 미술운동연구소 [Institute of the Fine Art Movement for the Abolishment of the Demilitarized Zone, a Sub-institute of the Federation of Artists and Naturalists for DMZ Conservation].

Hong, Seunghei Clara. 2015. "Silenced in Memoriam: Consuming Memory at the Nogŭnri Peace Park." *Cross-Currents: East Asian History and Culture Review* 14: 178–203.

Hurh, Won Moo. 2011. *"I Will Shoot Them from My Loving Heart": Memoir of a South Korean Officer in the Korean War*. Jefferson, NC: MacFarland.

Hwang, Eun-Ju. 2013. "DMZ Eco-belt Initiative and the Global Trust." Seoul: Korea Legislation Research Institute.

Ingold, Tim. 2011. *Being Alive: Essays on Movement, Knowledge and Description*. Abingdon, UK: Routledge.

Ingold, Tim. 2018. "Anthropology between Art and Science: An Essay on the Meaning of Research." *Field: A Journal of Socially-Engaged Art Criticism* 11. Accessed October 12, 2021. http://field-journal.com/issue-11/anthropology-between-art-and-science-an -essay-on-the-meaning-of-research.

International Campaign to Ban Landmines. 2013. "Landmine and Cluster Munition Monitor. Country Profile: Korea, South." Accessed March 12, 2021. http:// www.the-monitor.org/en-gb/MonitorSearch?year=2013&report=Country%20 Profile&section=&country=Korea,%20Republic%20of.

Jager, Sheila Miyoshi, and Jiyul Kim. 2007. "The Korean War after the Cold War: Commemorating the Armistice Agreement in South Korea." In *Ruptured Histories: War, Memory, and the Post-Cold War in Asia*, edited by Rana Mitter and Sheila Miyoshi Jager, 233–65. Cambridge, MA: Harvard University Press.

Jo Chun Sok. 1966. "A Bird from His Son." *Korean Nature: Association for Nature Conservation of the Democratic People's Republic of Korea* 3: 14.

Johnson, Chalmers. 2001. *Blowback: The Costs and Consequences of American Empire*. New York: Henry Holt.

Ju, Jaehyoung, Jae Hyun Kim, and Seung Ho Kim. 2016. "Habitat Fragmentation by a Levee and Its Impact on Frog Population in the Civilian Control Zone." *Journal of Wetlands Research* 18 (2): 113–20.

Jung, Jin-Heon. 2015. *Migration and Religion in East Asia: North Korean Migrants' Evangelical Encounters*. London: Palgrave.

Jusionyte, Ieva. 2018. *Threshold; Emergency Responders on the U.S.-Mexico Border*. Berkeley: University of California Press.

Kang Yung Sun [강영선]. 1974. 개관 [Synopsis]. Reports on the Scientific Survey Near the DMZ, 25–29. 자연자원보전위원회 [Korean Association for the Conservation of Nature], Bureau of Cultural Property, South Korean Ministry of Culture and Information.

Kang Yung Sun [강영선]. 1975. "비무장지대 인접지역의 생물 자연" ["The Biological Nature of Areas Adjacent to the DMZ"]. 북한 [*North Korea*] 4,3,39: 78–88.

Kim Chae-Han [김재한]. 2006. DMZ 평화 담사: 남북 평화와 남남 화해를 위해 [*Exploring the DMZ: InterKorean Peace and Intra-Korean Accommodation*]. Seoul: Oruem.

Kim Chae-Han [김재한]. 2011. "DMZ 연구의 오해와 논재" ["Controversy and Misconception in DMZ Research"]. 통일 문제 연구 [*Journal of Unification Studies*] 56: 107–45.

Kim, Ch'ang-hwan [김창환]. 2011. DMZ 지리 이야기 [Stories of the DMZ's Geology]. Seoul: 살림터 [Sallimt'ŏ].

Kim Chin-hwan [김진환]. 2012. DMZ의 미래와 인문학: 시각과 과제 [The DMZ's Future and the Humanities: Perspectives and Tasks]. 통일 문제 연구 [*Journal of Unification Studies*] 57: 154–85.

Kim, Eleana J. 2010. *Adopted Territory: Transnational Korean Adoptees and the Politics of Belonging.* Durham, NC: Duke University Press.

Kim, Eleana J. 2014. "The Flight of the Cranes: Militarized Nature at the North Korea–South Korea Border." *RCC Perspectives* 3: 65–70.

Kim, Eleana J. 2019. "Metabolic Relations: Korean Red Ginseng and the Ecologies of Modern Life." In *How Nature Works: Rethinking Labor on a Troubled Planet*, edited by Sarah Besky and Alex Blanchettte, 115–30. Santa Fe, NM: School for Advanced Research.

Kim, Eleana J. n.d. "Cold War's Nature: Midcentury American Science and the Ecologization of the Korean Demilitarized Zone, 1966–1968." Unpublished manuscript.

Kim, Eunjung. 2017. *Curative Violence: Rehabilitating Disability, Gender, and Sexuality in Modern Korea.* Durham, NC: Duke University Press.

Kim, GoWoon, Wanmo Kang, Dowon Lee, Rahul Teku Vaswani, and Jinhyung Chon. 2019. "A Spatial Approach to Climate-Resilient Infrastructure in Coastal Social-Ecological Systems: The Case of *Dumbeong* in Goseong County, South Korea." *Environment International* 131: 105032.

Kim, Hyun Mee. 2012. "The Emergence of the 'Multicultural Family' and Gendered Citizenship in South Korea." In *Contested Citizenship in East Asia: Development Politics, National Unity, and Globalization*, edited by Kyung-sup Chang and Bryan S. Turner, 203–17. Oxon, UK: Routledge.

Kim, Jae Hyun, Hyun Yong Chung, Kim Seung Ho, and Jae Geun Kim. 2016. "The Influence of Water Characteristics on the Aquatic Insect and Plant Assemblage in Small Irrigation Ponds in Civilian Control Zone, Korea." *Journal of Wetlands Research* 18 (4): 331–41.

Kim, Jodi. 2010. *Ends of Empire: Asian American Critique and the Cold War.* Minneapolis: University of Minnesota Press.

Kim Ke Chung. 1995. "Korea Peace Bioreserves System: A Process toward a New 'Keum-Su-Kang-San.'" In 비무장지대: 과거 현재 미래 [*Front DMZ: Past, Present, and Future*] edited by Lee Bann, 412–18. Seoul: 비무장지대 예술문화운동협의회 부설 비무장지대 미술운동연구소 [Institute of the Fine Art Movement for the Abolishment of the Demilitarized Zone, a Sub-institute of the Federation of Artists and Naturalists for DMZ Conservation].

Kim Ke Chung. 1997. "Preserving Biodiversity in Korea's Demilitarized Zone." *Science* 278: 242–43.

Kim Ke Chung. 2007. "Preserving Korea's Demilitarized Corridor for Conservation: A Green Approach to Conflict Resolution." In *Peace Parks: Conservation and Conflict Resolution*, edited by S. H. Ali, 239–60. Cambridge, MA: MIT Press.

Kim, Kwi-gon [김귀곤]. 2010. 평화와 생명의 땅 DMZ. [*DMZ: Land of Peace and Life*]. Seoul: 드림 미디어 [Dream Media].

Kim, Minjeong. 2018. *Elusive Belonging: Marriage Immigrants and "Multiculturalism" in Rural South Korea.* Honolulu: University of Hawai'i Press.

Kim, Myunghyun, L. Choe, S. Choi, J. Eo, M. Han, and H. Bang. 2016. "Studies into the Management and Restoration of Paddy Ecosystems to Enhance Biodiversity in South Korea." National Institute for Agro-Environmental Sciences (NIAES), Series 6: 149–58.

Kim, Nan. 2017. *Memory, Reconciliation, and Reunions in South Korea: Crossing the Divide*. Washington, DC: Lexington Books.

Kim Sang-Wook [김상욱]. 2006. "선형분광혼합화소분석을 이용한 서부지역 DMZ의 토지피복 변화 탐지" ["Land-Cover Change Detection of Western DMZ and Vicinity Using Spectral Mixture Analysis of Landsat Imagery"]. 한국지리정보학회지 [*Bulletin of the Korea GIS Association*] 9 (1): 158–67.

Kim Seung Ho, Jae Hyun Kim, and Jae Geun Kim [김승호, 김재현, 김재근]. 2011. "서부 민간인 통제구역에 존재하는 둠벙의 유형분류" ["Classification of Small Irrigation Ponds in Western Civilian Control Zone in Korea"]. 한국습지학회지 [*Korean Journal of Wetlands Research*] 13 (2): 275–89.

Kim, Suk-Young. 2011. "Staging the 'Cartography of Paradox': The DMZ Special Exhibition at the Korean War Memorial, Seoul." *Theatre Journal* 63 (3): 381–402.

Kim, Suk-Young. 2014. *DMZ Crossing: Performing Emotional Citizenship along the Korean Border*. New York: Columbia University Press.

Kirksey, Eben. 2015. *Emergent Ecologies*. Durham, NC: Duke University Press.

Kirksey, Eben, and Stefan Helmreich. 2010. "The Emergence of Multispecies Ethnography." *Cultural Anthropology* 25 (4): 545–76.

Klein, Naomi. 2014. *This Changes Everything: Capitalism vs. the Climate*. New York: Simon and Schuster.

Ko, Yekang, Derek K. Schubert, and Randolph T. Hester. 2011. "A Conflict of Greens: Green Development versus Habitat Preservation—the Case of Incheon, South Korea." *Environment: Science and Policy for Sustainable Development* 53 (3): 3–17.

Korean Broadcasting Service. 2004. 환경 스페셜 둠벙 ["Environmental Special: Dumbeong"].

Korean Campaign to Ban Landmines (KCBL). 1999. "지뢰 피해자 현주소" ["The Current Situation of Landmine Victims"]. March 24. http://psakorea.org/board/index.html?id=report&page=3&no=12.

Korean Landmine Removal Research Center [한국지뢰제거연구소]. 2008. "통일후 DMZ의 평화적 이용을 위한 지뢰제거에 관한 연구" ["Research on Landmine Removal for the Peaceful Utilization of the DMZ Following Reunification"]. Seoul.

Ku, Do-wan. 2009. "The Emergence of Ecological Alternative Movement in Korea." *Korea Social Science Journal* 36 (2): 35–66.

Lachman, Beth E., A. Wong, and S. A. Reseter. 2007. *The Thin Green Line: An Assessment of DoD's Readiness and Environmental Protection Initiative to Buffer Installation Encroachment*. Santa Monica, CA: RAND Corporation.

Larkin, Brian. 2013. "The Politics and Poetics of Infrastructure." *Annual Review of Anthropology* 42: 327–43.

Latour, Bruno. 1999. *Pandora's Hope: Essays on the Reality of Science Studies*. Cambridge, MA: Harvard University Press.

Latour, Bruno. 2002. *War of the Worlds: What about Peace?* Chicago: Prickly Paradigm Press.

Law, John. 2004. "Enacting Naturecultures: A Note from STS." Lancaster, UK: Centre for Science Studies, Lancaster University. Accessed March 30, 2016. http://www.comp.lancs.ac.uk/sociology/papers/law-enacting-naturecultures.pdf.

Lawrence, Michael J., Holly L. J. Stemberger, Aaron Zolderdo, Daniel P. Struthers, and Steven J. Cooke. 2015. "The Effects of Modern War and Military Activities on Biodiversity and the Environment." *Environmental Reviews* 23 (4): 443–60.

Lee Bann [이반]. 1990. "DMZ를 기념자연공원으로" ["Toward Making the DMZ a Monumental Peace Park"]. 공간 [*Space*] 273 (May): 60.

Lee Bann [이반], ed. 1996. 비무장지대 과거 현재 미래 [*Front DMZ: Past, Present, and Future*]. Seoul: 비무장지대 예술문화운동협의회 부설 비무장지대 미술운동연구소 [Institute of the Fine Arts Movement for the Abolishment of the Demilitarized Zone, a Subinstitute of the Federation of Artists and Naturalists for DMZ Conservation].

Lee, Chang-seok, Young-han You, and George R. Robinson. 2002. "Secondary Succession and Natural Habitat Restoration in Abandoned Rice Fields of Central Korea." *Restoration Ecology* 10 (2): 306–14.

Lee, Jang-hie. 2001. "International Legal Issues in the Peaceful Utilization of the Korean DMZ." In *The Korean DMZ: Reverting beyond Division*, edited by Chae-Han Kim, 127–56. Seoul: Sowha.

Lee, Katherine In-Young. 2018. "Space and the Big Bang." In *Dynamic Korea and Rhythmic Form*, 11–31. Middletown, CT: Wesleyan University Press.

Lee, Namhee. 2007. *The Making of Minjung: Democracy and Politics of Representation in South Korea*. Ithaca, NY: Cornell University Press.

Lee, Namhee. 2019. "Social Memories of the 1980s: Unpacking the Regime of Discontinuity." In *Revisiting Minjung: New Perspectives on the Cultural History of 1980s South Korea*, edited by Sun Young Park, 17–45. Ann Arbor: University of Michigan Press.

Lee, Seung-Ook, Najeeb Jan, and Joel Wainwright. 2014. "Agamben, Postcoloniality, and Sovereignty in South Korea." *Antipode* 46 (3): 650–68.

Lee, Sohl C. 2015. "Virtual Space and National Division: Crow's Eye View: The Korean Peninsula at the Venice Architecture Biennale." *Journal of Korean Studies* 20 (2): 291–332.

Lee, Steven. 2013. "The Korean Armistice and the End of Peace: The US–UN Coalition and the Dynamics of War-Making in Korea, 1953–76." *Journal of Korean Studies* 18 (2): 183–224.

Lefebvre, Henri. 1991. *The Production of Space*. Translated by Donald Nicholson-Smith. London: Wiley.

Lennon, John, and Malcolm Foley. 2000. *Dark Tourism: The Attraction of Death and Disaster*. London: Continuum.

Leopold, Aldo. 1989 [1949]. *A Sand County Almanac, and Sketches Here and There*. London: Oxford University Press.

Lévi-Strauss, Claude. 1966. *The Savage Mind*. Chicago: University of Chicago Press.

Lewis, Michael L. 2004. *Inventing Global Ecology: Tracking the Biodiversity Ideal in India, 1947–1997*. Athens: Ohio University Press.

Lorimer, Jamie. 2007. "Nonhuman Charisma." *Environment and Planning D: Society and Space* 25 (5): 911–32.

Lunstrum, Elizabeth. 2014. "Green Militarization: Anti-poaching Efforts and the Spatial Contours of Kruger National Park." *Annals of the American Association of Geographers* 104 (4): 816–32.

Lutz, Catherine. 2007. "Militarization." In *A Companion to the Anthropology of Politics*, edited by David Nugent and Joan Vincent, 318–31. Malden, MA: Blackwell.

Malkki, Liisa. 2015. *The Need to Help: The Domestic Arts of International Humanitarianism*. Durham, NC: Duke University Press.

Marshall, Colin. 2016. "Paju Book City, the Korean Town All about Reading (and Publishing, Printing, Browsing, Buying…)." *LA Review of Books*. Accessed February 10, 2017. https://blog.lareviewofbooks.org/the-korea-blog/paju-book-city-korean-town-reading-publishing-printing-browsing-buying/.

Masco, Joseph. 2004. "Mutant Ecologies: Radioactive Life in Post–Cold War New Mexico." *Cultural Anthropology* 19 (4): 517–50.

Matsuda, Haruka. 2007. "A Clash of Empires in East Asia: The Geneva Conference on Korea, 1954." *Seoul Journal of Korean Studies* 20 (2): 193–211.

Mauss, Marcel. 1990 [1924]. *The Gift*. London: Routledge Classics.

McCaffrey, Katherine. 2009. "Environmental Struggle after the Cold War: New Forms of Resistance to the U.S. Military in Vieques, Puerto Rico." In *The Bases of Empire*, edited by Catherine Lutz, 218–42. New York: New York University Press.

Merleau-Ponty, Maurice. 2003. *Nature: Course Notes from the Collège de France*. Translated by R. Vallier. Chicago: Northwestern University Press.

Miura, Hiroki, and Sunyoung Bak. 2011. "The Peaceful Use of the Korean DMZ Area: Transnational Interactions and South Korea's Policy Development (1990–2009)." *Korea Observer* 42 (3): 491–519.

Miyazaki, Hirokazu. 2006. "Economy of Dreams." *Cultural Anthropology* 21 (2): 147–72.

Miyazaki, Hirokazu. 2017. "Introduction: The Economy of Hope." In *The Economy of Hope*, edited by Hirokazu Miyazaki and Richard Swedberg, 1–36. Philadelphia: University of Pennsylvania Press.

Mol, Annemarie. 2002. *The Body Multiple: Ontology in Medical Practice*. Durham, NC: Duke University Press.

Moon, Manyong. 2012. "Becoming a Biologist in Colonial Korea: Cultural Nationalism in a Teacher-cum-Biologist." *East Asian Science, Technology and Society: An International Journal* 6 (1): 65–82.

Moon, Seungsook. 2010. "In the U.S. Army but Not Quite of It: Contesting the Imperial Power in a Discourse of KATUSAs." In *Over There: Living with the U.S. Military Empire from World War Two to the Present*, edited by Maria Höhn and Seungsook Moon, 231–57. Durham, NC: Duke University Press.

Navaro-Yashin, Yael. 2012. *The Make-Believe Space: Affective Geography in a Postwar Polity*. Durham, NC: Duke University Press.

Nixon, Rob. 2007. "Of Landmines and Cluster Bombs." *Cultural Critique* 67 (1): 160–74.

Nixon, Rob. 2011. *Slow Violence and the Environmentalism of the Poor*. Cambridge, MA: Harvard University Press.

Nixon, Rob. 2014. "The Anthropocene: The Promise and Pitfalls of an Epochal Idea." *Edge Effects*. Accessed December 12, 2014. https://edgeeffects.net/anthropocene-promise-and-pitfalls/.

Oliver, Kelly. 2009. *Animal Lessons: How They Teach Us to Be Human*. New York: Columbia University Press.

Oppenheim, Robert M. 2016. *An Asian Frontier: American Anthropology and Korea, 1882–1945*. Lincoln: University of Nebraska Press.

Paglen, Trevor. 2010. *Blank Spots on the Map: The Dark Geography of the Pentagon's Secret World*. New York: Berkley.

Pai, Hyung Il. 2013. *Heritage Management in Korea and Japan: The Politics of Antiquity and Identity*. Seattle: University of Washington Press.

Paik Nak-chung. 2011 [1995]. "The Ecological Imagination in Overcoming the Division System." Reprinted in *The Division System in Crisis: Essays on Contemporary Korea*, translated by Kim Myung-hwan, Sol June-Kyu, Song Seung-cheol, and Ryu Young-joo in collaboration with the author, 68–76. Berkeley: University of California Press.

Paik Nak-chung. 2013. "South Korean Democracy and Korea's Division System." *Inter-Asia Cultural Studies* 14 (1): 156–69.

Park, Eun-Jin [박은진]. 2011. "민통선지역 생태계 훼손요인 및 영향 저감방안 연구" ["Damaging Factors to the CCZ Ecosystems and the Mitigation of Their Impacts"]. Suwon: 경기개발연구원 [Gyeonggi Research Institute].

Park, Eun-Jin [박은진]. 2012. "DMZ생태평화마을 조성을 위한 기초조사 및 발전방향" ["DMZ Eco-peace Villages: Basic Survey and Development Strategies"]. Suwon: 경기개발연구원 [Gyeonggi Research Institute].

Park, Eun-Jin. 2013a. "Changes in the DMZ's Status and Preparations for Reunification." In *Whispers of the DMZ: All about the DMZ, a Symbol of Peace and Nature*, edited by Eun-Jin Park, 229–54. Goyang, South Korea: Wisdomhouse.

Park, Eun-Jin [박은진]. 2013b. "DMZ의 자연 환경" ["The Environment of the DMZ"]. In DMZ의 미래 [*The Future of the DMZ*], 31–43. Paju: 하늘 아카데미 [Hanŭl Academy].

Park, Eun-Jin, ed. 2013c. *Whispers of the DMZ: All about the DMZ, a Symbol of Peace and Nature*. Goyang, South Korea: Wisdomhouse.

Park, Eun-Jin, and Mi-A Nam [박은진, 남미아]. 2013. "민통선 이북지역의 토지피복 및 인삼 재배면적 변화분석" ["Changes in Land Cover and the Cultivation Area of Ginseng in the Civilian Control Zone: Paju City and Yeoncheon County"]. 한국환경생태학회지 [*Korean Journal of Environmental Ecology*] 27 (4): 507–15.

Park, Hyun Ok. 2015. *The Capitalist Unconscious: From Korean Unification to Transnational Korea*. New York: Columbia University Press.

Park, Kyong. 2020. "We Just Have to Wait a Little Longer." In "At the Border," *e-flux architecture*. Accessed May 11, 2020. https://www.e-flux.com/architecture/at-the -border/325760/we-just-have-to-wait-a-little-longer/.

Park, So Jin, and Nancy Abelmann. 2004. "Class and Cosmopolitan Striving: Mothers' Management of English Education in South Korea." *Anthropological Quarterly* 77 (4): 645–72.

Pearson, Chris, Peter Coates, and Tim Cole. 2010. *Militarized Landscapes: From Gettysburg to Salisbury Plain*. London: Continuum.

Petroski, Henry. 2009. "Engineering: Infrastructure." *American Scientist* 97 (5): 370–74.

Pettyjohn, Stacie L. 2012. *U.S. Global Defense Posture, 1783–2011*. Santa Monica, CA: RAND Corporation.

Public Papers of the Presidents of the United States. 1997. William J. Clinton, Book II, 1183–86. Washington, DC: US Government Printing Office.

Pugliese, Joseph. 2020. *Biopolitics of the More-Than-Human: Forensic Ecologies of Violence*. Durham, NC: Duke University Press.

Ra, J. Y. 1999. "The Politics of Conference: The Political Conference on Korea in Geneva, 26 April–15 June 1954." *Journal of Contemporary History* 34 (3): 399–416.

Rhee, Tae-yoon [이태윤]. 2010. DMZ, 생물 다양성의 HLZ (Handicapped Life Zone) [DMZ, Biodiversity of the HLZ (Handicapped Life Zone)]. 코리아 접경 포럼 제2 차 워크숍 [Proceedings of the Second Workshop, Korea Border Forum], 74–80. May 28–29. 통일연구원 [Korea Institute for National Unification].

Runge, Claire A., James E. M. Watson, Stuart H. M. Butchart, Jeffrey O. Hanson, Hugh P. Possingham, and Richard A. Fuller. 2015. "Protected Areas and Global Conservation of Migratory Birds." *Science* 350 (6265): 1255–28.

Russell, Edmund. 2010. "Afterword: Militarized Landscapes." In *Militarized Landscapes: From Gettysburg to Salisbury Plain*, edited by Chris Pearson, Peter Coates, and Tim Cole, 229–37. London: Continuum.

Schwenkel, Christina. 2006. "Recombinant History: Transnational Politics of Memory and Knowledge Production in Contemporary Vietnam." *Cultural Anthropology* 21 (1): 3–30.

Schwenkel, Christina. 2013. "War Debris in Postwar Society: Managing Risk and Uncertainty in the DMZ." In *Interactions with a Violent Past: Reading Post-Conflict Landscapes in Cambodia, Laos, and Vietnam*, edited by Vatthana Pholsena and Oliver Tappe, 135–56. Singapore: NUS Press in association with IRASEC.

Seo, Alex Young-Il. 2018. "From Disorderly Dispersion to Orderly Concentration; Frontier Villages at the Korean Border 1951–1973." *Scroope: Cambridge Architecture Journal* 27: 43–58.

Serres, Michel. 1990. *The Natural Contract*. Translated by E. MacArther and W. Paulson. Ann Arbor: University of Michigan Press.

Serres, Michel. 2006. *Revisiting the Natural Contract: 1000 Days of Theory*. Translated by A. Feenberg-Dibon. Accessed September 20, 2021. https://journals.uvic.ca/index .php/ctheory/article/view/14482/5325.

Seth, Michael. 2002. *Education Fever: Society, Politics, and the Pursuit of Schooling in South Korea*. Honolulu: University of Hawai'i Press.

Shigematsu, Setsu, and Keith L. Camacho. 2010. *Militarized Currents: Toward a Decolonized Future in Asia and the Pacific*. Minneapolis: University of Minnesota Press.

Shim Youngkyu. 2014. "Seize the DMZ!" *Space* 555 (February): 74–79.

Shin, D. 2017. "North Korea's Perspectives in Its Argument for a Peace Treaty." *Asian Affairs* 48: 510–28.

Sloterdijk, Peter. 2011. *Bubbles: Spheres*. Vol. 1, *Microspherology*. Translated by W. Hoban. Los Angeles: Semiotext(e).

Smith, Herbert L. 1972. "Landmine and Countermine Warfare: Korea 1950–54." Washington, DC: Department of Defense, Department of the Army, Corps of Engineers, Engineer Agency for Resources Inventories.

So Hŭng-yŏl [소흥열]. 1980. DMZ 기념 자연 공원을 위한 계획 [A Proposal for a DMZ Monumental Park]. 공간 [*Space*] 153 (March): 16–19.

Son Gi-Woong [손기웅]. 2011. DMZ 총람: 가요, 정치 군사적 현황. [DMZ Survey: Summary of the Current Political and Military Conditions]. 통일연구원 [Korea Institute for National Unification]. KINU Policy Research Series 11-06.

Song, Annie Young, and James Hastings. 2020. "Engaging North Korea: Environmental Cooperation in Peacebuilding." *Third World Quarterly* 41 (11): 1809–27.

Space [공간]. 1980. "DMZ를 기념 자연공원으로: Let's Make a Monumental Park in DMZ." 153 (March): 14–15.

Space [공간]. 1989. "DMZ를 기념 자연공원으로: Let's Make a Monumental Park in DMZ." 259 (March): 34–35.

Space [공간]. 1990. "DMZ를 기념 자연공원으로" ["Toward a Monumental Park in the DMZ"]. 273 (May): 60.

Space [공간]. 2014. "Resurrection of the DMZ Peace Park." 555 (February): 54–55.

Space [공간]. 2017. "Dreaming Once Again—DMZ." 601 (December): 44–45.

Stengers, Isabelle. 2005. "The Cosmopolitical Proposition." In *Making Things Public: Atmospheres of Democracy*, edited by B. Latour and P. Weibel, 994–1003. Cambridge, MA: MIT Press.

Stengers, Isabelle. 2014. "Gaia, the Urgency to Think (and Feel)." *Os Mil Nomes de Gaia: Do Antropoceno à Idade da Terra*. Accessed April 3, 2016. http://www .osmilnomesdegaia.eco.br.

Stoler, Ann Laura, and David Bond. 2006. "Refractions off Empire: Untimely Comparisons in Harsh Times." *Radical History Review* 95: 93–107.

Stoler, Ann Laura, and Carole McGranahan. 2007. "Imperial Formations: Refiguring Imperial Terrains." In *Imperial Formations*, edited by Ann L. Stoler, Carole McGranahan, and Peter C. Perdue, 3–42. Santa Fe, NM: School for Advanced Research Press.

Takacs, David. 1996. *The Idea of Biodiversity: Philosophies of Paradise*. Baltimore: Johns Hopkins University Press.

Thomas, Julia Adenay. 2009. "The Exquisite Corpses of Nature and History: The Case of the Korean DMZ." *Asia Pacific Journal* 7 (43): 3242.

Tsing, Anna Lowenhaupt. 2005. *Friction: An Ethnography of Global Connection*. Princeton, NJ: Princeton University Press.

Tsing, Anna Lowenhaupt, for the Matsutake Worlds Research Group. 2014. "Blasted Landscapes (and the Gentle Arts of Mushroom Picking)." In *The Multispecies Salon*, edited by Eben Kirksey, 87–109. Durham, NC: Duke University Press.

Ueta, Mutsuyuki, David S. Melville, Ying Wang, Kiyoaki Ozaki, Yutaka Kanai, Paul J. Leader, Chia-Chi Wang, and Chen-Yue Kuo. 2002. "Discovery of the Breeding Sites and Migration Routes of Black-Faced Spoonbills *Platalea minor*." *Ibis* 144: 340–43.

Ueta, Mutsuyuki, R. Kurosawa, and D. Allen, eds. 2000. *Conservation and Research of Black-Faced Spoonbills and Their Habitats*. Tokyo: Wild Bird Society of Japan.

UNEP (United Nations Environment Programme) and CMS (Convention on Migratory Species). 2012. "A Bird's Eye View on Flyways: A Brief Tour by the Convention on the Conservation of Migratory Species of Wild Animals." 2nd ed. Bonn: UNEP/CMS Secretariat.

Unruh, Jon D., Nikolas C. Heynen, and Peter Hossler. 2003. "The Political Ecology of Recovery from Armed Conflict: The Case of Landmines in Mozambique." *Political Geography* 22 (8): 841–61.

US Department of State. 2014. "US Landmine Policy." Accessed September 20, 2021. https://2009-2017.state.gov/t/pm/wra/c11735.htm.

van Dooren, Thom. 2014. *Flight Ways: Life and Loss at the Edge of Extinction*. New York: Columbia University Press.

Vine, David. 2009. *Island of Shame*. Princeton, NJ: Princeton University Press.

Wapner, P. 2010. *Living through the End of Nature: The Future of American Environmentalism*. Cambridge, MA: MIT Press.

Warkentin, Traci. 2011. "Interspecies Etiquette in Place: Ethical Affordances in Swim-with-Dolphins Programs." *Ethics and the Environment* 16 (1): 99–122.

Watson, Iain. 2014. "Rethinking Peace Parks in Korea." *Peace Review: A Journal of Social Justice* 26 (1): 102–11.

Watson, Matthew C. 2016. "On Multispecies Mythology: A Critique of Animal Anthropology." *Theory, Culture and Society* 33 (5): 159–72.

Weisman, Alan. 2007. *The World without Us*. New York: Picador.

Weiss, Erica. 2012. "Principle or Pathology? Adjudicating the Right to Conscience in the Israeli Military." *American Anthropologist* 114 (1): 81–94.

Weston, Kath. 2016. *Animate Planet: Making Visceral Sense of Living in a High-Tech Ecologically Damaged World*. Durham, NC: Duke University Press.

Westover, John G. 1987. *Combat Support in Korea*. Washington, DC: Center of Military History.

Whitney, Kristoffer. 2014. "Domesticating Nature? Surveillance and Conservation of Migratory Shorebirds in the 'Atlantic Flyway.'" *Studies in History and Philosophy of Science Part C: Studies in History and Philosophy of Biological and Biomedical Sciences* 45: 78–87.

Willerslev, Rane. 2007. *Soul Hunters: Hunting, Animism, and Personhood among the Siberian Yukaghirs*. Berkeley: University of California Press.

Williams, Raymond. 1976. *Keywords: A Vocabulary of Culture and Society*. New York: Oxford University Press.

Wilson, Robert M. 2010. *Seeking Refuge: Birds and Landscapes of the Pacific Flyway*. Seattle: University of Washington Press.

Won, Hong Gu. 1966. "Black-Faced Spoonbill and Its Protection." *Korean Nature: Association for Nature Conservation of the Democratic People's Republic of Korea* 1: 8–11.

Won, Pyong-Oh. 1966. "The Present Status of Some Threatened and Rarer Birds in Korea, 1962–1966." Smithsonian Institution Archives. Ecology Program Records. Record Unit 271, Box 16, Folder: "Korea: Ecological Studies 1965–66."

Wood, Chris, Hiroshi Tomida, Kim Jin-han, Ki-sup Lee, Hyong-ju Cho, Shin Nishida, Jamaluddin Ibrahim,Wee-haeng Hur, Hwa-jung Kim, Sung-hyun Kim, Hiroko Koike, Go Fujita, Hiroyoshi Higuchi, and Tetsukazu Yahara. 2013. "New Perspectives on Habitat Selection by the Black-Faced Spoonbill *Platalea minor* Based upon Satellite Telemetry." *Bird Conservation International* 23 (4): 495–501.

Woodward, Rachel. 2014. "Military Landscapes: Agendas and Approaches for Future Research." *Progress in Human Geography* 38 (1): 40–61.

Youatt, Rafi. 2015. *Counting Species: Biodiversity in Global Environmental Politics*. Minneapolis: University of Minnesota Press.

Zani, Leah. 2019. *Bomb Children: Life in the Former Battlefields of Laos*. Durham, NC: Duke University Press.

Index

The letter *f* following a page number denotes a figure; the letter *m*, a map; the letter *t*, a table.

Chun Doo-hwan, 34, 38
Chung Hyun-yong, 79
Civilian Control Line (CCL), x, xi, 11, 124m;
    north-facing villages, 72, 138
Civilian Control Zone. *See* CCZ
civil society movements, 37, 126. *See also* ICBL
Clark, Don, 164n17
climate change, 3, 8, 47, 80, 84; and bird
    wintering sites, 79, 98, 105, 117
Clinton, Bill, 10, 145, 175n20
Cold War, 8–9, 10, 12; biopolitics, 90; continu-
    ation of, 35–36, 37–38; retro aesthetics, 42;
    science, 90, 91; US military expansion,
    155. *See also* landmines; US-ROK alliance
Collins, Samuel, 15
colonial period, 25, 39–40, 69, 87, 169n5,
    175n19
Comprehensive Plan for Border Development
    (2011), 21
Convention on Biological Diversity, 170n7
Convention on the Conservation of Migra-
    tory Species, "Bird's Eye View on
    Flyways," 93
Coolidge, Harold, 72
coronavirus pandemic, 156
cosmopolitanism, 116, 117
cosmopolitics, 14, 19–20, 27, 116
cranes: banding, 96; endangered migratory,
    78; as flagship species, 96; habitats, 46,
    79, 84, 85, 103, 168n24; habituation to
    humans and animals, 96, 171n13; red-
    crowned, 70, 90, 96, 102, 103, 122, 166n7,
    169n3; white-naped, 70, 85, 169n3
Cuban Missile Crisis, 135
Cumings, Bruce, 155

Daeseong-dong (Freedom Village), 72
decommissioned military sites, 100, 133, 154–55
deforestation, 70, 72, 80, 164n20, 168n18;
    North Korea, 3, 44
de la Cadena, Marisol, 84
Deleuze, Gilles, 101
DeLoughery, Elizabeth, 175n3
Demilitarized Zone. *See* CCZ (Civilian Con-
    trol Zone); DMZ
democracy movement, 37, 38, 40
Democratic People's Republic of Korea
    (DPRK). *See* North Korea
democratization, 34–35

Denali National Park, 117–18
denuclearization, 37
DERI (DMZ Ecology Research Institute), 19;
    cross-border Ramsar wetlands village
    project, 84–85; data collection, 74, 75–76,
    82; *dumbeong*-as-commons, 81–82, 84;
    members, 74–75, 81, 125, 168n20; pond
    work, 62–63, 65; programs for high school
    students, 73–74; research activities, 20, 75,
    77–79; scientific reputation and publica-
    tions, 75–76, 77. *See also* Heo Young; Kim
    Seung Ho; Rhee T'ae-yoon, Dr.
Derrida, Jacques, 16, 116
Despret, Vinciane, ethical "enacting," 20, 92
Diamond Mountain Resort, 163–64n14,
    167n9
Diego Garcia island, 154–55
division: infrastructure of, 22, 139; making
    peace with, 152; meantime of, 27, 82, 124,
    152
DMZ (Demilitarized Zone): as brand, 24,
    47, 48, 49, 50, 146, 150–51; as Cold War
    holdover, 22, 50; as conservation area,
    5, 18, 44–45, 49, 68, 159n4; defined, x, xi,
    8–11; before democratization of South, 34;
    GIS Landsat data, 164n20; governance, 9,
    71, 160n10; guard posts, 22, 160n9; hetero-
    topic nature of, 15, 124, 134, 147; as "living
    museum," 31–32; as peace zone, 5–6, 32,
    38, 159n4, 67–68; plans and proposals
    for, 6t, 17, 21, 22–23, 26, 38–41, 47–48, 68,
    159n4, 161n18; as "post-war ecosystem,"
    66; promotion "as gold mine of nature,"
    150–51, 150f; shrinking of, 10–11; wildlife,
    4, 26, 33, 75, 115, 159n2, 169n3. *See also*
    DMZ tourism; double bind; ecologi-
    cal exceptionalism; peace and nature
    preservation
DMZ barrier system, 119–20
DMZ Ecology Research Institute. *See* DERI
DMZ Forum, 5, 44, 165n26
DMZ Geopark, 122, 151
"DMZ Lives, The" (television documentary
    series), 16
DMZ Marathon, 165n26
DMZ National Trust, 82
"DMZ: Peace Economy" conference, 165n26
DMZ Peace Forum, 46–47
DMZ Peace Train, 32, 33f

200